MEGASCIENCE: THE OECD FORUM

MEGASCIENCE POLICY ISSUES

ORGANISATION FOR ECONOMIC CO-OPERATION AND DEVELOPMENT

ORGANISATION FOR ECONOMIC CO-OPERATION AND DEVELOPMENT

Pursuant to Article 1 of the Convention signed in Paris on 14th December 1960, and which came into force on 30th September 1961, the Organisation for Economic Co-operation and Development (OECD) shall promote policies designed:

- to achieve the highest sustainable economic growth and employment and a rising standard of living in Member countries, while maintaining financial stability, and thus to contribute to the development of the world economy;
- to contribute to sound economic expansion in Member as well as non-member countries in the process of economic development; and
- to contribute to the expansion of world trade on a multilateral, non-discriminatory basis in accordance with international obligations.

The original Member countries of the OECD are Austria, Belgium, Canada, Denmark, France, Germany, Greece, Iceland, Ireland, Italy, Luxembourg, the Netherlands, Norway, Portugal, Spain, Sweden, Switzerland, Turkey, the United Kingdom and the United States. The following countries became Members subsequently through accession at the dates indicated hereafter: Japan (28th April 1964), Finland (28th January 1969), Australia (7th June 1971), New Zealand (29th May 1973) and Mexico (18th May 1994). The Commission of the European Communities takes part in the work of the OECD (Article 13 of the OECD Convention).

Publié en français sous le titre :
POLITIQUES DE LA MÉGASCIENCE

FOREWORD

The Megascience Forum was established on 1 June 1992 by the Council of the OECD as a subsidiary body of the Committee for Science and Technological Policy. The goal of the Forum, in the context of the work programme of the Directorate for Science, Technology and Industry, is to help ensure the exchange of information and open and substantive discussion of issues relating to existing and potential megascience projects among Member country governments and the scientific communities involved in very large scientific undertakings. In this context, six expert meetings were held from 1992 to 1994 in disciplines making significant use of megascience; the results have appeared in the Megascience Forum series. These meetings also raised horizontal issues, issues concerning all disciplines and megascience policy. The Forum has, as a result, discussed these issues at its meetings, after requesting eminent experts to prepare the discussions.

The Forum has considered and discussed in depth the following topics, as they relate to megascience and stronger international co-operation:

- foresight/forward planning in megascience (July 1994);
- national decision-making processes in big science (January 1994);
- intergovernmental and international consultations and legal co-operation mechanisms in megascience (July 1994);
- implications of hosting an international scientific facility (June 1995);
- cost, funding and budget issues: the case of the United States (January 1995).

The five chapters in this publication contain the papers prepared on each of these themes by five authors who have both drawn on their personal experience and taken account of many of the points raised during Forum discussions. In many respects, therefore, this is a collective exercise which reflects the concerns of science policy makers when planning, deciding, funding and setting up a very large facility or equipment.

Chapter 1 describes the stages of a megascience project from its initial conception by the scientific community, which engages in debate and finally reaches a consensus, up to the decision-making phase. Then, four case studies of international co-operation projects bring out approaches that lead reliably to a successful project, as opposed to those that prove unsatisfactory. Finally, the chapter makes a few suggestions for world-scale projects.

Chapter 2 analyses the national decision-making processes and the specific selection strategies for megascience, which is nearly always financed through public funding. The evolution of these decision-making modes during the brief history of megascience (essentially the past 50 years) also brings to light the directions taken by public policy over the same period. The constraints arising from the internationalisation of projects are then investigated, as are the features of megascience that make it possible to view it as a public good in economic terms.

Chapter 3 develops and systematically describes the issues arising when a large scientific project to be implemented through international co-operation reaches the intergovernmental consultation phase. The author draws on his own experience as negotiator to point out all the traps and obstacles that invariably arise and to draw 20 lessons aimed at helping government officials responsible for the negotiations.

Chapter 4 reviews the few studies available on the problems encountered by a country that hosts an international science facility. It begins by listing the benefits which the host country hopes to reap and then considers the actual benefits and drawbacks. It seems certain that the host country always derives more benefits than disadvantages. Finally, the chapter considers the best ways of ensuring an adequate return, *i.e.* a quantifiable one, for all the partners of a very large facility under international co-operation.

Chapter 5 is a case study. It is not possible to present an overall view of the issues raised by the funding of megascience projects in the various countries that build them, as each country has its own budgetary practices and timings. The example of the United States is presented, although other analyses may follow. In addition to describing the US system, the author suggests improvements to the United States budgetary system, especially with a view to more frequent international co-operation.

It is important to emphasise the novelty of the work done by the Megascience Forum, which has studied the various obstacles to be removed if megascience co-operation is to expand – as most countries wish it to do – and become interregional, if not global.

The present volume is published on the responsibility of the Secretary-General of the OECD.

Table of contents

Chapter 3

INTERGOVERNMENTAL AND INTERNATIONAL CONSULTATIONS/AGREEMENTS AND LEGAL CO-OPERATION MECHANISMS IN MEGASCIENCE EXPERIENCES, ASPECTS AND IDEAS

Chapter 4

THE IMPLICATIONS OF HOSTING INTERNATIONAL SCIENTIFIC FACILITIES

Chapter 5

COST, FUNDING, AND BUDGET ISSUES IN MEGASCIENCE PROJECTS: THE CASE OF THE UNITED STATES

List of tables

List of figures

Chapter 1

GENERIC MEGASCIENCE POLICY ISSUES

FORESIGHT AND FORWARD PLANNING IN MEGASCIENCE

by

W.J.McG. Tegart

Visiting Professor and Director,
Australian Network for Research and Technology Policy
University of Canberra, Australia

Executive summary

Case studies of several megascience projects clearly indicate that successful projects are those for which a well-defined research foresight exercise has been undertaken. This process allows for clear definition of the scope, scale, and location of a project, for identification of possible alternatives, and for identification of potential difficulties.

Specific arrangements for carrying out and managing megascience projects, including arranging for resources, creating an appropriate organisational structure, and selecting a site are among the major issues for forward planning covered in the foresight exercise. A foresight exercise has three phases: pre-foresight, main foresight, and post-foresight. Forward planning activity starts from the latter half of the main foresight phase, at which point the issues have become clearer.

1. Pre-foresight: the bottom-up conception of projects.
   This stage can be said to begin when scientists recognise the need for a new facility or programme in order to advance the frontiers of their field. It requires active consultation within the scientific community, and it entails developing the concept and the means of realising it. Once there is a groundswell of interest, the project enters the domain of research foresight.

2. Main foresight: defining projects and linking bottom-up to top-down.
   The main task of foresight is to define the project. While this phase is initiated by scientists who take a purely scientific view, it soon becomes necessary to link bottom-up to top-down views.

- The definition of projects
  This phase involves a more organised effort to refine the project. The procedures include: establishing scientific review panels, with representation from all the countries and bodies involved; obtaining information on related facilities and their evolution; interviewing potential users; identifying the role that the facility would play in the short and the medium term in meeting clearly stated scientific and technological goals. At this stage, a project's scientific merits must be fully discussed in order to optimise the scientific goals.
  Several different types of research foresight currently exist. They are conducted in various ways: within a scientific discipline (*e.g.* at the request of NSF in the United States); by governmental or intergovernmental bodies [*e.g.* the DG XII of the European Commission (CEC)]; within agencies [*e.g.* the European Space Agency (ESA)].
- Linking bottom-up to top-down
  At this stage, it becomes extremely important to include governments in research foresight activities, because these bodies should be aware of long-term goals at an early stage, and because the scientific merit of a megaproject or megaprogramme is to little avail if it does not have support at high governmental levels.

One of the most efficient means of linking bottom-up scientific initiatives to top-down political support is through input into the national agencies most directly concerned with scientific research. These are often government-supported agencies or academies that serve an advisory or co-ordinating role on matters of scientific policy. They can often mediate between the scientific community and the governmental and funding bodies and help shape the project for presentation to the non-scientific decision-making bodies.

Because of the nature of megascience today, such decisions inevitably become political decisions; that is, they involve consideration of factors beyond the scientific merit or feasibility of a proposal, particularly when selection of proposals involves different disciplines. However, scientific merit and feasibility must remain the primary criteria.

Linking bottom-up to top-down procedures requires shaping the programme so that the two main types of criteria are kept in mind: internal (scientific and technological aspects) and external (the usefulness of the proposal in social, economic, environmental or political terms). Various means have been proposed to facilitate this process.

At this stage, the forward planning exercise can be said to begin.

3. Post-foresight: forward planning, decision making, implementation, and execution.

The project that emerges from the main foresight phase becomes the actual project at the forward planning stage. Here, the project is examined in terms of: available budgetary, human, and technical resources; best mixture of existing and new projects; balance between big and small sciences in the field; appropriate organisational structure; and site selection. Finally, if the project looks feasible, it enters the implementation phase.

In general, when proposals come before governments for decision, they do not generally arrive there through a well-ordered process. Often, events unrelated to the proposals are determining: forthcoming elections and the need to gain political mileage, discreet or overt lobbying, or the influence of champions. For national projects, it has been recognised that there is considerable merit in having a body outside the day-to-day processes of government that can encourage the definition of big science projects through organised foresight exercises. These are carried out, for example, in France, Japan, and the United States. At the European scale, the advantages of the foresight exercises carried out by ESA, the European Organisation for Nuclear Physics (CERN) and the European Science Foundation (ESF) have been clearly recognised, and there are moves to strengthen this regional approach to new facilities.

It is recognised that such a body is needed at world scale when considering supra-national projects. Particle physics has the European Committee for Future Accelerators (ECFA) and the Intergovernmental Committee for Future Accelerators (ICFA), although they need some improvement. Other areas (*e.g.* space, astronomy) need to form such organisations. ICSU could be a key player in global foresight exercises; several of its member bodies have already moved in that direction. Such organisations require adequate resources for carrying research foresight exercises through the three phases noted above.

1.   Introduction

The concept of big science, or megascience as it is now more commonly called, has been discussed at length in a number of recent publications (Galison and Hevly, 1992; Irvine, 1994; Krige, 1992; Hicks *et al.*, 1991; President's Council, 1992; and OECD, 1993). While megascience can be superficially categorised in terms of expenditure – Weinberg (1967) defined big science as any scientific project large enough to demand a noticeable portion of the gross national product – it is now clear that this is insufficient, even though politicians and bureaucrats tend to focus on costs when taking political decisions (OECD, 1991).

As Hevly (1992) points out, several important features aside from high costs set "big" science apart from "small" science. First, the resources devoted to it have been increasingly concentrated in a decreasing number of research centres with special facilities dedicated to specific goals. Second, within these specialised institutions, the work force has specialised: laboratories have been divided not only into theoreticians, experimenters, and instrument builders but also into group leaders, laboratory managers, and business co-ordinators. Third, big science, drawing on earlier rhetoric concerning science and power, has to attach social and political significance to scientific projects. Fourth, megascience is potentially international in nature.

It is only relatively recently, and largely as a result of studies by historians and sociologists, that these characteristics have been recognised and, in particular, that the links between science and politics have been understood. Scientists tend to look far ahead to see how their field is likely to evolve and to define what means are needed to undertake the required research. Recognising the need for a major new facility or programme in the process of research foresight constitutes the bottom-up input and provides the driving force for a proposal for a new megaproject.[1] However, scientific support of a megaproject or a megaprogramme is of little consequence if it is not supported in the political process which provides the funding for its realisation. This is the top-down input. It is now clear that linking bottom-up to top-down is perhaps the most critical step in the development of a very large project.

Achieving this linking is difficult at the national level and can be even more so at the international level. As Skolnikoff (1993) has remarked, international science and technology has seen an important shift away from national security goals and towards international economic ones, but there has been little change in the strongly national basis of decision-making. However, resource constraints will increase the attractiveness of international scientific co-operation to share costs, although the economic pressures on governments will limit the number and scale of these projects. Further, the opportunities and needs for international co-operation will increase as interdependence increases. Nevertheless, very large facilities or programmes remain symbols of power; therefore, the main obstacles to co-operation are ideological (*i.e.* prestige) and economic (*i.e.* control of the relevant science and the technology flowing from it).

The following sections examine the concepts of research foresight (Section 2) and its application to megascience (Section 3). Then a number of case studies of megaprojects are presented (Section 4). Section 5 draws out the elements of successful foresight and forward planning in megascience.

2. Concepts of research foresight

Given the long-term nature of many investments in scientific infrastructure, it is increasingly recognised that prospective studies and technological forecasting can play a valuable role in framing future policies for science and technology. Research foresight may be used not only to formulate hypotheses about the possible or probable evolution of different areas of science, to assess promising paths of development, and to identify possible modifications, but also to assess likely needs for new instruments and experimental techniques and to identify significant technical bottlenecks that may block further progress in research (Papon, 1994).

Martin and Irvine (1989) have studied closely the foresight process. In considering the concept of foresight, they point out the importance of unambiguous terminology and recommend the definition developed by Coates (1985):

"A process by which one comes to a fuller understanding of the forces shaping the long-term future which should be taken into account in policy formulation, planning and decision making.... Foresight involves qualitative and quantitative means for monitoring clues and indicators of evolving trends and developments and is best and most useful when directly linked to the analysis of policy implications.... Foresight is not planning – merely a step in planning."

This definition has several implications:

- Foresight is a process rather than a set of techniques and involves consultation and interaction among the scientific community, research users and policy makers.
- Foresight is concerned not so much to predict the details and timing of specific developments as to outline the range of possible futures which emerge from alternative sets of assumptions about emerging trends and opportunities.
- The foresight process must be transparent and make the underlying assumptions, analytical framework, and data inputs available for external scrutiny. Such openness also makes it possible to give non-conformist views equal weight with conventional ones and to identify emerging paradigms.
- Foresight is neither simple nor unproblematic; it provides an input to the decision-making process but does not provide a definitive solution.

In short it is clear that research foresight cannot be equated with forecasting, nor with long-term research planning; rather, it denotes a specific conception of the role of prospective analysis in policy-making.

Martin and Irvine have characterised four levels of decision making at which foresight is relevant:

1. holistic, *e.g.* Cabinet or broad national decisions, where prospective analysis is used to gain an overview of possible future directions for the national research effort;
2. macro level, *e.g.* government department or sectoral decisions, where foresight is focused on a limited number of research fields;
3. meso level, *e.g.* the board of a research agency or decisions within a major research establishment, where foresight is concerned with a single scientific or technology sector;
4. micro level, *e.g.* research committees or universities or decisions to prefer one programme to another, where foresight is used at the level of projects or scientific specialties.

Examples of all of these have been documented (Martin and Irvine, 1989; OECD, 1991; ASTEC, 1990; see also Chapter 2 of the present volume), and the principles are now well established (Figure 1). Martin and Irvine distinguish three phases in a foresight exercise, namely, *pre-foresight* (an explicit decision to initiate the process, followed by preparatory activities); *main foresight* (detailed design of the process, strategic analysis, definition of options, diffusion of results); and *post-foresight* (implementation, project definition, programme execution).

A critical aspect of a foresight exercise is defining the aim, since this determines how it is linked with the decision-making process. Martin and Irvine set out six possible aims:

1. direction setting – broad guidelines in science policy and development of an agenda of options;

15

Figure 1. **Elements and stages in foresight for priority setting
(including implementation)**

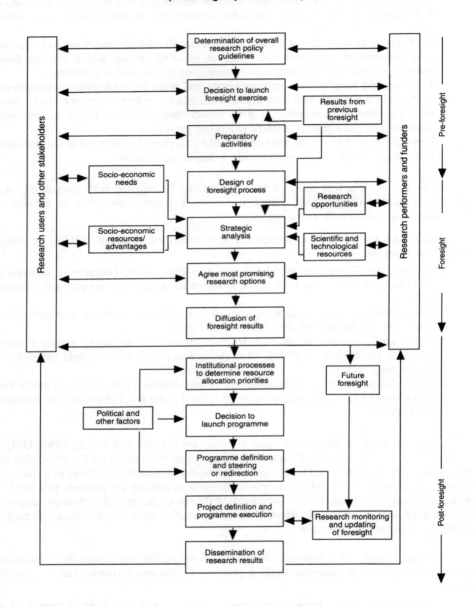

Source: Martin and Irvine (1989).

2. determining priorities – perhaps the most important aim of foresight and the driving force in most of the documented country studies, owing to resource constraints and increasing demand from researchers;
3. anticipatory intelligence – identification of emerging trends with major implications for future policy making;
4. consensus generation – promotion of greater agreement on identified needs or opportunities among scientists, funding agencies, and research users;
5. advocacy – promotion of policy decisions in line with preferences of specific stakeholders in the R&D system;
6. communication and education – promotion of internal communication within the scientific community, promotion of external communication with users of research, and wider education of the general public, politicians, and bureaucrats.

In practice, it is extremely difficult to separate these various aims, and a successful exercise has elements of all of them (see, for example, ASTEC, 1991). Experience shows that the essential features of a successful foresight exercise are:
– research users, producers, and funders are all involved;
– at least as much attention is paid to the top-down as to the bottom-up flow of views;
– decisions taken in the process can, and will, be implemented;
– the process is sensitive to the unexpected, so that plans can be modified.

3.   Foresight and forward planning in megascience

In tackling new problems, scientists tend to think about the feasibility of using either scaled-up versions of existing facilities or new custom-built facilities. In the former case, existing technology makes it possible to estimate the benefits and outcomes from a new investment of resources. In the latter case, the information output is highly uncertain or unknown, so that the investment involves a greater gamble (see Faucher and Fitzgibbons, 1993). This situation is exacerbated in the case of megaprojects that address scientific problems of such significance, scope and complexity that they require completely new approaches and involve unusually large-scale collaborative efforts on an international scale. Foresight can play a major role in reducing uncertainties in such projects.

Section 2 distinguished three phases in the foresight process: pre-foresight, main foresight and post-foresight. However, it should be borne in mind that the boundaries between these stages are somewhat blurred.

Pre-foresight – the bottom-up conception of projects

Scientists, looking well into the future when they think about the evolution of their discipline, may recognise the need for a new facility or programme in order to advance its frontiers. Here, the research foresight process can be said to begin. For megascience, whatever the source of the initial and indispensable bottom-up impetus, the magnitude of

17

the effort will require both strong scientific rationale and broad-based scientific consensus.

As noted above, active consultation within the scientific community is essential throughout the foresight process. Some disciplines have developed quite effective means of attaining this goal. Discussion may begin informally, at international scientific conferences, in conversations or communications among peers, in meetings of scientific organisations, learned societies, or academies. Once a groundswell of interest has been identified, the idea enters the domain of research foresight.

The natural trajectories of discovery may dictate that only one research approach will generate the information required, but, in general, some information can be gained, if perhaps less elegantly, through other approaches. Foresight activities clarify the feasible approaches and play a crucial role in the evolution of scientific disciplines.

Papon (1994) points out the importance of the growing multi-disciplinary use of scientific instrumentation. For example, condensed matter physics, surface chemistry, the chemistry of molecular structures, and molecular biology have all come to rely on experimentation using neutron reactors and synchrotron sources. The diffusion of instrumentation and techniques is invariably fruitful and can be an important source of scientific progress. Large facilities that are conducive to such interaction, such as the Institut Laue-Langevin (ILL) in Grenoble or the Photon Factory in Tsukuba, can stimulate interdisciplinary studies.

Foresight by the scientific community can often lead to new concepts with implications for megascience. For example, recent work with super-intense lasers suggests the feasibility of a new generation of particle accelerators with energies comparable to those of the largest existing accelerator rings (*e.g.* at CERN) over distances of a few metres (Burgess and Hutchinson, 1993). Further development of this technology could make it possible to replace the present generation of accelerators by accelerators that are cheaper and require less energy.

Main foresight – defining projects and linking bottom-up to top-down

Defining projects

This phase entails a more organised effort to refine the project. Particularly in disciplines requiring large facilities, procedures for research foresight are often well established. These procedures include: establishing scientific review panels, with representation from all the countries and bodies involved; obtaining information on related facilities and their evolution; interviewing potential users; and identifying the role that the facility would play in the short and the medium term. Scientists in the field are interviewed, and workshops are organised to discuss needs and findings. The merits of a project must be fully discussed at a purely scientific level in order to meet the scientific goals of the scientific community concerned.

There are different means of engaging in research foresight. One type takes place within the scientific discipline, with or without the collaboration of national scientific research agencies [*e.g.* the US National Science Foundation (NSF) or the French National

Centre for Scientific Research (CNRS)]. A second type is undertaken by governmental or intergovernmental bodies which have scientific programmes (*e.g.* the DG XII of the European Commission). A third type is undertaken within agencies (*e.g.* ESF) that bring together research councils [*e.g.* the United Kingdom's Science and Engineering Research Council (SERC), France's CNRS, Italy's National Research Council (CNR)]but also call on experts.

CERN can serve as an example of the first type. In its role as international organisation in charge of big science, it has long practised research foresight. Scientific planning for the Large Hadron Collider (LHC) at CERN began in 1984, at a seminar organised by ECFA and CERN. This was followed in 1987 by a more detailed study of the most promising options. Parallel R&D activities were undertaken by the Working Group on the S&T Future. Studies were made of cost-effectiveness, customers, uses to which the facility would be put, and comparison with other facilities. Final approval was given at the end of 1994 and completion will take at last ten years.

A more recent and more innovative example of the first type of research foresight has been undertaken by the joint action of several unions and interdisciplinary committees of ICSU for the large programmes concerning planet Earth, namely the World Climate Research Programme (WRCP) and the International Geosphere-Biosphere Programme (IGBP).

The Framework Programme of the European Commission's DG XII, which recently studied European scientists' main needs for large facilities in a number of fields (neutron beam sources, large magnetic fields, hydraulics, combustion techniques, earthquake engineering, oceanography and high-powered lasers) in the next ten years, is an example of the second type (CEC, 1991). This type of research foresight, with the participation of the scientific disciplines involved, is a regular part of the Commission's work.

The Nuclear Physics European Collaboration Committee (NuPECC), an ESF committee that has succeeded in creating a European research foresight process for nuclear physics, is an example of the third type. In its recent foresight effort, it formed six groups consisting of five to seven experts, including non-NuPECC members. Each group prepared an analysis of a particular sub-field, on the basis of proposals from individuals and laboratories and of meetings at local and national level. The working documents analysed the equipment available, as well as equipment under development and proposed. Following a general week-long meeting, which brought together the members of all the groups, other experts, and the members of NuPECC, NuPECC formulated detailed recommendations and circulated them within the scientific community. Final recommendations were then proposed in a publication to be used as input to the decision-making processes of funding agencies. The next step is submitting a proposal to the governments of the concerned countries for a facility to be built in collaboration.

Linking bottom-up to top-down

The scientific merit of a megaproject or megaprogramme is to little avail if it does not have support at high government levels. One of the most important means of linking bottom-up scientific initiatives to top-down political support is through input into the national agencies most directly concerned with scientific research. These are often government-supported agencies or academies that serve an advisory or co-ordinating role on matters of scientific policy. Because governments should be aware of long-term goals at an early stage, it is extremely important to include these bodies in research foresight activities. They can often mediate between the scientific community and the governmental and funding bodies and help shape the project for presentation to the non-scientific decision-making bodies.

Decisions about the investment of the very large sums of money needed for megascience facilities inevitably become political decisions; that is, they involve consideration of factors that go beyond the scientific merit or feasibility of the proposal alone. This is particularly so when selection among proposals involves different disciplines. The benefits that might derive from investing in one research area, such as the Space Station, are not easy to measure or to compare with those that might accrue from a similar investment in another area, such as the Human Genome project.

However, scientific merit and feasibility (including considerations such as timeliness and cost-effectiveness) are clearly the primary criteria. It is not possible to justify government investments in major facilities or programmes which require large-scale co-operation unless the research is at the leading edge of international science and technology. Only by extending the frontiers of knowledge can broad scientific and social benefits be realised.

Criteria for assessing proposals for major research facilities or programmes can be grouped under two main headings: those that measure the scientific and technological aspects of the proposal (internal criteria) and those that gauge the wider social, economic, environmental, or political impact or utility of the proposal (external criteria). The first set determines whether the proposal is good scientific and technological research, while the second set assesses whether it is good for the nation.

Various criteria have been proposed (Weinberg, 1963; Dutton and Crowe, 1988; and OECD, 1987), but the most comprehensive appear to be the sets developed by the Australian Science and Technology Council (ASTEC) for assessing potential major research facilities for Australia (ASTEC, 1992). The criteria are framed as questions but could equally well be formulated as statements; they are reproduced in full in Tables 1 and 2. While they incorporate features specifically related to Australia's size and geographical isolation, they are a basis for developing criteria that can be used by any country to assess its participation in an international megascience project. Possible sets derived from these are given in Tables 3 and 4.

In most countries, different governmental science and technology bodies [such as the CNRS in France, the Science and Technology Agency (STA) in Japan, SERC in the United Kingdom, the National Research Council (NRC) and the NSF in the United States, and ASTEC in Australia]engage in research foresight (Martine and Irvine, 1989). These bodies have significant scientific input and serve to bring together the interests of scientific communities and policy makers. In the United States, for example, the NRC convenes expert disciplinary panels in a number of areas approximately once every ten years. An Advisory Panel on High Energy Physics has reported since the 1960s to what is now the Department of Energy, considering trends and recommending priorities for federal support. Astronomy has also been reported on for several decades, and a recent

Table 1. Criteria for assigning priorities for major national research facilities (benefits to science and technology)

Scientific objectives and their significance

1. Areas of research
Does the proposal develop an area of scientific or engineering research of great importance to Australia, and which is at the leading edge of international research?

2. Key scientific questions
What are the key scientific questions that can be answered by having access to the proposed national facility?

3. Significance for Australian science and technology
Why are the answers to the questions significant for Australian science and technology?

4. Availability to outside researchers
Will the proposed national facility be made available to outside researchers subject to independent peer views?

Established need

5. Australia's national priorities
Is the case for the proposed national facility appropriate in terms of Australia's current national priorities?

6. Major source of expenditure
Does the proposal involve a major source of expenditure on a piece or pieces of physical equipment of a scale such that it could not be developed incrementally or funded by an institution or consortium of institutions without serious disruption to other commitments of equal or higher priority?

7. Community of scientists and technologists
Is there a community of outstanding Australian scientists and technologists committed to the success of the proposed national facility?

Unique characteristics

8. Unique characteristics
Are there characteristics of the proposed national facility that are uniquely appropriate for Australia?

Degree of impact

9. Interdisciplinary research
What impact will the proposed national facility have on fostering interdisciplinary research?

10. Doctoral and post-doctoral training
Will the proposed national facility provide new opportunities for doctoral and post-doctoral training in research?

11. National prestige
Will the proposed facility contribute to public pride and the prestige of Australia's science and technology?

International characteristics

12. International scientific collaboration
Will the proposed national facility encourage international scientific collaboration by attracting researchers from overseas to spend time in Australia?

13. Advantages of overseas locations
Could the proposed national facility be located with advantage overseas in partnership with one or more other countries?

14. Attractiveness to international partners
Would the proposed national facility, if located in Australia, attract international partners?

Source: ASTEC, 1992.

**Table 2.   Criteria for assigning priorities for major national research facilities
(benefits to the nation)**

Industry objectives and their significance

1. Technological stimulus to Australian industry — Will the construction of the proposed national facility provide a technological stimulus to Australian industry?
2. Unique services of benefit to Australia — Will the proposed national facility provide unique services of benefit to Australian industry?
3. Linkage between research and industry — Could the proposed national facility lead to better linkages between academic and research institutions and industry?
4. New Australian enterprises — Will the research output from the proposed national facility foster the development of new Australian enterprises?
5. Technology training and skills — What contribution will the proposed national facility make to enhancing the skills base and training level of Australian technology?

Social objectives and their significance

6. Advancement of knowledge, growth, economic health, welfare or national security — Is the proposed national facility of high national priority for the advancement of knowledge, economic growth, health, welfare or national security?
7. Environmental management — Does the proposed national facility contribute to a better understanding and management of our environment?
8. Community appreciation of science and technology — Will the proposed national facility lead to an improved understanding and appreciation by the Australian community of the accomplishments of science and technology?

International standing

9. Image as a technologically advanced nation — Will the proposed national facility project and enhance Australia's image as a technologically advanced nation?
10. International negotiating position — Will Australia's position in international negotiations be strengthened as a result of the proposed national facility?

Source: ASTEC, 1992.

NRC panel on astronomy and astrophysics has proposed a menu of priorities for ground-based and space astronomy for the 1990s. In the area of space research, the Centre national d'études spatiales (CNES) in France, STA in Japan, and the National Aeronautics and Space Administration (NASA) in the United States regularly prepare research documents. In Australia, ASTEC has proposed priorities for astronomy for the next decade, as well as for other major national research facilities.

In Europe, international bodies with both scientific and policy responsibilities undertake research foresight in several fields. The documents prepared for these disciplinary studies serve both to set out scientific goals and to inform policy makers on the state and needs of the discipline involved. As noted earlier, CERN carries out research foresight in high energy physics in conjunction with ECFA. ESA began research foresight for space research with the Horizon 2000 and Horizon 2000 Plus Programmes (see Section 4). To a lesser degree, the ESF responds to specific requests from its constituency of research councils: it conducted its first major study for the European Synchrotron Radiation

**Table 3. Criteria for assigning priorities for participating in
an international megascience facility
(benefits to science and technology)**

Scientific objectives and their significance

1. Areas of research — Does the proposal develop an area of scientific or engineering research which is at the leading edge of international research?

2. Key scientific questions — What are the key scientific questions that can be answered by having access to the proposed megascience facility?

3. Significance for national science and technology — Are the answers to these questions significant for national science and technology?

4. Availability to outside researchers — Will the proposed international facility be made available to researchers of non-participating nations subject to independent peer review?

Established need

5. National priorities — Is the case for the proposed international facility appropriate in terms of current national priorities?

6. Major source of expenditure — Does the proposal involve major expenditure on a facility of a scale such that it could not be developed nationally?

7. Community of scientists and technologists — Is there a community of outstanding national scientists and technologists committed to the success of the proposed international facility?

Unique characteristics

8. Unique characteristics — Are there characteristics of the proposed international facility that are unique?

Degree of impact

9. Interdisciplinary research — What impact will the proposed international facility have on fostering national interdisciplinary research?

10. Doctoral and post-doctoral training — Will the proposed international facility provide new opportunity for doctoral and post-doctoral training in research?

11. National prestige — Will participation in the proposed international facility contribute to the national prestige of science and technology?

Source: Author.

Facility (ESRF) (see Section 4); and NuPECC's previously mentioned recent report constitutes another important example of research foresight.

Post-foresight – decision making, implementation, and execution

The scale and complexity of megaprojects generally means that the answers to the questions posed in Tables 3 and 4 will not be unambiguous, and, while the answers may be useful, they may not decisively influence either the decision or policy. It is clear that time is an essential element in the megascience decision-making process. The process can

Table 4. Criteria for assigning priorities for participating in an international megascience facility (benefits to the nation)

Industry objectives and their significance

1.	Technological benefit to national industry	Will the construction of the proposed international facility provide a technological stimulus to national industry?
2.	Unique services of benefit to the nation	Will the proposed international facility provide unique services of benefit to national industry?
3.	Linkage between research and industry	Could the proposed international facility lead to better linkages between academic and research institutions and industry?
4.	New enterprises	Will the research output from the proposed international facility foster the development of new enterprises?
5.	Technology training and skills	What contribution will the proposed international facility make to enhancing the skills base and training level of national technology?

Social objectives and their significance

6.	Advancement of knowledge, growth, economic health, welfare or national security	Is the proposed international facility of high national priority for the advancement of knowledge, economic growth, health, welfare or national security?
7.	Environmental management	Does the proposed international facility contribute to a better understanding and management of the national environment?
8.	Community appreciation of science and technology	Will participation in the proposed international facility lead to an improved understanding and appreciation of the accomplishments of science and technology?

International standing

9.	Image as a technologically advanced nation	Will participation in the proposed international facility enhance the national image as a technologically advanced nation?
10.	International negotiating position	Will the national position in international negotiations be strengthened as a result of participation in the proposed international facility?

Source: Author.

be seen as a series of micro-decisions, each of which limits future manoeuvrability. The final product is the last (small) choice in the series.

Several authors have suggested ways to improve the process. Averch (1993) has developed a set of rules for improving the inevitably political process of choosing megaprojects (Table 5). His rules also contain elements needed for forward planning and control of megaprojects. If costs are not controlled at an early stage, expensive technologies can rapidly become entrenched. As Williams (1988) has remarked, "It is in the nature of big projects that they are relatively inflexible". He sets out a number of questions which complement Averch's rules. These issues must be addressed as part of the careful forward planning that is an essential part of the foresight process and will be further discussed in Section 5.

Table 5. **Rules to improve the megaproject selection process**

Rule 1:	Face consideration of cost as well as requirements at the very earliest stages of choice.
Rule 2:	For comparing megaprojects, estimate the budget levels at which information returns will start to diminish.
Rule 3:	When multiple research technologies are available to generate desired information, start more than one track and monitor costs and identify and reduce uncertainties about technological and economic performance.
Rule 3.1:	If a ''go'' decision turns out to be appropriate, select the alternative that gives lower costs or less uncertainty based on actual operating experience.
Rule 4:	Once a given set of megaprojects has been selected, carry out real-time, formative evaluations and give rapid feedback to those involved.
Rule 5:	Widen the composition of advisory groups to include more kinds of expertise and interests than research-performing scientists and engineers.
Rule 6:	Design the construction of a megaproject with sufficient flexibility and modularity so that experts can be reconvened periodically with updated information.
Rule 7:	Take predictive track record into account when selecting experts.
Rule 8:	Megaprojects that can be cost-shared internationally should be preferred to those that cannot be.

Source: Averch, 1993.

The decision-making process is extensively dealt with in Chapter 2 of the present volume. Of particular interest in the present context is the new emphasis that the expansion of megascience has placed on shared responsibilities and costs within international structures. There are various formulae for these forms of co-operation:

- the participation of various countries in one agency, such as CERN, to which they contribute in proportion to their resources;
- the creation of special companies to manage facilities jointly funded by several countries, such as ESRF or ILL;
- specific co-operation agreements between countries or representative agencies, as for a space astronomy mission;
- the establishment of a world-wide project for which all the interested countries sign an agreement, as in the International Thermonuclear Experimental Reactor (ITER) project;
- the creation of new co-operative structures, as for the large-scale climate and ocean exploration programmes.

As Atkinson (1993) has pointed out, Europe has gradually learned to draw up fundamental agreements for co-operation in megascience projects. Following the CERN Convention, there have been the European Southern Observatory (ESO) and the European Space Research Organisation (ESRO) Convention which led to the ESA Convention. Most recent is the ESRF Convention, which drew heavily on past experience, while improving the basic rules for collaboration.

Despite the clear scientific merit of a project, decision making for and final agreement on co-operation are often extremely difficult owing to the intervention of political factors. In general, the bigger the project, the higher the political profile. When senior political figures become involved, decisions on a particular project become part of a larger range of issues, as very large projects are symbols of power and the main obstacles to co-operation are ideological (*i.e.* prestige) and economic (*i.e.* the potential loss of benefits from the project and its associated technology).

4. Some megascience case studies

The expert meetings organised by the Megascience Forum, and the resulting publications, have been extremely useful in identifying many of the issues associated with big projects in astronomy (OECD, 1993*a*), deep drilling (OECD, 1993*b*), global change (OECD, 1994*a*), oceanography (OECD, 1994*b*), reactors and synchrotrons (OECD, 1994*c*), and particle physics (1995). Detailed studies of big science projects in these fields and others are very important for identifying the features that affect their success or failure. Since a long time often elapses between inception and implementation, it is hard for those involved to appreciate properly which factors influenced the course of events, especially since many factors contribute to the difficulty – the size of the installations, the number of institutions involved, the magnitude of budgets, the importance of politics, the sophistication of management, and the numbers of scientists from different institutions.

It is only relatively recently that historians and sociologists of science have begun to analyse in detail the course of big science in the post-Second World War period (see, for example, Galison and Hevly, 1992; Krige, 1992; and Smith, 1993). Publications on the history of CERN (Hermann *et al.*, 1987, 1990, and 1994) are an outstanding example of a study of big science. A similar series is being written on the history of ESA (Krige *et al.*, 1994). Such studies reveal the complexities of the political processes that inevitably determine the final fate of such projects and the role that scientific champions have played in linking the scientific community to the political process.

Below, several case studies are presented. They show the role of foresight and forward planning in megascience and, in particular, the need for successful linkage between the bottom-up scientific approach and the top-down political approach. Multinational examples have been chosen, as being representative of megascience today; they are mostly European, since Europe has been most active in bringing national interests together for a multinational project, largely, it must be said, as a means of combating technological pressures from the United States, Russia, and Japan.

Case study no. 1

The Scientific Programme of the European Space Agency

ESA was constituted in 1975, some time after space activities had started in Europe. (The information contained in this section draws largely on Cavallo, 1993; see also ESA, 1984.) Originally, European space activities were organised through two different organisations established in 1964: ESRO and the European Space Vehicle Launcher

Development Organisation (ELDO). ESRO covered space research and ELDO development of launch capability. ESA was formed to assure more coherent development on a broader base, and to allow for expanding into fields requiring longer development times, which could be separated off as commercial activities without ties to ESA.

ESA is by convention only allowed to develop space activities for strictly peaceful purposes. It has therefore always been fully funded from civil sources. In general, its programmes fall into two different classes:

1. Mandatory programmes, for which funding is a fixed fraction of the gross national product (GNP) of each of the member countries. These are covered by the General Budget and the Scientific Programme.
2. Optional programmes, which are funded by direct subscription to specific activities by the member countries. These are the Telecommunications programme, the Earth Observations programme, Space Transportation Systems, the Space Station, the Microgravity programme, and the European Astronauts Centre.

In 1994, ESA's Scientific Programme had a budget of 331 MAU, or approximately 11 per cent of ESA's total budget. The programme is managed with the support of an external advisory structure representing the European space science community. Decisions are taken by the Science Programme Committee (SPC) on which all member countries are represented.

In the first years of ESA, it was not possible to develop many new concepts, as it was necessary first to set in place the infrastructure that would permit proper selection and subsequent smooth development of new projects. Therefore, ESA's early projects were a natural continuation of projects already conceived under ESRO. Because of the uncertainties and exploratory nature of early space research, no general framework was established. Missions were selected on an *ad hoc* and competitive basis, as and when funds became available. Despite its then *ad hoc* nature, the Scientific Programme was extremely successful; it launched and operated 17 missions, five of which are still in orbit.

With the appointment of Dr. R.-M. Bonnet as Director of the Scientific Programme in 1983, a move was made to place the programme on a long-term footing, on the basis of a carefully planned foresight exercise by European space scientists, supported by industrialists, the ESA Executive, and the political actors in the member countries. The resulting programme, "Horizon 2000", reflected two major policy considerations – the European viewpoint and relations with agencies outside Europe.

The European viewpoint reflected the recognition that only by pooling its resources could Europe expect to have an independent programme capable of matching the larger programmes of NASA and others. While there were national programmes in Europe that contributed significantly to the space effort, a simple comparison of resources made it obvious that national programmes could only be competitive on a world-wide scale in limited areas and must eventually find their place within an overall European endeavour able to optimise the European space research effort. Co-ordination between ESA and national programmes required defining a long-term strategy. This could then lead to establishing a frame of reference for European space research as a whole, within which the ESA programme and the national programmes could progress in a co-ordinated fashion.

With respect to relations with other agencies, and in particular NASA, co-ordinating the European programme with those of agencies outside Europe was thought to be in the best interests of European scientists. This would give them additional possibilities, would avoid wasteful duplication, and would increase the scientific return on total investment. A long-term European programme was a prerequisite for such co-ordination, so that relations with other programmes could be evaluated *a priori* and thereby avoid the intrinsic weaknesses and risks of *a posteriori* reactions to events beyond European control.

In the light of these considerations, an independent European long-term programme was to meet the following criteria:

- *Scientific standard.* This is the paramount criterion. Cultural heritage and scientific tradition demand that Europe's scientific goals be set at the highest standard.
- *A suitable mix of large and smaller projects.* Large projects tend to be complex and expensive; they should be versatile and serve a broad community of users. A facility requires preparation by the scientific community and prior scientific and technical development. It is necessary to include in the overall programme smaller projects with more specialised scientific aims and/or as stepping stones towards the larger facility. National programmes could play an important role here and for relevant technologies.
- *Flexibility and versatility to match the scientific evolution.* Plans for missions and design of instruments tend to be frozen many years in advance, in particular for large complex missions. Setting up these long-term programmes requires lengthy preparation at the scientific, technological, and policy levels. It is thus essential that, where possible, large and complex facilities should be carefully identified, and the rigidity they introduce into the programme should be accepted. Having established the major missions as the cornerstones of the programme, provision needs to be made for a number of typical, but unidentified, small and medium-sized missions to ensure flexibility and to keep pace with the shifting needs of science. Identification and selection of these smaller missions should be made at an appropriate time and follow the established competitive procedure.
- *Continuity of effort by scientific institutes and industry.* This is of fundamental importance for the development of a coherent and successful scientific programme. Considering the number of scientific institutes and the distribution of industries in Europe, a total of some 12 to 15 missions over the next 15 years could be foreseen.
- *A high technological content.* The basic objective of a science programme is, of course, the benefit to the scientific disciplines themselves. It must, however, be recognised that there is a strong interrelationship between scientific development and technological advance. Scientific projects "pull" technology and vice versa: science blossoms in the wake of a new technological development. The programme must emphasise this close interrelationship.
- *Realistic budgetary limits.* It would be quite unrealistic to propose that Europe should devote as much as NASA to space research, even though the United States and Europe have similar GNPs, population, and space communities. On the other

28

hand, the ESA mandatory science budget of 1983, constrained by the boundaries established in 1971, was completely inadequate to meet the objectives stated above. At that level, ESA could only develop one small or medium-sized project every two years, with no prospect whatsoever of engaging in the larger projects being requested in most disciplines, other than as subordinate partners in missions conceived and developed by NASA. Such dependence on another agency's programmes was strongly felt not to be compatible either with the ambitions and role of Europe, or with its cultural heritage.

While an increase in the level of funding was seen necessary to achieve an autonomous programme of a high standard, the increase had to be realistic and feasible. It was proposed that the future programme should be contained within a new budget envelope of about 200 MAU a year in 1983/84 units, a figure that European industry had arrived at independently on the basis of its views of a reasonable frequency of development contracts for European countries. This amount, an increase of 50 per cent over the 1984 level of about 130 MAU per year, was to be reached progressively between 1985 and 1991. A 5 per cent annual increase of the science budget was later approved for the period 1991-94. The 1994 budget was about 331 MAU in 1994 units.

– *A proper balance between entirely European projects and co-operation with other agencies.* The European programme should be autonomous but not isolated. It should be well matched to world-wide plans to avoid wasteful duplication. A certain degree of interdependence by way of co-operative projects would be beneficial both because of the intrinsic scientific advantages and as a means to maintain project costs within the limits of European capabilities.

The Horizon 2000 programme was developed between October 1983 and July 1984 with the strong involvement of the European scientific community. At that time, some 2 000 European scientists were using results from space studies. The Director of the Scientific Programme announced a call for mission concepts in November 1983. There were 77 replies, and they covered the entire spectrum of scientific disciplines under consideration. A Survey Committee was set up, along with a number of teams and panels involving about 50 European scientists. The Survey Committee co-ordinated the entire effort. It was composed of the Space Scientific Advisory Committee members and invited scientists from other international scientific research organisations – CERN, ESO, ESF, and the International Astronomical Union (IAU). The teams and panels analysed the scientific priorities and requirements of the different research topics in the light of the mission concepts that were received and other information and identified means of realising them.

The Survey Committee, together with the chairmen of the teams and panels, discussed their findings, and, finally, in a three-day meeting in Venice, formulated, on the basis of the teams' analyses and priorities, a coherent overall programme for European space science for the following 15 to 20 years. Horizon 2000 has four major projects, the so-called "cornerstones" of the programme up to 2004, which cost about 400 MAU each (1984 economic conditions). The first is at the advanced development stage, and the second is in the advanced planning phase. They are complemented by four medium-sized missions, costing about 200 MAU each (1984 economic conditions), which provide flexibility. These are selected competitively. The original plan also envisaged a number of smaller projects, to be selected competitively, each costing not more than 100 MAU (of 1984). They were to respond to needs for frequent flight opportunities and to take quick advantage of opportunities; they were also to cover minor participation in other ESA programmes, *e.g.* space platforms, or in the programmes of other agencies. Horizon 2000 offered only modest opportunities to use ESA space platforms, and small projects were mostly annual extensions of existing missions, *e.g.* the International Ultra-violet Explorer, or the Giotto Extender Mission, which used the Giotto spacecraft in 1992 to encounter a second comet after Halley. The issue of ESA's role in small missions remains open (see below).

Following its approval by the ESA Council in 1985, Horizon 2000 has become the reference for the planning of most space science activities in Europe. The success of the approach prompted the Space Science Advisory Committee (SSAC) in early 1993 to propose extending ESA's long-term scientific space plan a further ten years (Horizon 2000 Plus Programme). The SSAC felt that the cornerstones should remain mainly under ESA leadership and should favour long-term missions, even if these were not necessarily the most ambitious projects; co-operation with non-European partners could increase the mission capabilities but should in no way cause dependence, since ESA must remain in charge of the essential components of its long-term plan.

For medium-sized missions, on the other hand, such considerations should be less pressing. For small missions, the SSAC took the concerns of the scientific community over the selection process under advisement and proposed to study this area more thoroughly in the light of experience with earlier projects.

The process for extending Horizon 2000 essentially followed the earlier pattern. A call for mission concepts by October 1993 was announced. The proposals were to include a general description of the mission, an assessment of the technological and scientific developments needed to carry it out, of possible avenues for international co-operation, and of the budgetary level required. They were examined by scientific working groups and then put before a committee composed of the SSAC and experts from the scientific community. By the summer of 1994, the committee had defined a science strategy and a coherent plan based on these proposals.

Lessons from the case study

The successful elements of Horizon 2000 appear to be:
- a committed leader with clearly defined policy objectives and criteria for achieving these objectives;
- a carefully planned foresight exercise;
- clearly defined budgetary objectives that ensure a stable and balanced programme;
- from the start, the strong, albeit implicit, support of the European space scientific community;
- a broad-based scientific selection committee, which meant that scientists from other organisations were also committed to the outcome;

- strong support from European industry, which saw the virtues of a stable space programme for their forward planning;
- strong support of the national representatives on the ESA Science Programme Committee and the ESA Council, which reflected the consensus achieved in their respective scientific and industrial communities who then put pressure on their national governments to support the outcome.

This is an excellent example of the linkage of the bottom-up impetus from the scientific community with the top-down support within the political process, a linkage firmly cemented by the full support of industry, represented in both groups.

Case study no. 2

The International Space Station

An impetus behind Horizon 2000 was the desire to co-ordinate the European space science effort in order to create more effective links with the work of agencies outside Europe, notably in the United States and the former USSR. The International Space Station, instead, illustrates the problems that arise when international megascience projects proceed without proper foresight and forward planning (on all this, see Hayward, 1993; see also Logsdon, 1992; and Kay, 1994).

In the early 1980s, interest in a major international space programme developed both at NASA and, on a more modest scale, at ESA. Both put forward plans for a space station that would be a permanent manned laboratory for developing space technology and applications. While NASA had a clear technological lead in space technology, especially manned space, ESA had the Ariane launcher programme well underway and plans for a more powerful version (Ariane 5) to put a manned shuttle (later named Hermes) into orbit. Although much the junior in terms of space technology, ESA's success in moulding European space activities, combined with France's determination to press for regional autonomy in space, encouraged a move towards co-operation with the United States.

The negotiations were protracted and difficult, particularly since the United States involved Canada and Japan as additional partners during the process. The United States' primary motives in opening up the US national space programme to international participation were money and politics. NASA felt that it could defray some of its rising costs by external inputs and that internationalisation would help to maintain national political support for its programmes.

From the European viewpoint, participation in the US programme offered substantial benefits. European design work on a space station had been hampered by lack of experience with manned space systems, and the US project could offer a relatively cheap route to manned space. This would boost European technology so that it could compete in world markets.

After an "in principle" agreement was signed in 1984, negotiations continued on a formal agreement. Questions of management of the programme and the facility, technology transfer, the use of the space station (particularly its potential military use) bedevilled the discussions. The United States maintained that, since it would be bearing the major share of the funding (ESA would fund $4.5 billion against the US contribution of $14 billion), it should control the programme. Positions changed on both sides during the period of the discussions but finally, in late 1988, the parties signed a Memorandum of Understanding.

Over this period, design studies had been undertaken. An ambitious initial design was estimated at $8 billion but a more modest design rapidly rose to $17 billion. Estimates tended to be shaped more by what was likely to be politically acceptable than by a realistic technical appraisal of the tasks involved. The unstable nature of the NASA budget, owing to the fact that the US political process is geared to an annual budget cycle with no commitment to long-term support, constituted a major problem (see Chapter 5). This gave rise to considerable uncertainty in Europe about the prospects for collaboration, particularly in the early 1990s.

At that time, Europeans also began to experience problems of rising costs and declining political support for manned space programmes. In 1992, ESA's manned space activities were cut back. The Hermes project essentially became a technology demonstration programme, so that ESA's only substantial commitment to manned space was its role in the Space Station. Thus, after a decade of national and collaborative effort and the expenditure of $7.7 billion in the United States and $2 billion in Europe, the future of the International Space Station was far from assured. However, in mid-1993, President Clinton decided to go ahead with a scaled-down version, in an effort to cut $4 billion from the programme over five years.

Later in 1993, plans evolved further. The Space Station project now includes a Russian contribution in hardware, has been renamed ''Alpha'', and fulfils the essentially political goal of ensuring more co-operation between the United States and Russia.

Lessons from the case study

The unsuccessful elements of the International Space Station appear to be:

- an *ad hoc* approach to international collaboration driven by political processes in the United States and Europe;
- a lack of foresight on a co-operative basis to define the technical parameters of the project at an early stage;
- consequently, an inability to define the budget for the project with any degree of certainty;
- a lack of balance of skills and resources between the major partners leading to unrealistic expectations on both sides;
- an inability to carry out rational forward planning due to the unpredictability of the political processes, particularly in the United States, where active presidential support is necessary to success.

By contrast with the first case study, this shows a lack of top-down and bottom-up linkage, which led to a poor result for a large expenditure of money. Foresight studies on a collaborative basis from the beginning could have revealed potential problems well before the political process took over and drove the programme in an unplanned fashion.

Case study no. 3

Synchrotron radiation in Europe

Synchrotron radiation is a brilliant light which is emitted when electrons from a high energy accelerator are forced to travel in a circular orbit in a strong magnetic field. It has been described as the "ultimate searchlight"; it is much more potent than the most high-powered lasers and is also the most powerful available source of X-rays.

Since it was first used in the 1960s, synchrotron radiation has experienced rapid growth as a research tool. The discovery that radiation is emitted over a broad spectrum has created communities of users in the ultraviolet and soft X-ray range, as well as in the hard X-ray range. Synchrotron radiation is now a major factor in the scientific landscape and is expanding rapidly. It should be stressed that the present expansion in research in this field is accompanied by (and dependent on) major technical advances in machine physics. Since dedicated storage rings were first used for synchrotron radiation research in the 1970s, successive generations of design have led to the proposed third generation of super-brilliant sources.

Implicit or explicit foresight studies carried out by the scientific community over the last two decades indicate a clear trajectory. The first generation of synchrotron radiation sources were high energy physics accelerators converted to furnish electron energies of 0.8-2 GeV and produce soft X-rays. The circumference of the storage ring was typically 350 m. The second generation – the Photon Factory at Tsukuba and the Daresbury Laboratory in the United Kingdom – were dedicated machines which incorporated straight sections in the ring to make it possible to use emission devices with a range of wavelengths, but they still only produced electron energies of 1.5-2.5 GeV. The third generation – ESRF at Grenoble, the Advanced Photon Source (APS) in the United States and SPring-8 in Japan – are machines with larger storage rings, from 850 m to 1.5 km in circumference, which incorporate optimised straight sections and specialised emission devices, have electron energies of 6-8 GeV and produce hard X-rays. It is recognised that research with synchrotron radiation is highly specialised and that different storage rings have different characteristics and different beamlines and instrumentation so that no one facility can satisfy the needs of all users.

The European investment in synchrotron radiation has been significant, but, even so, only about half of the European Union countries have synchrotron radiation facilities of their own; in the other half, the intensity of usage is lower by a factor of about ten. Potential demand is extremely large (see European Science Foundation, 1989; and, for more recent information, OECD, 1994c).

As part of the continuing development of European facilities to meet this steadily rising demand, a study of a European synchrotron radiation facility was initiated by ESF in 1977.[2] At the ESF's General Assembly in November, the report of a working party chaired by Professor H. Maier-Leibniz entitled "Synchrotron Radiation – A Perspective View for Europe" was formally approved. An *ad hoc* committee on synchrotron radiation was set up to prepare a feasibility study. Thus, the pre-foresight phase was endorsed and carried through to a main foresight phase.

The *ad hoc* committee, chaired by Professor Y. Farge of France, set up two sub-groups, one chaired by Dr. D.J. Thompson of the United Kingdom and the other by Professor B. Buras of Denmark, to deal with work on the machine and instrumentation. The *ad hoc* committee and the subgroups included directors or representatives from the main laboratories and scientific organisations in Europe. They set about developing the scientific case for the facility by organising some 12 workshops in Europe between February 1978 and May 1979. Topics covered were: preparation of the scientific case, wiggler, application of Mössbauer spectroscopy, atomic and molecular physics, molecular dynamics and photochemistry, X-ray diffraction, X-ray emission spectroscopy, life sciences, radiometry, non-biological X-ray crystallography, X-ray radiography, and X-ray Compton scattering. There was also a final workshop. About 120 scientists were involved in these discussions, which resulted in the development of a strong consensus on applications and methods.

The *ad hoc* committee presented its report in 1979 (ESF, 1979), and the ESF General Assembly endorsed the concept. The main foresight phase continued as a team carried out a detailed machine design in order to estimate costs. The team was based at CERN where European countries were already involved in strong co-operation and where expertise on machine design could be readily pooled. The team produced its report in 1984.

The project now entered the post-foresight phase. The initiative was taken up at intergovernmental level by a group chaired by Professor Levaux of Belgium. Considerable lobbying of governments occurred, and problems arose in particular over the question of site, with France, Germany, Denmark, Belgium, and the Netherlands all putting forward strong claims. At the same time, the aeronautical engineering community was pressing forward a proposal for another large experimental facility – the European Wind Tunnel (EWT) (see Chapter 3 of the present volume). In this case, France, Germany, and the Netherlands were interested in serving as host nation. After considerable negotiation, a deal was struck: France gained the ESRF and Germany the EWT, and both countries were to make special contributions to capital and operating costs (Anon., 1984). For ESRF, a major internal struggle then ensued between a site at Strasbourg and a site at Grenoble adjacent to ILL. The latter prevailed, and the first steps towards implementing ESRF were taken in 1985. France, Germany, Italy, and the United Kingdom gave firm commitments to fund the project, and negotiations commenced with other countries. In the early stages, the link with ILL proved invaluable, and the latter's strong support in the development of instrumentation has been significant in ensuring the success of the facility.

A provisional Council was formed in 1986, and negotiations on participation continued. The text of the Convention, signed by the member countries in 1988, was ratified by the French Parliament on 24 November 1989; the contract between ESRF and its multinational building consortium was signed on 1 December 1989. The Convention marked a major step in European co-operation in megascience; 12 countries are participating, some grouped in consortia owing to a minimum contribution of 4 per cent. The major share of construction and operating costs are being met by France, Germany, Italy, and the United Kingdom, with smaller contributions from the Benelux countries (Belgium,

Netherlands), Spain, Switzerland, and the Nordic countries (Denmark, Norway, Sweden, and Finland). Construction began in 1988 and ESRF was operational in 1994.

Lessons from the case study

The successful elements of ESRF appear to be:
- a carefully planned foresight exercise;
- a succession of champions who kept the project alive over an extended period;
- the strong support of the European scientific community from the start of the process;
- the broad-based nature of the *ad hoc* committee and the strong support of all the European national laboratories;
- ESF's important role in supporting the development of the concept and providing the political linkages to enable the project to advance;
- the scientific and political involvement, from the start, of both large and small countries, which led to a truly European facility.

This is an excellent example of bottom-up and top-down linkage.

Case study no. 4

AUSTRON – A pulsed neutron source for the future?

The OECD expert meeting on synchrotron radiation sources and neutron beams, held at Risø in late 1993 (OECD, 1994c), highlighted the problem of the ageing research reactors in Europe and the urgent need for planning new neutron sources to support the growing European research community, including Eastern Europe. Two types of facilities are used by the neutron scattering community, research reactors and spallation sources. In the first type, neutrons are generated, at a constant rate, through fission, and the process generates energy within the facility of approximately 80 MeV per neutron. The spallation process is quite different. Here, proton beams are accelerated to high energy, typically 1-2 GeV, and then directed to a heavy metal target. The neutrons are produced by the collisions between the very energetic protons and the nuclei of the target material. Typically, approximately 25 MeV are required to produce one neutron. The neutrons produced by spallation usually show a pulsed distribution.

As a consequence of the methods of production, the experimental techniques adopted at the two classes of facilities are quite different. The traditional view is that the two classes are complementary, with spallation facilities excelling at higher neutron energies and reactors providing better performance at low energies. In fact, with the rapid improvements in accelerator performance, spallation sources are becoming very competitive even at low energies. To put the performance of spallation and reactor beams into perspective, the performance of the world's premier reactor facility, the ILL reactor at Grenoble, at 57 MW, is similar to that of the premier spallation source, the ISIS facility at the Rutherford-Appleton Laboratory in the United Kingdom, with a beam power of 130 kW.

Against this background, the European physics community, particularly in central Europe which lacks major facilities, has been considering possible options for neutron sources. In 1990, Professor M. Regler, together with a number of other Austrian and European scientists, decided to propose the concept of a regional neutron source based in Austria. Regler is an experimental particle physicist who worked for ten years at CERN and is head of the experimental department of the only large institute for experimental high energy physics in Austria. In Bratislava in October 1990, Regler presented the concept to a group of Central European scientists and asked them to consider whether they would find a pulsed neutron spallation source or a synchrotron a more valuable instrument. This can be considered as the pre-foresight stage of the project.

During his tenure at CERN, Regler had established a strong link with Dr. C. Rubbia (a Nobel Prize winner and Director-General of CERN). He discussed the concept with Rubbia in January 1991 and received his support, since it fitted in well with Rubbia's plans for the reorganisation of research in Central Europe. Armed with this support, Regler attended another meeting in Bratislava at which Rubbia and the Czechoslovak Minister for Science and Research were present. At this meeting, a decision was made to proceed with the development of AUSTRON, a neutron spallation source based on a rapid cycling proton synchrotron.

The project then entered the main foresight phase; it was given impetus by a meeting hosted by Rubbia at CERN in October 1991 at which 30 leading European scientists representing more than 50 research institutes unanimously endorsed the proposal and defined the main parameters of the AUSTRON project. In Regler's words, "AUSTRON will join eastern and western European countries in a collaborative scientific effort".

To be attractive, a new neutron spallation source must offer performance equal to or better than that of the ISIS facility. The AUSTRON concept is an accelerator with a specially tailored design that makes it possible to achieve a high beam power while maintaining a relatively simple target based on an edge-cooled design. The available peak neutron flux will be comparable to what is currently available at ISIS.

In the ensuing months, with the support of several directors of Austrian research institutes, Regler and Professor P. Skalicky, Rector of the Technical University of Vienna and a member of the *ad hoc* feasibility study for ESRF, intensively lobbied the Austrian Government. The case for AUSTRON was strengthened when it was designated as one of the three major projects of the "Centres of Excellence" project of the Central European Initiative, the others being the ELETTRA synchrotron in Trieste and the new research reactor in Budapest. Rubbia's strong support also helped convince Dr. E. Busek, the Austrian Vice-Chancellor and Minister for Science and Technology, of the worth of the project. At the end of December 1992, Dr. Busek officially declared that the Austrian Government would support AUSTRON on the basis of an Austrian contribution of one-third of the total project cost, estimated at Sch 3 billion or ECU 220 million, provided that partner countries shared the remaining cost. A town in lower Austria offered a site and the necessary infrastructure.

Discussions then began with potential partners in other countries, and a major meeting was organised by the proponents of AUSTRON in Vienna in May 1992. Called "The International Meeting on an Advanced Spallation Neutron Source", the meeting was hosted by the Federal Economic Chamber of Austria, thereby demonstrating the support of the Austrian industrial community. It was attended by senior Austrian government officials and some 100 scientists from 15 countries, including heads of major laboratories. Technical presentations on AUSTRON's structure and research goals were presented. At the meeting, the Austrian Ministry for Science and Research supported the establishment of an AUSTRON Planning Office in Vienna and an Accelerator Study Group hosted by CERN to carry out the development of technical parameters.

The international status of the project was emphasised by the creation of an International Steering Committee in Vienna in October 1993. The committee was chaired by Dr. A. Furrer of Switzerland and its members included distinguished scientists from countries in western and central Europe.

The work on AUSTRON's technical features has continued, with the support of the teams in Vienna and CERN and the members of the International Steering Committee. The current organisational structure is shown in Figure 2, which illustrates the complex structure needed to advance a megascience project. Of vital importance is the AUSTRON team, which provides a strong link between the scientific community and the political stakeholders. Further, there is significant input from experts from other international facilities. With the assistance of personnel from ISIS and SINQ (the Swiss continuous neutron spallation source currently under construction at Villigen), a pre-feasibility study was completed by October 1993. During these studies, it became clear that the beam power could be doubled relatively cheaply to make it a more powerful source and that AUSTRON would also be able to supply ion beams for cancer therapy, making it a much more versatile facility than originally envisaged. A detailed feasibility study was completed in November 1994. Governments will now decide about participation in the light of advice from their scientific communities and the continuing discussions and presentations that have taken place at government level in a number of countries as the project has developed.

Lessons from the case study

While it is still too early to say whether AUSTRON will be a successful mega-science project, it has so far appeared to have the right elements:
- committed scientists as champions;
- the support of leading national and European scientists from the start of the process through pre-foresight to the main foresight phase;
- the strong support of Austrian industry;
- a strong commitment from the Austrian Government to fund one-third of the cost, provided that the remainder can be found internationally;
- a determination to ensure linking of the bottom-up and top-down processes from the inception of the project;
- systematic forward planning from the early stages.

Figure 2. AUSTRON feasibility study: organisation chart

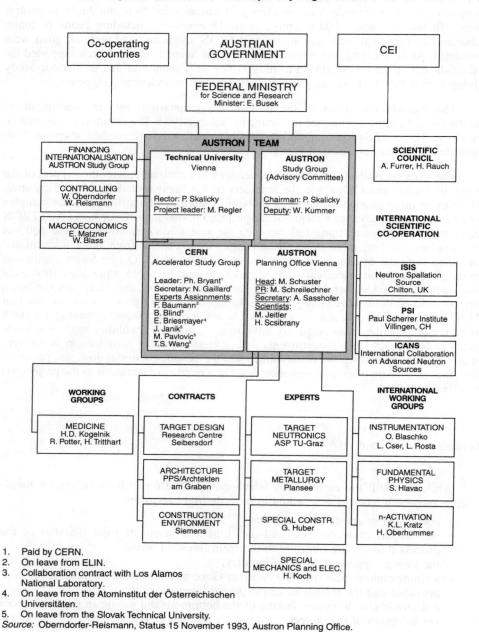

1. Paid by CERN.
2. On leave from ELIN.
3. Collaboration contract with Los Alamos National Laboratory.
4. On leave from the Atominstitut der Österreichischen Universitäten.
5. On leave from the Slovak Technical University.

Source: Oberndorfer-Reismann, Status 15 November 1993, Austron Planning Office.

5.   Framework for successful megaprojects on an international scale

In elaborating the principles discussed in Sections 2 and 3, the case studies make manifest a number of elements essential for successful megaprojects on an international scale. They are: 1) the need for a foresight process; 2) the need for a forum outside government to carry out foresight and to advance projects; 3) the need for the support of national governments; 4) the significant role of champions; 5) the need for forward planning.

The need for a foresight process

Successful megascience projects are clearly those for which a well-defined research foresight exercise has taken place. Such an exercise is a necessary but not sufficient condition for success. Without a clear definition of the scope, scale, and location of a project or identification of possible alternatives or possible difficulties, the project will advance with difficulty, if at all, and the outcome will be less than optimal. The case study of the International Space Station illustrates the need for a foresight process at an early stage in the development of an international megaproject. The European High Performance Laser Facility discussed in Chapter 2 of the present volume offers a further example. Horizon 2000, ESRF, and AUSTRON show instead how a foresight process can dramatically improve the chances that a multinational megascience project will succeed.

A significant point that emerges from the case studies is the role that small countries can play in developing megascience projects. In several of the early megascience projects, the principal role was taken by one or more major countries, and the facilities were set up as bilateral or trilateral projects. Subsequently, other countries, particularly small countries, have been allowed to use such facilities, on a peer review basis and usually as members of international consortia. However, pressures on national budgets have forced partner countries increasingly to restrict free access and to seek payment in cash or kind for use of facilities. At CERN, for example, small countries have been allowed to join at reduced rates, while at ILL, the three partners (France, Germany, and the United Kingdom) have allowed Austria, Spain, and Switzerland to use the facilities on payment of a small fee (a few per cent of annual operating expenses) as so-called scientific members.

To take full advantage of such participation, small countries must have a national capacity to train students and plan proposals. The need to plan on the basis of smaller budgets often leads to novel approaches to developing equipment and facilities. Involving small countries in foresight exercises for megaprojects from the early stages might therefore provide useful inputs. The experience of ESRF and now of AUSTRON indicates that such an approach is manageable and, indeed, desirable when considering new megascience proposals.

The need for an extra-governmental forum to carry out foresight and advance projects

In general, proposals come before governments for decision not through perfectly rational processes but shaped by events unrelated to the proposals, *e.g.* forthcoming elections and the need to gain political mileage, discreet or overt lobbying, or the influence of champions. For national projects, it has been recognised that there is considerable merit in having a body outside the day-to-day processes of government which can stimulate the definition of big science projects through the organised foresight exercises described in Section 3.

Such a body has been recognised as even more essential for supra-national projects. Thus, a Carnegie Commission report on science, technology and government (Kenyan, 1991) argued that the United States needed a forum outside government to study policy questions created by international scientific and technological co-operation (some 20 US government agencies engage in such co-operation). A report from the House of Lords Select Committee on Science and Technology (1991) in the United Kingdom also drew attention to the absence of a supranational forum capable of taking "a strategic overview of the work of large facilities and their development in the context of work done in national facilities".

In such a body, the scientific community must play the major role in determining priorities for megascience projects. The quality of projects must be determined by a bottom-up merit review process linked to structured foresight exercises.

As noted in Section 3, CERN has been active in promoting research foresight in high energy physics in Europe. It encouraged the formation of ECFA, which is essentially independent of CERN and provides a forum in which all European laboratories can make known their views about needs and future developments.[3] ECFA makes biennial surveys of personnel and budgets in particle physics in Europe, arranges exchange of information on specific topics such as detector technology, and provides input to CERN on the need for services, such as data networks, to the community.

On the broader international scene for high energy physics, ICFA was set up in 1976 under the auspices of the "Particles and Fields" Committee of the International Union of Pure and Applied Physics (IUPAP). Its task is to promote international co-operation on the construction and operation of new very high energy accelerators and to exchange information on regional installation projects. ICFA's 15 members are the directors of the world's major laboratories. ICFA organises workshops on topical subjects, and every three years, it holds a seminar on future perspectives in high energy physics.

ICFA has no direct powers and in the past has been unable to play a significant role when new national projects are being considered. However, at its meeting in Hamburg in May 1993, it took a more active stance with a strong statement on international collaboration (see OECD, 1995; and Anon., 1993*a* and 1993*b*). This statement argues that collaboration must start during the early stages of planning for large-scale facilities with a unique scientific potential, of which only one should exist (pre-foresight stage). Such facilities should be planned, designed, and, where appropriate, built in international collaboration.

There should be an agreement on an appropriate structure for the scientific community to review the scientific proposal for a such a facility (main foresight stage) before formal approaches are made to government. Governments must be kept informed of progress, but projects should not be put to governments until the world scientific community has agreed on the technical parameters and on the site. This statement clearly takes a step forward, but ICFA needs to follow it up by taking a stronger role as the international body carrying out foresight exercises in international high energy physics. This would mean a strengthened secretariat and a more formal structure, one to which governments should probably agree to give direct powers.

Other areas, *e.g.* space, astronomy, lasers, etc., also need better co-ordination. Perhaps the relevant international unions could set up bodies akin to ICFA with strengthened secretariats and formal structures to carry out foresight exercises. Precedents for collaborative international foresight and forward planning exercises already exist for global distributed programmes [*e.g.* WCRP, World Ocean Circulation Experiment (WOCE), the Ocean Drilling Program (ODP), etc.]

On the European scene, there has recently been a move to strengthen the role of ESF, which is composed of 54 member organisations from 20 countries, in foresight and forward planning for European science. ESF's role in the processes leading to ESRF (see Section 4) is an excellent illustration of the role that can be played by an extra-governmental body. Its moves to develop links to the European Union recognise the need for a European science policy forum capable of playing a key role in shaping European research by defining future requirements for major scientific facilities in Europe, in assessing long-term prospects for scientific developments, and in monitoring the scientific output of major national and European laboratories (Abbott, 1993*a* and 1993*b*; and ESF, 1993). Such a role had been foreshadowed earlier (Papon, 1994). Discussions are still continuing on the clearly recognised need for a focal point for European science.

The need for the support of national governments

National governments play a critical role in megascience because of the scale of the cost and risk elements involved. They have three distinct options: 1) they can reject proposals, modify them, or even discourage modified ones; 2) they can agree to underwrite the whole or part of the projected costs, either of the project proposed or of a modified one; 3) they can decide that the cost and risk elements are such that, despite the worth of the proposal, the only safe route is bilateral or multilateral co-operation. What happens in any given case depends crucially on the particular country and the political orientation of its government, the nature of the project, and the timing. The substantial international collaboration in science and technology that has taken place in Europe in recent decades, for example, often predisposes European governments to look for solutions that are still quite foreign to American administrations, which still tend to prefer independent action (Williams, 1988).

When considering their role in megascience projects, governments must consider elements beyond scientific value; the social and political significance of a project, whether for its contribution to economic development, industrial potential or national

41

prestige, influences their final decision. The need to link the scientific undertaking to these concerns affects how scientists present proposals to governments, and foresight processes must therefore ensure that big science is placed in a broader context that includes social aspects.

The scientist's world is essentially a technological one, and technological needs and opportunities arising from megascience can strongly influence a government's perceptions of the worth of a proposal. Cost/benefit studies of big projects at CERN (Schmied, 1975; also, Bianchi-Streit *et al.*, 1985) and ESA (ESA, 1980) show that an economic utility multiplier effect, at work through industrial contractors who create new products, reduce costs and increase sales of high technology items, can result in significant economic gains (see also Chapter 4). While this cannot be construed as the major justification for large multinational scientific enterprises, it is clearly a potentially significant factor when governments consider their participation.

As Sections 3 and 4 show, the bigger the project, the higher the political profile. When political leaders become involved and national prestige is seen to be at stake, the decision-making process can become protracted and difficult, particularly in democratic societies. As Kay (1994) points out, under the prevailing norms of democratic decision making – whether defined as popular consent or as agreement among elites – megaprojects present politicians and bureaucrats with a dilemma. Large-scale, expensive, risky, and uncertain projects cannot be undertaken without broad political consensus. However, the development of such a consensus inevitably leads to increases of scale and expense as well as attempts to reduce risk and uncertainty, and all this jeopardises the project's chances of political acceptance, as in the case of the International Space Station discussed above. In extreme cases, senior political figures determine the shelving or reducing of major programmes (Williams, 1988). The linking of the bottom-up and top-down processes must be effective if political support is to be secured. While R&D elites are often unused to dealing with the political process, it is now a fact of life that they must do so to ensure the success of a megaproject. The case studies of Horizon 2000, ESRF and AUSTRON (Section 4) are examples of how bottom-up/top-down interaction helps gain support from national governments.

Even when a megascience project is decided upon and is in operation, the actions of partner governments can affect its success. A change of government may bring to power a political party with different fiscal priorities; large expenditures in megascience projects may be criticised and commitments may be called into question. For CERN, for example, Krige (1991) has documented the conflict between the United Kingdom and France over the limitation of the CERN budget proposed by the United Kingdom in the late 1950s and early 1960s. In this case, the will of the group prevailed, and the United Kingdom was forced to continue funding at an appropriate level.

Despite these problems, there are many outstanding examples of international megascience projects for which difficulties have been resolved and consensus has been reached on funding, location, operation, etc. ILL and ESRF both stand at the forefront of scientific excellence, with facilities that no single nation could afford as well as harmonious management and funding arrangements.

The role of champions

Success in creating new megascience projects, like other major human achievements, often owes much and sometimes everything to a single individual who by some mixture of competence, conviction, and force of persuasion succeeds in securing the necessary resources, wins sufficient time and overcomes all obstacles. These champions play a significant part in dealing with governments in situations where personal prestige, diplomatic talent, and personal or professional links can play a decisive role. For Horizon 2000, Bonnet was the champion, for ESRF, it was Farge, and for AUSTRON it was Regler.

These individuals are all Europeans, because the case studies presented above mainly concerned European megaprojects, but there are many examples of champions for US megascience projects. As Pestre and Krige (1992) point out, there was a fusion of pure science, technology, and engineering in post-war US high energy physics. This symbiosis produced individuals with scientific, engineering, and entrepreneurial qualities who led the growth of US big science, following the earlier example of E.O. Lawrence. The US system for advanced education, which links graduate instruction with direct research experience, is justly regarded as a uniquely effective way to train creative and productive scientists, and US megascience projects have provided them with invaluable training and experience in critical fields.

This symbiosis developed more slowly in Europe owing to the traditional separation of pure science from applied science and engineering. In Europe, the engineers were the drivers. However, with time, European scientists have become skilful in handling big projects. There is, for example, Carlo Rubbia who played a very significant role in the development of CERN. As mentioned with respect to AUSTRON, he has also been able to exert significant influence on the development of science in Eastern Europe.

The scientific champion's role is well illustrated in the case of Le Nautile, a manned submersible vehicle for deep-sea observation and experimentation at depths of up to 6 000 m (Papon, 1994). It was conceived in 1980 by a small group of scientists in the French *Centre national pour l'exploitation des océans,* under the leadership of Prof. X. Le Pichon. Despite open scepticism from the majority of French marine scientists, who saw the project as severe competition for the limited funds available, Le Pichon was able to pilot it through the bureaucratic process by winning support at ministerial level and securing the necessary funding. Le Nautile was launched in 1985 and proved to be extremely successful, as shown by the fact that there is now not enough time available at depth to satisfy demands from the scientific community. In this case, the research foresight process was somewhat informal and the role of the champion was paramount.

The importance of the post-foresight phase

The specific arrangements for carrying out and managing megascience projects are one of the factors that potential funding bodies weigh when deciding on commitment. This is a much more important aspect today than it would have been two decades ago when there was much less experience with major projects. Given the scale of megascience and big technology programmes, one might think that decisions were always taken following an extremely thorough analysis, and after a system providing for both real time and *ex post facto* evaluations was set up to monitor progress. The extensive literature shows that, historically, this has often not been the case, particularly for large technology projects (Williams, 1988; Averch, 1993; and Faucher and Fitzgibbons, 1993).

Such large-scale projects have high risks – technological, economic, and political – particularly when a technological breakthrough or the construction of a new technology is involved. Institutional responses to risk management will increasingly determine technological choice and commitment. Megascience projects require the mobilisation of ever greater human and technical resources and thus the creation of an appropriate organisational structure. Inappropriate organisational arrangements are as much a cause for failure as insufficient financing or irreconcilable political opposition. A new international megascience project therefore requires careful forward planning, particularly for an appropriate organisational structure. Western Europe has the most experience of international megafacility organisation (*e.g.* CERN, ILL, ESRF), but there are more and more examples of distributed projects linked at an international scale through appropriate structures (*e.g.* WCRP, ODP).

The question of site selection is clearly an important factor in the forward planning process. When a suitable site has been identified in the foresight process and has the strong support of the scientific community, and if possible of the national scientific organisations, this helps smooth out problems that may arise in the post-foresight phase when political considerations become significant. If this issue is not resolved early, the project will fail, as did the European High Performance Laser Facility. The successful linking of two major facilities on one site, as for ILL and ESRF at Grenoble, raises interesting questions about the future siting of megascience facilities. The possibility of drawing on a skilled work force with an established infrastructure may become a significant factor. Cost reductions achieved by sharing personnel and facilities will be increasingly significant as the costs of megascience facilities increase. Unless there are excellent scientific reasons for a greenfield site in a remote area, *e.g.* the construction of a new telescope in Chile to realise the best viewing conditions, it is likely that megascience facilities will tend to cluster in established areas.

It is clear that some megascience projects are best pursued at world level. Research on fusion for generating thermonuclear energy is one of these, and there is extensive interaction among the scientific communities concerned in Europe, the United States, Japan, and Russia. However, the formulation of a single world programme with a single location for a particular machine will require a completely new approach to organisational structure. In 1991, the four parties agreed to carry out design studies for ITER; these should be completed by 1997. Construction costs have been estimated at about $5 billion (in 1992 dollars). Forward planning will be essential to the development and operation of a successful world fusion facility.

Notes

1. The corresponding French term, *prospective*, differs in certain respects from "research fore-sight" (see Godet, 1986; Papon, 1988; and Martin and Irvine, 1989). However, the differences are relatively minor, so that research foresight can be used as the nearest English equivalent.
2. Professor J. White of the Australian National University, a former director of ILL, and Dr. G. Stirling, of the Engineering and Physical Sciences Research Council, kindly supplied information on the early days of the ESRF project.
3. See OECD, 1995, for a detailed discussion of ECFA and ICFA. I am also grateful to Dr. G. Stirling (United Kingdom) for information on these bodies.

References

ANON. (1984), "France in a Stew over Synchrotron Decision", *New Scientist*, 29 November, p. 7.

ANON. (1993*a*), "Guidelines Stress Collaboration at an Early Stage" *Europhysics News*, Vol. 24, p. 83.

ANON. (1993*b*), "ICFA On International Collaboration", *CERN Courier*, pp. 1–2.

ABBOTT, A. (1993*a*), "Brussels Gives Bigger Role to European Science Foundation", *Nature*, Vol. 366, p. 396.

ABBOTT, A. (1993*b*), "Foundation Seeks Enhanced Role in Europe", *Nature*, Vol. 366, 18 November, p. 193.

ASTEC (1990), *Setting Directions for Australian Research*, AGPS, Canberra.

ASTEC (1991), *Research and Technology: Future Directions*, AGPS, Canberra.

ASTEC (1992), *Major National Research Facilities – A National Program*, AGPS, Canberra.

ATKINSON, H. (1993), "Conclusions", in *The Implementation of the ESA Convention – Lessons from the Past*, Proceedings of an international colloquium held in Florence, October 1993, Martinus Nijhoff Publishers, Dordecht, pp. 223-229.

AVERCH, H.A. (1993), "Criteria and Rules for Evaluating Competing Megascience Projects", *Science and Public Policy*, Vol. 20, pp. 105-113.

BIANCHI-STREIT, M., N. BLACKBURNE, R. BUDDLE, H. REITZ, B. SAGNELL, H. SCHMIED, and B. SCHORR (1985), *Utilité économique des contrats du CERN*, 2nd study, CERN, Geneva.

BURCH, G.J. and G. TEGART (1994), "Big Science for Small Nations: Evaluating Options to Invest in Research Facilities", in J. Irvine, ed., *Equipping Science for the 21st Century*, forthcoming.

BURGESS, D. and H. HUTCHINSON (1993), "Stronger than Atoms", *New Scientist*, 20 November, pp. 28-33.

CAVALLO, G. (1993), personal communication.

COATES, J.F. (1985), "Foresight in Federal Government Policy Making", *Futures Research Quarterly*, Vol. 1, pp. 29-53.

COMMISSION OF THE EUROPEAN COMMUNITIES (1991), *Large Installations Plan (1989-1992): Reports of the Study Panels*, EUR-13539, CEC, Brussels.

DUTTON, A. and L. Crowe (1988), "Setting Priorities Among Scientific Initiatives", *American Scientist*, Vol. 76, pp. 599-603.

ESA (1984), *European Space Science: Horizon 2000*, SP-1070, ESA, Paris.

ESA (1990), *Les effets économiques indirects des programmes du ESA* BR-63, ESA, Paris.

EUROPEAN SCIENCE FOUNDATION (ESF) (1979), *European Synchrotron Radiation Facility*; Part 1, *The Feasibility Study*, presented by Y. Farge; Supplement 1, *The Scientific Case*, Y. Farge and P.J. Duke, eds.; Supplement 2, *The Machine*, D.J. Thompson and M.W. Poole, eds.; Supplement 3, *Instrumentation*, B. Buras and G.V. Marr, eds., European Science Foundation, Strasbourg.

ESF (1989), *The Status of Research with Synchrotron Radiation in Europe: 1: VUV/XUV*, No. SCI-1021, ESF, Strasbourg.

ESF (1993), *ESF: The Next Decade: A Reappraisal of ESF's Strategic Mission*, Final Draft Report, November, ESF, Strasbourg.

FAUCHER, P. and K. FITZGIBBONS (1993), "Public Demand and the Management of Technological Risk in Large-Scale Projects", *Science and Public Policy*, Vol. 20, pp. 173-185.

GALISON, P. and B. HEVLY, eds. (1992), *Big Science*, Stanford University Press, Stanford, California.

GODET, M. (1986), "Introduction to la Prospective", *Futures*, Vol. 18, pp. 134-157.

HAYWARD, K. (1993), "International Collaboration in Space: The Case of the International Space Station Freedom", *Science and Public Policy*, Vol. 20, pp. 333-341.

HERMANN, A., J. KRIGE, U. MERSITS and D. PESTRE (1987-1994), *History of CERN*, Vol. I, *Launching the European Organisation for Nuclear Research* (1987); Vol. II, *Building and Running the Laboratory 1954-1965* (1990); Vol. III, J. Krige, ed., *The Years of Consolidation 1966-80* (1994), North Holland, Amsterdam.

HEVLY, B. (1992), "Reflections on Big Science and Big History", in Galison and Hevly, eds., *Big Science*, pp. 345-363, Stanford University Press, Stanford, California.

HICKS, E.K. and W. van ROSSUM, eds. (1991), *Policy Development and Big Science*, Proceedings of colloquium held in Amsterdam, September 1989, North Holland, Amsterdam.

HOUSE OF LORDS SELECT COMMITTEE ON SCIENCE AND TECHNOLOGY (1990-91), Second Report, *International Scientific Programmes*, HMSO, London.

IRVINE, J., ed. (1994), *Equipping Science for the 21st Century*, Proceedings of the conference held in Amsterdam, October 1992, forthcoming./p>

KAY, W.D. (1994), "Democracy and Super Technologies: The Politics of the Space Shuttle and Space Station Freedom", *Science, Technology and Human Values*, Vol. 19, pp. 131-151.

KENYAN, A. (1991), *"The United States as a Partner in Scientific and Technological Co-operation: Some Perspectives from Across the Atlantic*, Carnegie Commission on Science, Technology and Government, New York.

KRIGE, J. (1991), "Changing National Policies on Acceptable Levels in the CERN Budget: An Historical Case Study of Two Turning Points", in E. K. Hicks and E. van Rossum, eds., *Policy Development and Big Science*, Proceedings of a colloquium held in Amsterdam, September 1989, pp. 8–14, North Holland, Amsterdam.

KRIGE, J., ed. (1992), "Choosing Big Technologies: A Comparative Analysis", *History and Technology*, Vol. 9:1-4. Reprinted as: Krige, J., ed. (1993), *Choosing Big Technologies*, Harwood Academic Publishers, Chur, Switzerland.

LOGSDON, J.M. (1992), "Choosing Big Technologies: Examples from the US Space Program", *History and Technology*, Vol. 9:1-4, pp. 139-150.

MARTIN, B.R. and J. IRVINE (1989), *Research Foresight: Priority Setting in Science*, Pinter Publishers, London.

OECD (1987), *Evaluation of Research: A Selection of Current Practices*, Paris.

OECD (1991), *Choosing Priorities in Science and Technology*, Paris.

OECD (1993*a*), *Astronomy*, The Megascience Forum series, Paris.

OECD (1993*b*), *Deep Drilling*, The Megascience Forum series,Paris.

OECD (1993*c*), *Megascience and Its Background*, The Megascience Forum series, Paris.

OECD (1994*a*), *Global Change of Planet Earth*, The Megascience Forum series, Paris.

OECD (1994*b*), *Oceanography*, The Megascience Forum series, Paris.

OECD (1994*c*), *Neutron Beams and Synchrotron Radiation Sources*, The Megascience Forum series, Paris.

OECD (1995), *Particle Physics*, The Megascience Forum series, Paris.

PAPON, P. (1994), "Long-Term Planning for the Equipment of Science: The Contributions of Research Foresight and Technological Forecasting" in Irvine, *Equipping Science for the 21st Century*, forthcoming.

PAPON, P. (1988), "Is a Prospective of Science Feasible?", *Futures*, Vol. 20, pp. 402-409.

PESTRE, D. and J. KRIGE (1992), "Some Early Thoughts on the History of CERN", in P. Galison and B. Hevly, eds., *Big Science*, pp. 78-99, Stanford University Press, Stanford.

PRESIDENT'S COUNCIL OF ADVISORS ON SCIENCE AND TECHNOLOGY (1992), *Megaprojects in the Sciences*, OSTP, Washington, D.C.

SCHMIED, H. (1975), *A Study of Economic Utility Resulting From CERN Contracts*, CERN, Geneva.

SKOLNIKOFF, E. (1993), "New International Trends Affecting Science and Technology", *Science and Public Policy*, Vol. 20, pp. 115-125.

SMITH, R.W. (1993), "The History of Big Science", in OECD, *Megascience and Its Background*, pp. 9–23, The Megascience Forum serie, Paris.

WEINBERG, A.M. (1963), "Criteria for Scientific Choice", *Minerva*, Vol. 1, pp. 159-71.

WEINBERG, A.M. (1967), *Reflections on Big Science*, The MIT Press, Cambridge, Mass.

WILLIAMS, R. (1988), "Choosing Big Technologies: The Core Issues", *History and Technology*, Vol. 9:1-4, pp. 223-234.

Chapter 2

MEGASCIENCE AND NATIONAL DECISION-MAKING PROCESSES

by

François Jacq
Centre de sociologie de l'innovation, Paris

Executive summary

1.   The role of decision making in megascience

Although decision-making processes have always been important in megascience, four factors contribute to reinforcing their role:

- rising costs, which, in conjunction with new budgetary constraints, require making more difficult choices;
- the size and complexity of facilities, which call for specific procedures for managing decisions;
- the need for investments to be both scientifically and economically viable;
- internationalisation, the result of the two preceding factors, which means greater intergovernmental co-operation for building facilities.

These factors have made decision making more complex, and it now involves processes commensurate with the size of the project. Decisions can no longer be viewed as a linear sequence: provision has to be made for adaptation and for promoting project flexibility.

Thus, it is during the decision-making process that major choices affecting the future of the project are made.

2. Definition of megascience and impact on decision-making modes

Criteria for defining megascience

The OECD Megascience Forum has proposed a definition of a megascience project as "a scientific initiative encompassing the facilities, instruments, human resources, and logistic support required to address a set of scientific problems of such significance, scope and complexity as to require an unusually large-scale collaborative effort".

A number of other elements are also important:

– the amount of funding required;
– the unique character of the installation;
– the nature of the programme (fixed-site or distributed).

However, there is no universal criterion for identifying a megascience project. As a result, the decision-making process will be very different, depending on the element that seems most significant.

Diversity in the handling of decisions

A comparative review of the situation in various member countries of the Forum shows a great deal of diversity. First, some countries recognise the category and some do not. Second, the small or medium-sized countries systematically set their policy in an international framework, while others concentrate on a national balance. Third, there may or may not be specific procedures for examining projects for major facilities.

Divergent approaches

The absence of any uniform approach to decision making stems from the diversity of the actors involved in the different countries. As a first approximation, four separate approaches can be identified:

– The deliberately international approach supported by medium-sized countries, whereby megascience is regarded as international and procedures are devised accordingly.
– An "agency" approach, in which the agencies remain in control and take on the task of promoting new projects as part of their existing activities. Megascience is seen as fitting into the ordinary decision-making process and emphasis is placed on local equilibria, occasionally to the detriment of overall coherence.
– A national science policy approach, based upon choices made in terms of national independence. Preference will sometimes be given to smaller projects set up within the country rather than to a major international project.
– A purely scientific approach, which emphasises the development of the different disciplines in their own right, with no interdisciplinary review.

In any particular country, one or another of these options will predominate. This explains why certain countries hesitate to embark upon an overall review of megascience projects based on uniform rules. These different positions have to be taken into account when interpreting the difficulties encountered in reaching certain decisions or in coming to an agreement.

3. The evolution of decision making

A brief historical overview

The history of big science can be approximately divided into three periods. Before the Second World War, major facilities were of limited significance. They were either set up by individual entrepreneurs who had managed to interest and persuade a wide variety of collaborators or they stemmed from large-scale government initiatives in which many projects competed for consideration. The former model stressed engineering and originality, the latter conventionality and enormous size.

With the recognition of the importance of big science, the Second World War ushered in a new era. Over two decades (1940-60), science and government had a tacit understanding which quite explicitly encouraged the expansion of new scientific fields such as nuclear physics, high energy physics, and radio astronomy. During this period, scientific entrepreneurs still played an important role in decision making, but they had increasingly to submit to a competitive process arbitrated by committees which tended to prefer the safest solutions.

In the early 1960s, questions were first raised about big science, and projects had to provide more solid justification. Individual entrepreneurs gradually gave way to powerful agencies set up to support particular scientific and technical fields; the growth of CERN in the 1960s offers an excellent example. Decision-making procedures began to favour projects that had been formulated gradually within the agencies' own structures as component parts of their programme. During this period, the race for facilities was still marked by stiff competition, but the scientific communities became considerably more structured and more attention was paid to technically innovative projects. This was a way of responding to the weakening of the tacit covenant between science and government. Finally, international co-operation in various fields began in Europe, in the form of agencies with a number of member countries: CERN (European Organisation for Nuclear Physics), ESA (European Space Agency), ESO (European Southern Observatory).

A transition

The last few years have probably been a period of transition. Initially, constraints on big science intensified. Budget cuts, the questioning of scientific undertakings, and the increasing size of facilities all have made big science an issue.

Policy for major facilities has tended to shift from the national to the international level; despite the problems involved, as well as the hesitancy of certain countries, it is indeed becoming increasingly difficult to conceive of a purely national facility for research at the knowledge frontier.

Moreover, governments now seek to make the best possible use of their funds and to satisfy the broadest scientific communities. Questions are also being asked about the future of big science (industrialisation, distribution of work, mobilisation of large resources in certain fields), about new priorities, such as incorporating decision making into a framework of concerted development, reviewing projects in a longer-term perspective, emphasising communities of users, and involving a number of design teams at an early stage.

Finally, distributed big science programmes (such as climate studies) need specific forms of intergovernmental co-operation and hence decision-making procedures designed explicitly as a means of co-ordination.

These different factors mean that decision-making procedures now incorporate new criteria. They also draw attention to the need to encourage greater flexibility and to involve the largest possible number of partners.

4. Major trends in decision-making processes

The impact of internationalisation

Internationalisation has become a major constraint on decision making in megascience. Every government urges its scientists to form alliances, and this makes decision making more complex. Indeed, it is a delicate matter to maintain a balance between national policy and a choice for international co-operation. As things stand, internationalisation can have an adverse effect by creating greater uncertainty around projects. The number of obstacles increases with the need to:

- find an appropriate structure;
- establish ''fair return'' clauses and sharing of economic spinoff;
- harmonise the needs of the different partners;
- develop data interpretation resources;
- establish training facilities for national researchers.

The decision-making process must provide an adequate forum for handling these tensions and for avoiding any opportunist or short-sighted behaviour by the different partners. In particular, the monitoring organisations or committees need to consider these issues at a very early stage.

Internationalisation is nevertheless a positive factor. There is no doubt that it complicates decision making, but beyond the sharing of costs, it also serves to promote scientific dynamism, by bringing together different scientific groups which, through their collaboration, produce many innovations. Therefore, specific procedures and incentives should exist to support this trend.

Decision-making processes as a means of co-ordination

Because of their enormous size, certain megascience facilities are unique. Yet, in the past, scientific practice was based on the replication of experiments. To compensate for the lack of replication and to make sure that major facilities are in fact valid, the various potential users and the technical and political partners must come to agreement during the decision-making process. It is no longer a matter of procuring a single decision, but of endorsing a whole series of choices (scientific, technical, and economic) and of guaranteeing the kind of scientific practice that the chosen instrument will ensure. In this way, countries have a solid guarantee that the proposed activities have a sound basis.

Only by reaching a consensus is it possible to guard against a tendency for projects to get out of control, carried along only by the momentum of the growth of megascience. However, consensus is not a static equilibrium. Consensus should be seen in terms of a debate in which all who take part formulate their needs and interests, and where these are gradually incorporated into the shape of the project. It is therefore extremely important to keep a close watch on this process. Decisions in big science, properly managed, may in fact be good examples of democratic consultation processes.

Procedures instrumental in decision making

Procedures model projects to a considerable extent. They determine the form the projects take and have a regulating role which should logically favour the emergence of the widest and richest consensus possible. The principal elements are:
- the way in which the proposals are reviewed;
- the committees involved;
- the implicit and explicit rules governing project follow-up.

The criteria that are set up constitute the standards to which the actors will conform. However, they also indicate the margins for negotiation and reformulation which the teams involved may use as they try to respond as best they can to the need to make a convincing case.

As an instrument for regulation, procedures – or their absence – orient the decision-making processes. The possibility of adverse effects should be stressed: for example, if international co-operation is simply advocated without working out specific details, then it may turn out to be merely for show, a shaky combination of miscellaneous teams, and the project may fail. Accordingly, norms and procedures must be examined with care.

What form of decision-making process?

As megascience has evolved, the various constraints affecting decisions have made the decision-making process more complex. There are three main requirements.

With the weakening of the tacit understanding between science and government, science today no longer enjoys the privilege of "extraterritoriality" and must confront other social and economic priorities. Against this background, the decision-making process must adopt procedures which guarantee to the political authorities that the undertakings envisaged are relevant.

If the decision-making process is to work properly, it is essential that all concerned, particularly governments and the political authorities, should be brought together at an early stage. It should be related to an overall review of megascience operations.

More generally, decision making must become a flexible process, accommodating development and reorientation, and therefore made up of a large number of feedback loops involving scientific needs, political desires, technical development, and social effects. This will ensure that projects are implemented efficiently.

5. The elements of decision making

Analysis of the decision

Having identified the major features of decision-making processes, stressed their essential role, and shown that they influence significantly the nature of projects, the discussion turns to an examination of the elements that help crystallise decisions and the nature of their influence. What opinions and interpretations matter in decision making? How are decision making modes structured, and what are the consequences to be expected from particular patterns?

Parameters and arguments entering the decision

This section analyses a series of factors which make it possible to take decisions more or less quickly and diminish the risks involved.

The scientific programme and its development

A prerequisite for all projects, and one which is now fairly well satisfied, is the definition of a serious scientific programme accepted by the community as a whole. Unanimity is built through research foresight seminars, meetings of scientific committees, and exchanges between scientists. The decisive criteria are related to the dynamics of the programme proposed and its modularity.

On the first point, all good programmes are usually innovative. They may produce a very great variety of results, but they are not necessarily capable of creating the broadest prospects for the evolution of the field. A distinction can therefore be drawn between highly dynamic and conventional programmes. As an example of the latter, some of the accelerators used in particle physics offer very rich programmes, but they may appear not to be very open to new fields, so that over the longer term, there is a risk of stagnation.

On the second point, a programme very closely focused on a particular field does not allow for involving various groups of researchers who can explore complementary aspects of the questions studied. There is a spontaneous tendency to prefer conventional programmes which are less dynamic and not very modular, an attitude which can be dangerous. It would seem appropriate to recommend the opposite attitude.

Expected spinoffs and economic contribution

A distinction should be drawn between research based upon pure curiosity and research aimed at immediate application. Arguments that draw attention to direct spinoff play an important role upstream in the process, but only affect the few disciplines that can attest to immediate results and that clearly receive preferential status (*e.g.* the exploration of the human genome).

On the other hand, peripheral spinoff comes into play much later in the definition and elaboration of projects and offers means of attracting important actors, such as financial authorities and industrialists. Increasing attention is then given to the development of specific industrial technologies.

The danger of such approaches, in particular for strongly oriented programmes such as the genome, remains the focus on a few narrow technologies; this is a source of long-term impoverishment and works against possibilities for later redeployment.

Cost and budgetary constraints

The cost of facilities enters the decision-making processes in various ways.

In each country, the cost of the facility must be integrated into the national budget and into the planned development of its resources. As a result, projects are sometimes defined in terms of what can be obtained with a given financial envelope.

The cost must fit into a planning approach in order to smooth out expenditure peaks and contingencies. A discipline will obtain better results if it can show the need for an investment at a particular moment.

Cost sharing is clearly advantageous to a project, although it can lead to creating "monsters" that ultimately do not cost less, because they are difficult to manage, when efficient co-ordination mechanisms among partners do not exist. Ensuring efficiency depends on establishing effective co-ordination procedures.

Finally, the cumulative costs of megascience projects cause concern at times and can help increase public deficits. A guarantee that expenditure will be strictly controlled has become an essential condition. It requires, in particular, a body of preparatory work and technical and industrial studies as the decision-making process proceeds.

The role of competition and alternative prospects

The traditional pattern, in which a project threatened by foreign competition easily succeeded, is tending to die out. The existence of the LHC was not enough to save the SSC, which suffered from other weaknesses. Similarly, when there are many projects in a particular field, decision-makers will be cautious and tend to postpone the decision. In the present transitional phase, competition plays an ambiguous role: it encourages postponement of decisions while favouring rather hasty compromises in order to resolve conflicts. From a normative point of view, it is essential to support the incorporation of several complementary perspectives in a project, a process which can only enrich it. The danger, of course, lies in unsatisfactory compromises.

Integration in global science policy

The internationalisation of megascience raises the delicate problem of the relation between national policy and the development of new projects. As far as possible, each project fits into the general framework of national concerns and thus acquires additional support. However, governments accord particular importance to:

– directly contributing to a national priority, such as health or environment;
– sustaining the development of national communities.

A project that meets these criteria, although perhaps of lesser interest with respect to others, will tend to obtain a favourable decision in the absence of a balanced review of all priorities involving the various responsible authorities and the other disciplines. In particular, when there is no such review of megascience projects, certain high-profile sectors may have the advantage (this was once the case of high energy physics and today probably applies to molecular biology).

Community of users

Examining the link between the required investment and the number of potential users has become an important waypoint in decision making processes. Public authorities want to ensure that the installations are put to the best possible use, so it is important to bring together and mobilise groups of users at various levels – local, national, and international – and to take their wishes into account. Facility sharing and maximum use have become the rule. Thus, it is important to put forward projects of interest to a variety of users.

Project evolution: balancing planning and continuity

The evaluation of a megascience project requires precise assessment of how the project will evolve and, in particular, the investments it may require at a later stage. The project must be integrated into the multi-annual resource planning of a discipline.

The project must also incorporate longer-term considerations about the evolution of the communities concerned and possible changes to the facilities and teams. This highlights the need to foresee the funds that may be required to close down certain facilities and to link this question to the opening of any new facility. As this raises difficult problems, it is frequently neglected.

Status of technology and industrial alliances

If a megascience project is to proceed satisfactorily, complex technologies may have to be brought into play, with all the risks that this implies. To mitigate the latter, it is important to undertake a series of full-scale preparatory trials to test the reliability of the solutions adopted.

The more a project can demonstrate its proficiency in this area, the more support it will receive. Since long-term economic spinoff is also a matter of concern to governments, this preparatory phase also allows them to obtain industry's views on the knowledge and experience it is acquiring and thus sharpen their views on the project.

The role of procedures

Procedures affect the form that projects take. For example, when a single committee reviews a number of competing projects, it will often prefer the most conventional project and the technologies that draw on the most powerful industrial systems. It is therefore important that procedures are available for controlling and orienting the decision-making process, so that it offers the various actors in the scientific, technical, industrial, and political communities the necessary opportunities for reaching consensus.

The role of the actors and the means of bringing them together

Because the decision-making process should encourage the various actors to become associated and to enter into discussions, one way of assessing a project is to examine how and how carefully it has brought them together (see above, for the role of procedures). In particular, the presence of political actors at an early stage can increase their awareness of the project's importance.

Influence of the finance ministries

In reviewing a project, the financial authorities use a different approach from the one used for scientific endorsement. They give greater emphasis to comparative aspects, and also tend to work towards defining a stable means of long-term financial review. They also seek to have a clear financial analysis that can be adjusted according to various objectives, and will prefer projects which offer possibilities for downward revision.

Duration and irreversibility

The overlap in the review procedures and the relative lack of formal decision-making procedures tend to increase the role of time and irreversibilities. A feeling of urgency leads to giving preference to the apparently most convenient solutions, often without undertaking an in-depth examination. As a result, any changes of direction may be costly.

To avoid an ultimately decisive irreversibility (choice of technology for a component, refusal to involve a particular partner, lack of funding for a particular year), the solution is the formation of feedback loops, which make it possible to review the project in the light of new constraints.

Structure of decision-making processes and lessons to be learned

Section 9 (Recommendations closely linked to the decision-making process) points out, in what is probably too general a way, several normative aspects which should be emphasized.

It is during the decision-making processes that megascience projects are definitively worked out. Many characteristic features that are found at a later stage may have their origin in this period. For each of these topics, several options are possible; their consequences, and the potential risks involved, are summarised above.

6. Follow-up to the decision

Implementation structures

There are four different types of partners:
- the body charged with building the installation or setting up the structures of a project;
- the body or structure to be charged with managing the project in the long term, which may be the one described above;
- the body holding and managing the funds assigned to the project;
- the body responsible for the undertaking, when it is not the one just mentioned.

The main problem is to clarify the relationships between these different partners, avoid redundancy, and ensure financial transparency. One frequent obstacle appears to be the lack of connection between the provider of funds and the body responsible for the project.

Three different patterns can be described:
- Fixed-site international projects, which raise, for the various countries involved, the problem of monitoring and the most suitable form of international agreement. For example, the flexibility of the memorandum of understanding may conceal serious risks to the subsequent stability of projects.
- Major distributed international programmes, still a fairly new category, for which the problem of setting up monitoring committees and finding original forms of co-operation has yet to be fully resolved.
- National or multilateral facilities, for which intergovernmental agencies probably provide one of the most satisfactory solutions.

The problem of financial management

Budgeting is an important part of the work. Although the budget share devoted to megascience is not as huge as has been claimed, the necessary concentration of resources in space and time does raise specific questions.

What is needed, in fact, is relatively uniform planning over time so that contingencies do not result in additional costs. In order to demonstrate rigorous management, it is necessary to establish long-term programming and close control over the growth in expenditure.

More practically, centralised funding allocations and concerted review would obviate the problem of wasted funds. Similarly, the institution of review structures that would systematically inform the authorities would allow them to avoid risky expenditures. Finally, special assistance to project managers would permit them to improve the allocation of expenditure.

Technical implementation

Like financing, technical implementation looks back to the decision-making process and the harmonisation of the relevant teams. Dispersal is a potential risk, if the construction of facilities is poorly co-ordinated and there is uncertainty about the availability of the proposed techniques. Two points deserve emphasis:

- A construction plan and a schedule which indicate the main technical should be established; it should be submitted with the budgetary review.
- Care should be taken to co-ordinate the work and preserve the modularity of the facility.

Conclusion

In the follow-up to the decision, there are inadequate links among:

- budgetary monitoring by the authorities or agencies involved;
- scientific monitoring by the scientific committees;
- technical implementation.

All countries try to strengthen the cohesion of these three often divergent forces to some extent. They do so especially because, in cases where megascience is not identified as a special category, there is a tendency to use methods similar to those used for small-science disciplines, which tolerate these divergent tendencies somewhat better.

The effects of budgetary approximations in megascience are much more perceptible. This explains the prickly reactions to big science: the announcement of huge cost overruns inevitably gives rise to arguments about the effectiveness of such machines. The uncertainties involved are not very different from those encountered in other laboratories, and the approximations are probably not greater than the sum of those for the latter, but big science irreversibilities make the errors more damaging. The co-ordination procedures already well established in the megascience scientific communities need to be extended to include regular monitoring of expenditure and the management of funding over time.

7. The model of science as a public good

Here this issue is the role that megascience can play in the development of science. Questioning of the primacy of big science as a development tool and revision of the tacit agreement between big science and government raise new questions about its place in scientific development. To some extent, big science has been tied to the cold war and very narrow objectives. Here, this view is discounted and economic considerations are taken as a point of departure in order to stress the importance of megascience, as well as its potential deflection.

Science as a public good

Economists define a public good in terms of three main characteristics:
- non-appropriability, under normal conditions, of information (no one can have the sole use of a public good);
- non-rivalry (the use of a good by an individual does not limit its use by other individuals);
- durability (the good is stable and does not change).

On the surface, science satisfies these three criteria: the knowledge produced cannot be appropriated by a given group, the use of a scientific statement by one group does not limit its use by others, and finally, the results do not change. A closer look shows that this is only apparent. When scientific statements are closely linked to highly expensive machines, as in the case of high energy physics, and are only interesting when they can be used, they have traits resembling those of a private good.

Without a suitable instrument and very specific know-how, the scientific statement can only be used by teams possessing these advantages. Moreover, budgetary constraints make it necessary to choose certain options, and the use of statements can thus become rival (a group obtains funding to explore a statement in one way and thus becomes a rival of the group that is not funded). Finally, the durability of scientific statements assumes that they continue to be used, and this implies maintaining means of educating, training, and developing scientific communities. Science can thus become a private good.

The culmination of this trend may be concentration on a small number of objectives which give an immediate return. The trend is even stronger when there are increasing returns. Given the amount of effort invested, a particular field can become much more attractive than its neighbours because it has concentrated all the resources. (The effect is similar to that of a network: with only two users it is of little interest, but every additional user considerably increases its strength.)

The risk in this approach is the possibility of eliminating scientific diversity. Disciplines will always tend to focus on a strong and immediate return, but this results in loss of skills and a lack of dynamism. The point is not, of course, to encourage unbridled fundamental research on all possible subjects, but to avoid becoming locked into scientific undertakings which are difficult to redirect and which can restrict innovation.

Naturally, maintaining diversity has a price: maintaining science as a public good implies a public responsibility and considerable investment. The latter must, however, be concentrated on the development of very novel undertakings and original combinations.

Megascience as a public good

At first glance, megascience seems to oppose the notion of science as a public good. It tends to reduce scientific diversity markedly. Recent developments in particle physics and molecular biology have demonstrated tendencies to hegemony and to the transformation of science into a kind of private good. These are, however, deviations from the general position of megascience. In fact, the study of decision-making processes as a means of co-ordination has shown that megascience could be an ideal theatre for sharing scientific information and maintaining the diversity of scientific undertakings. Megascience can become, albeit at a substantial price, a public good as well as an opportunity for scientific and technical development, subject to certain conditions: that projects are modular, that those with the strongest scientific dynamism are selected, that association of all possible users is encouraged, and that industrial and political partners are involved.

8. Phases of the decision-making process and methodological rules

This section proposes a model decision-making process. It will clearly not be suitable in every case, but it can nevertheless serve to identify a number of methodological rules. There are three main phases.

Proliferation phase

This phase essentially takes place in the scientific communities, but it should be monitored and encouraged by the public authorities, who will have recognised what is at stake. The main idea is to permit the emergence of the greatest possible number of proposals, to preserve the diversity of scientific research. At this stage, the decision-making process has two aspects: on the one hand, the initiative of the scientists and, on the other, vigilance on the part of the public authorities and agencies to ensure that all the conditions necessary for proper discussion are met.

Association-extension phase

Here, the main idea is to establish the maximum number of firm links among scientists, technicians, funding bodies, and industry. It is also the moment for working out the technical plan, the outlook for using the machine, and funding and support structures. Special attention should be paid to the decision-making criteria for adjusting the project and imposing reviews of the conception of the project (discussed in Section 5). Emphasis should also be placed on the importance of users.

Convergence phase

This phase corresponds to the finalisation of the project, the definitive setting up of its host structures and the international agreement. Particular emphasis is placed on repeated examination by national and international committees in the decision process.

9. Recommendations

These few recommendations are based on Sections 5 and 7. They do not claim to provide a complete solution to the enormous problem of modes of decision making but merely draw attention to certain factors.

General recommendations

1. As many scientific groups as possible should be associated with the project. This makes a bigger contribution to project quality than any excessively *a priori* selection principle. Contrary to expectations, the most profitable approach in the preparatory phase may be not selectivity but the multiplication of contacts and alternatives.
2. All new associations should be encouraged by urging participation in the general decision-making process. This is a matter both for the scientific communities and the public authorities. The latter can test the variety and strength of the links formed.
3. Among the important criteria in project reviews, attention must be paid to the likely dynamism of the project, such as the extent to which it avoids increasing returns and diminishing diversity. In this way, an attempt can be made to limit the influence of dominant disciplines which benefit from the momentum they acquired during their growth phase.
4. To maintain non-rivalry it is necessary to increase the modularity of projects. This assures them greater flexibility for future development. This point, together with the attention paid to the community of potential users, is a good indication of the openness of the project.
5. When the details of the project are being worked out, it is necessary to support and ensure close association of science, technology, and industry. Projects will be enriched by bringing their various skills together.
6. To ensure the renewal of the field concerned, it is worthwhile maintaining incentives for small megascience projects related to the reorientation of certain fields or the emergence of new trends.
7. Defining science as a public priority implies broad public debate of its orientations and options for diversification. These question should be submitted early to parliamentary and government authorities for cross-cutting review.

More specific administrative recommendations

1. It is important to encourage joint review of megascience projects and to propose procedural rules (of the type indicated earlier) to this end.
2. A clearly identified budgetary envelope for megascience is an advantage in managing the decision-making processes.
3. A choice in favour of international co-operation cannot accommodate hesitations and reversals in order to favour purely national options. It is important to resist inward-looking tendencies that might encourage certain groups or agencies to prefer national projects for opportunistic reasons.
4. Areas of national intervention must therefore be clearly defined and the resources to be devoted to them specified. Every megascience project should fit into balanced national planning. This means that the question of funding should be dealt with very early.
5. Every discipline needs a long-term programme, which covers the facilities to be built, those to be shut down, and those to be converted, both nationally and internationally.
6. It is essential to have a specific body charged with keeping a close watch on projects and their costs to guard against cost overruns and delays in implementation.
7. To avoid unsatisfactory sharing of responsibilities, it is preferable to adopt robust structures (such as international agencies) for carrying out projects.
8. Care must be taken from the outset to ensure that the various aspects of projects are divided appropriately among the partners, particularly as regards technical aspects and the problems of operating instruments and running projects.
9. It is important to establish procedures (still to be devised) for dealing with distributed megascience projects, which involve a much more delicate form of co-ordination among countries.

Recommendations closely linked to the decision-making process

These are based on the discussion in Section 5:
- Promote the most dynamic scientific programme possible.
- Integrate the financial parameters at a very early stage, with a review of national resources, and then explore the possible forms of association with potential partners.
- Ensure early association at international level.
- Work to achieve the broadest possible community of users.
- Encourage preliminary project work, particularly as regards technical aspects, so as to have several technical options and avoid blind alleys.
- Privilege project modularity and flexibility.
- Maintain feedback loops throughout the decision-making processes to permit adaptation as the process advances.
- Involve public decision-makers early.

– Take irreversibilities into account, with a regular review of the consequences of decision, the return to committees, the assessment of alternative schemes, comparing progress with timetable.

1. The role of decision making in megascience

The interest generated by decision-making processes in megascience stems from three points that could almost be described as self-evident. First, there is the fact, which has been recognised for some time, that large scientific projects, whether international or not, absorb a significant share of government funding for scientific research. It thus appeared essential, if scientific development in general was to proceed harmoniously, to monitor planning and decision making for such projects carefully, so as to make optimal use of available resources. However, this was done in a restricted framework, since it essentially involved an *ad hoc* review of each new project.

Second, in recent years, as constraints on government budgets have increased, science, particularly megascience, has not been spared. Indeed, funding restrictions have renewed questions about the relevance of megascience. There is still something of a consensus on the issue of the need to maintain and expand megascience activities, as a number of recent studies have shown (OECD, 1993b; Cohendet and Lebeau, 1987). On the other hand, the issue of resource allocation is now raised within a general framework rather than on a specific basis. The need to screen projects far more carefully means examining how decisions are taken and attempting to define a structure that could assist governments and scientific organisations in their deliberations. The decision-making processes become all the more crucial when it becomes necessary to choose among projects.

Finally, this more far-reaching review of megascience has also raised questions about the type of scientific activities it covers. A characteristic feature of this form of scientific endeavour is the emergence of enormous bodies which bring together scientific communities and groups, government agencies, decision makers, and instruments. The association of these varied forces does not occur spontaneously, but constitutes an essential stage in the genesis of a project, one which entails formulating a coherent and effective plan, involving the maximum number of partners, refining the project's objectives, testing the technical and scientific approaches envisaged, and determining how the project will ultimately function. While it cannot prejudge the inevitable contingencies attached to scientific activities, this process, which fairly closely overlaps the decision-making process, largely determines the characteristics of the future scientific project. In a word, megascience sets in motion decision-making processes on its own scale. Quite apart from the immediate financial and technological parameters, one of the major constraints of this extreme form of big science is the fact that the decision-making processes are now themselves extremely weighty, yet they are essential to the subsequent smooth running of the projects.

Given the stakes involved, megascience encourages a careful review of the decision-making processes, but, at the same time, it is partly defined by those processes. This being said, there remains the thorny question of where decision making actually occurs. Obviously, there is the fateful moment when formal approval of a project enables it to get started. In that case, focus would be placed on the final review by official bodies charged with giving a verdict. However, this would not provide a comprehensive and realistic view. Although these decisions are ultimately taken at the political or parliamentary level, the groundwork is done over a long period that involves preliminary soundings, expert committees, and many adjustments to the projects. In the case of the American SSC, a long series of negotiations and of unexpected developments linked to hostile votes in the Congress led eventually to a final refusal, all of which shows that it is very difficult to reduce decision making to a linear process.

An "eddying" model would appear to be much closer to reality. The decision-making process is far from necessarily involving a perfectly ordered series of events:
- concept;
- preparation of a preliminary project;
- formalisation by an agency or laboratory;
- review by an expert committee;
- executive approval (or rejection);
- a parliamentary vote.

Instead, it often mixes up the stages and involves various feedback loops in order to ensure coherence. Project reviews facilitate revisions and changes in design and the involvement of new partners at every stage. It is important to bear this general structure in mind as modes of decision making are analysed.

In the following sections, the position of megascience and the criteria usually employed to define it are described. Next, an historical review of how methods of decision-making have changed shows how different models have emerged. Then, the characteristic features of current decision-making processes are considered, before an attempt is made to identify the main factors involved in producing the decision and outlining a structure of decision-making modes. The follow-up to the decision and the procedures necessary for that stage are then examined. Finally, the role of megascience as a public good – to use the terminology of economics – receives attention, and an effort is made to define decision-making modes which, while not ideal, preserve effective megascience and public investments.

2. Definition of megascience and impact on decision-making modes

Criteria for defining megascience

Discussions of the importance of megascience have already highlighted the main criteria normally used for qualifying megascience projects. The OECD Megascience Forum, in its preliminary meetings, used a fairly broad definition which stipulated that a megascience project was "a scientific initiative encompassing the facilities, instruments, human resources, and logistic support required to address a set of scientific problems of such significance, scope and complexity as to require an unusually large-scale collaborative effort" (OECD, 1993b). Beyond this definition, the Forum looked for more operational criteria. First among them is the financial aspect, with megascience projects being identified by their cost thresholds. In addition, there are the size of installations or programmes, the need for international co-operation, the unique character of installations, and their radical innovativeness.

Other authors have defined megascience projects differently, using three convergent criteria: a total cost throughout the life of a project in excess of $1 billion, the deployment of extensive technological and scientific equipment, and radical uncertainty about the information to be obtained from the projects (Averch, 1993). This definition is not entirely well-founded. The extent of technical and managerial effort varies enormously from one project to another; in particular, the technical difficulties involved are often very different. Also, uncertainty about the results, apart from the inevitable unknowns, is not so different in megascience from what it is in "small" science. In the case of a synchrotron radiation machine, for example, uncertainty has more to do with the future users than with any particular feature of the machine. Similarly, in the case of large particle accelerators, a major share of the results are part of a coherent research programme, which substantially reduces the margin of uncertainty. This has to do with the decision-making processes for a megascience project: other things being equal, this kind of project is more precisely defined than smaller ones, as a result of the joint planning of programme techniques and objectives.

On the other hand, uniqueness does appear to be a relevant feature. For the most part, megascience projects cannot be duplicated, owing to their size and the resources involved, but also to the limited value of merely reproducing the results. It is important therefore to manage this aspect as well as possible by securing in advance the basic conditions that guarantee the reliability of the results. Compared with a theoretical model of science in which the reproduction of experiments and the dissemination of instruments is the principal resource (Shapin and Schaffer, 1985), megascience requires a new model, in both epistemological and practical terms. Discussion of the project and the comparison of programmes provide the necessary guarantee that the outcome will be acceptable to the scientific community and to the governments and funding agencies.

Thus, to the immediate criteria of cost and technological complexity must be added the constraints arising from the establishment of new forms of (scientific) bodies that have gradually acquired, particularly since the Second World War, an important place in the scientific field.

This point of view is reinforced by the distinction made between two types of megascience: fixed-site, which includes large accelerators or telescopes, for example; and distributed, which includes large-scale climate or ocean observation programmes which, by their very nature, require widely dispersed efforts (Praderie, 1993). In fact, for distributed megascience, decision making is affected more than ever by the need for co-operation and international agreements, the involvement of many partners, and the establishment of a coherent research programme.

Diversity in the handling of decisions

Although there is a degree of consensus on a small number of practical criteria for defining megascience projects, there is much greater variety in the practice of decision making. This can easily be seen from a brief survey of analyses of different national approaches, proposed by the countries concerned and summarised below.

The United States uses the megascience category to classify their largest projects or those in which they participate; however, it has not adopted a specific decision-making process (President's Council of Advisors on Science and Technology, 1992). Decisions are based on an *ad hoc* review of proposals; specifically American projects often arise from initiatives of scientists and big agencies such as NASA. However, the Congress plays a significant role in decision making, since it makes the final funding decision. The 1993 vote on the SSC project also marks the sudden realisation of the importance of a concerted megascience policy, in order to guard against financial overcommitment.

Australia is also studying megascience, particularly in terms of the respective advantages of having a national facility or participating in an international project. The increasing number of megascience projects has led to consideration of the criteria to be applied when assessing the suitability of projects (Burch and Tegart, 1992). At the moment, however, the existing procedure seeks less an examination in terms of megascience than an evaluation of the best policy for the country's scientific facilities. The question of taking part in international megascience projects is nevertheless a pressing one.

Japan's situation appears very different. Japan does not use the term "megascience". While the ITER or Space Station programmes are certainly regarded as megascience projects, the term is not used for other projects dealt with by the Japanese scientific and government authorities. Moreover, the Japanese authorities do not use cost thresholds to define megascience, because they feel that the financial criterion is inadequate. However, relevant projects are examined carefully by various advisory bodies before being submitted to the executive and parliamentary bodies.

France deals with these questions quite differently, through a body specifically charged with advising the political authorities on decisions about "very large facilities", which are defined very much like megascience projects. However, although the category is well identified as such, the role of the Council on Very Large Facilities (*Conseil des très grands équipements*) remains advisory; its opinion is given at the end of a decision-making process which involves scientists and bodies supporting research. However, the Council for Very Large Facilities reviews proposals for all new projects and monitors their implementation (Petiau, 1992; *Rapport du Conseil des TGE*, 1992).

Like France, Sweden identifies megascience projects and has been dealing with them in a specific manner since the beginning of the 1980s. They are generally funded from a particular budget and are handled as megascience projects by the advisory and executive bodies. This applies to the decision-making and implementation stages, after which they cease to be so considered.

Germany takes a middle ground. To some extent, it identifies megascience projects, since, in the past, the Pinkau and Mayer-Leibnitz Committees were set up to make recommendations on the megascience projects to be realised in the Federal Republic of Germany. More recently, the Grossmann Committee has reviewed German fundamental research across the board, with no special procedure for megascience. However, Germany sets financial thresholds for scientific facilities (DM 30 million and DM 100 million), beyond which much greater attention is paid to monitoring the progress of projects.

Canada is developing procedures for dealing with megascience. Megascience is acknowledged as an important category, and an attempt was made, at the interdepartmental level, to use joint review of proposals to unify the relevant decision-making processes. The approach proved too complicated; there is now a move towards a more focused review of megascience projects in each scientific discipline, and consideration is being given to setting up procedures specific to megascience to meet the need for a monitoring and harmonisation policy.

Although Russia has a fairly large number of megascience projects, the country has not set up specific decision-making structures. They are reviewed in the same way as other projects by the different ministries, with contributions from expert committees appointed for example by the Academy of Sciences.

Denmark does not have any specific criteria for identifying megascience projects. They are submitted for normal political and scientific study to the scientific community, the Ministry of Research, and various advisory bodies. On the other hand, there is a multi-annual budget programme. Denmark also emphasises the increasing demand for a careful follow-up for investments in megascience.

Switzerland presents still another point of view. Given the country's size and the investment needed for megascience projects, the category concerns the major international operations to which Switzerland contributes in the same way as other partners. It has in this case a procedure for reviewing proposals which is quite separate from decisions concerning large facilities (obviously of smaller size) at national level. The review procedure involves international experts and an examination of the relevance of Swiss participation in the undertaking concerned.

Finland's case is fairly similar, in that it regards megascience as involving international scientific co-operative undertakings which are reviewed by qualified expert committees. From this standpoint, the decision-making process differs from the normal review only in that additional care is taken.

Belgium has no specific mechanisms for megascience, a category which at present is little used in national procedures. Emphasis is placed both on participation in European programmes and on national initiatives in a variety of areas.

Finally, the Netherlands notes the difficulty of drawing a clear distinction between big science and megascience. The country uses the specific criterion of a threshold of ECU 1 million for identifying the largest facilities. These funds come from a specific budget, and credits for participation in international ventures are also separately identified. These two special arrangements are in fact based upon a decision taken in a specific framework.

The methods used for dealing with megascience are clearly fairly diverse. Although most countries acknowledge the existence of such projects in a practical and informal manner, few actually use this category when developing their scientific policy. On the other hand, they all follow a similar pattern, in which scientists make proposals for projects and advisory bodies responsible for scientific questions review the proposals, before the matter is passed on to the political, executive, and legislative side. However, the presence or absence of a concerted budgetary review for this type of project constitutes an important difference.

Impact on modes of decision making

The establishment of a partial equivalence between identifying problems related to megascience and establishing procedures for qualifying it and monitoring its development raises a difficulty. It is likely that several factors contribute to this relative distortion.

First, there are two aspects related to the circumstances under which megascience actually develops. The assessment of megascience projects clearly depends on the size of the countries concerned and their relative priorities. It is striking that for a number of medium-sized countries, "megascience" automatically implies "international". The scale of their resources prohibits these countries from embarking on their own on such undertakings, so that megascience is necessarily seen in a framework of bilateral or multilateral co-operation. Consequently, there is a fairly sharp distinction between these undertakings and projects for national facilities, owing to the very different orders of magnitude.

From the Netherlands' point of view, the level of ECU 1 million clearly refers to expensive facilities, but it has nothing in common with the $1 billion often used to define megascience. In the two cases, the decision-making processes will quite naturally be different. One involves the internal management of the research system within specialised bodies, the other involves from the start international negotiations in which the views of the scientific communities are solicited. This does not mean that decision making follows a set pattern, but that the questions are viewed in a different light.

For other countries, however, megascience projects remain a possible form of national science policy. This clearly applies to the United States or Russia, with their large numbers of strictly national projects. The case of Australia is significant because, while it claims a status of medium-sized nation in scientific terms, it places international undertakings and the construction of national facilities on the same footing. Hence, countries adopt fairly different approaches, depending on their perception of the scale of investment.

This divergence is, at a deeper level, related to the fact that countries and scientific communities are passing through a period of transition, which can be characterised briefly as a move from the national towards the international. Of course, countries have made many attempts to work together in the past, for example in European organisations for scientific co-operation, but in the last few years the political and financial context has brought attention to this phenomenon into sharper focus. Until recently, although megascience was generally regarded as an international venture, it remained an intermediate category, since the boundary between international megascience and national big science had not yet been clearly marked. Many countries could still strike a balance between taking part in a substantial international joint venture and the wish to maintain their own resources at home, thus duplicating the international initiatives.

This phenomenon can be compared with the "pyramid policy" recommended by the CERN (European Organisation for Nuclear Physics) in the 1960s. The watchword then was to build a very large accelerator in the framework of the European organisation, in parallel with the construction of large machines by individual countries, in order to establish a scientific network in high energy physics. The remains of this view are probably still alive. Megascience is still an emerging category, one that is poorly identified in national research policies which formerly essentially acted on big science, or its derivatives, at national level. More broadly, this ambiguity reflects certain countries' reticence to formulate specific orientations in megascience too clearly, for fear that they will lose leverage for domestic scientific development and be forced into uniform and even standardised co-ordination mechanisms at international level: in effect, the introduction of more or less standard procedures would give rise to a process of harmonisation that could be the death of projects of only medium utility, even if strongly supported by certain groups. There is also the fear that scientific practice would be made uniform and lose its diversity. Megascience thus conceived would focus on certain limited fields. This objection is related to the idea of science as a public good (discussed in Section 7).

Two other difficulties stand in the way of an overall evaluation of decision making in megascience. The first concerns the nature of the judgements to be made. In Canada, for example, an initial attempt to deal with these questions using an interdepartmental review procedure failed because it was too complicated. If megascience is recognised as having an independent status, then it is necessary to equate a number of projects and judge them in an analogous manner. Yet it is well known that scientific communities and expert groups are reluctant to undertake interdisciplinary evaluation. While appreciating the intrinsic qualities of a project may not raise major obstacles, explicit comparison of investment in astronomy and oceanography, for example, causes problems.

The second difficulty concerns the administrative machinery of the different countries involved. Recognising megascience as a category and setting up a specific review of decision making presupposes a horizontal structure, which may find itself in conflict with the various agencies or advisory bodies already responsible for the different disciplinary programmes. The lack of any administrative framework and agencies' desire to retain an independent decision-making framework for their own programmes thus constitute two obstacles to a common review of megascience projects. It is possible that those countries which do not employ the megascience category, or do not recognise it, are simply unwilling to interfere with the division of responsibilities among scientific agencies, ministries and advisory bodies and a local equilibrium in which each follows its own approach. It may be observed in passing that even where independent institutions do exist, they often run into the question of co-ordination among government agencies and the need for interdisciplinary arbitration.

These few elements show why the concept megascience, in particular in its relationship to actual political decision making, takes a variety of forms. Issues such as maintaining a national policy, the uncertain boundary between certain forms of national big science and megascience, the relative share of resources devoted to megascience, as well as countries' approaches to the decision-making process, result in a certain diversity in the responses to a problem recognised by all.

If megascience is not officially taken under consideration in decision making, there are obviously significant consequences. The emergence of megascience exerts a *de facto* influence on decision-making methods by forcing the different actors to work together more closely, by stressing association and the exploration of new approaches, by provoking a joint process for reviewing proposals, and by seeking the best way to share financing. Indeed, a successful megascience effort may be said to presuppose these characteristics. Certain of these principles are already at work, without necessarily being formalised. On the other hand, the difficulties encountered by certain projects reflect a decision-making process in which the search for partners comes too late and the means of co-ordination are somewhat ineffective.

Thus, megascience is making its mark. It is possible to imagine a different pattern in which this might not be so: a given agency might, using the normal decision-making process, manage to impose a large-scale project by assembling all the necessary support. But such a project would then inevitably impinge on the other activities requiring funding by severely restricting the available choices.

As things stand, megascience is an important category of scientific practice, even if it is treated in different ways in the decision making process. Four approaches can be distinguished. The first is the deliberately international approach supported by medium-sized countries, which places megascience on an international level and devises procedures accordingly. The project must allow for bringing together the greatest possible number of partners and working out modular participation.

The second model could be called the ''agency approach''. Here, the agencies remain in control and take on the task of promoting new projects as part of their existing activities. Megascience is seen as fitting into the ordinary decision-making process, and local equilibria receive preference, occasionally to the detriment of an overall logic.

A third model is the national science policy approach, based on judgements of the suitability of certain projects in terms of national independence. Here again, megascience may be treated very differently in different contexts, sometimes resulting in a preference for realising smaller projects on home ground.

Finally, there is the disciplinary approach, which prefers to review the projects in their disciplinary framework and thus avoid the problem of interdisciplinary arbitration. This approach clearly raises a number of problems for the implementation of a joint megascience process.

The interaction among these approaches explains the reluctance to take megascience as such into account in decision making. It also draws attention to the potentially harmful effects of not doing so, since, whether one likes it or not, megascience is imposing itself. And, where these four approaches meet, it is possible to see the outlines of a megascience decision-making structure, the historical emergence of which is traced below.

3.   The evolution of decision making: an historical analysis

The origins of megascience have been widely discussed and relatively well explored (for an overview and a few examples, see Smith, 1993; Hermann *et al.*, 1987 and 1990; et Edge and Mulkay, 1976). The following analysis does not attempt to retrace the history of big science and megascience as such, but to examine it from the standpoint of decision-making processes, showing how these have evolved and have relied upon different models.

Two paradigms: the period before the Second World War

The period before the second World War offers two interesting achievements which illustrate the possible approaches to decision making in big science. They are, first, the cyclotron built at Berkeley by Lawrence, often referred to as one of the primary sources of big science; the other is the large electromagnet of the French Academy of Sciences, built at Bellevue under the direction of Cotton (Heilbron and Seidel, 1989; Shinn, 1993).

The electromagnet corresponds well to the image of megascience today. The planned machine was enormous, extremely complicated to build, and had to produce fields of several tens of thousands of Gauss. It was expensive, at nearly FF 1 million at the time, and was the most important machine of its type anywhere in the world. It mobilised scientists and engineers and concerned a field regarded as important and promising: the use of intense magnetic fields for exploring matter or studying magnetic phenomena.

The decision-making process, however, appears fairly typical of a very hierarchical system. A number of eminent scientists, deeply involved in French scientific and political life, conceived the idea of a very powerful magnet that would substantially aid research on magnetism. This initiative was of interest to various scientific groups working on the question, but their efforts remained unco-ordinated. Several teams wished to build a large electromagnet and various projects began to take form. The issue was finally brought before the Academy of Sciences, which reviewed the various proposals and finally decided in favour of the one put forward by Cotton and Weiss. Weiss was among the promoters of the idea of a large magnet (Shinn, 1993*a* and 1993*b*).

The decision-making process calls for some comment. To begin with, there was the initiative from above, the virtually abstract decision to build a large magnet. Magnets were certainly starting to be used in scientific circles, but no effort had been made to pull together what were fairly heterogeneous tendencies. Thus, the decision to build the machine was, to some extent, detached from the development of the idea. The final decision was clouded by uncertainty, but various groups, each with a different construction scheme, were allowed to present their proposals. The discussion process was explicitly competitive and confrontational. The projects appeared to be mutually exclusive, and the groups tried more to discourage one another than to co-operate. While such competition may have been natural, it was never counterbalanced by incentives to collaborate.

Under those circumstances, the Cotton-Weiss project was chosen. It should be noted that it was the least innovative among them. It adopted the most conventional technical approaches and simply increased the scale of the machine. Moreover, no particular thought was given to the experimental zones inside the machine. Cotton, pursuing his own interest in the measurement of magnetic birefringence, wanted a magnet with the largest possible air gap and the most homogeneous field possible. He thus incorporated into the machine his own ideas as to what its experimental programme could be. In technical and scientific terms, the victory of the Weiss-Cotton team was that of the lowest common denominator. The biggest, the most traditional, the most reassuring project, the one that would involve the most conventional research, was the one chosen.

It is interesting to look further into what became of the great Bellevue electromagnet. As the decision to build it was taken on the eve of the First World War, its construction was postponed until after the war. It was then proposed to use the money collected for the national Pasteur fund to build the machine. Cotton was put in charge of construction and took up the pre-war design. After laborious preliminaries, the machine was gradually built and did in fact become the world's biggest magnet. The project was characterised by slow progress, disputes as to its relevance, and rising costs, issues that have also arisen in certain more recent situations.

With regard to the programme of work and the design of the instrument, there were two parallel trends. On the one hand, the team performed *ad nauseam* experiments to measure the effect of the field on aromatic substances but did not move into any new areas. On the other hand, Cotton concentrated on perfecting the instrument and strove continuously to improve its performance. As a result, the machine played an extremely passive role and did not contribute to organising or reorganising the research programmes and the scientific areas involved.

In the 1930s, a small group suggested using the magnet for low temperature physics. The proposal attracted little interest and nothing was done to adapt the machine to meet this new challenge. Thus, the decision-making process partly determined the ultimate fate of the machine. Because there was no effort to bring partners together, because neither the machine nor the project were regarded as active elements of scientific work, and because the experimental zones were either neglected or regarded as suitable for only one purpose, the project was condemned to die. It is significant that the decision-making method employed excluded co-operation, entrusted the evaluation, based upon a competitive approach, to a committee at the top of the scientific hierarchy, and led to the choice of the most conservative technical and experimental approach.

It is ironic and paradoxical that Cotton himself should have compared his project with Lawrence's project at Berkeley. In fact, in the latter case, the decision-making and implementation model is quite different (Heilbron and Seidel, 1989). Both cases, it is true, involved a passion for technology, but the role of the instrument was quite different. The first cyclotron was built in a university framework on the initiative of a single individual, Lawrence, but there the similarity ends.

To get his machine built, Lawrence did everything in his power to recruit the greatest possible number of partners. He naturally turned to his own institution but he also sought to interest powerful foundations in his project. The project he presented was a skilful mixture of technical and scientific needs. For example, particle acceleration was conceived partly as a tool of nuclear physics, partly as a research facility for the medical community, which could use it to obtain the radioisotopes needed for treating cancers. Lawrence succeeded by assigning the instrument a very different role: instead of being passive, it played an active part in organising research priorities and in bringing different communities together. The size and technical complexity of the installations were not abstract factors but the subject of negotiations by the various partners to define their scope and significance. The decision-making process, while it partly recalls Schumpeter's "individual entrepreneur" model, also illustrates the need to involve potential users in the designing of the instrument. Similarly, the stress placed on technology aimed at introducing relatively new solutions instead of simply reproducing confirmed technologies on a bigger scale. There is no need to dwell on the spinoff from the cyclotron and the consequences for nuclear physics. The contrast with the electromagnet is very clear.

The two instruments illustrate two trends in megascience decision making. They also provide a concrete illustration of the impact of decision-making processes and the way they are conducted on the nature and evolution of instruments, to say nothing of their relative effectiveness. Finally, they underline the need to take into account – in what was still only big science – the decisive role of the instrument in co-ordinating scientific groups and methods.

Reconciling the two models: 1940-60

The Second World War was an important period in the emergence of megascience. It was in fact the work done at that time on the atomic bomb and radar that brought home to governments the importance of large-scale scientific undertakings. Lawrence and his cyclotron were in the forefront during this period, since Lawrence proposed to build ever more powerful machines in order to separate the isotopes needed to produce the bomb. At the same time, the war made it possible to allocate funds out of all proportion to those previously available for physics (Kevles, 1988).

As scientific development entered a new phase, it offered the different communities new opportunities for expansion. Among the main ones were particle accelerators for nuclear physics, radio astronomy and the large antennas stemming from radar, experimental nuclear reactors and the neutron diffraction instrument, and shortly thereafter, the space programmes.

During this period, scientists and politicians came to realise what each had to offer the other. On the one hand, the scientists saw new avenues of research opening up. On the other, the politicians, with the military in the lead, grasped the essential role of science for the security and prestige of nations. One of the causes of the development of megascience is therefore the tacit agreement entered into by science and the powers that be. A contract more subtle than would appear, since the military, having learned a lesson from the story of nuclear physics and the atomic bomb, accepted the need to support research without any immediate concrete goal, on the grounds that it might very well produce sophisticated weapons at some time in the future. Thus, requests for new accelerators were favourably received, particularly in the United States. The situation was somewhat different in Europe, since CERN was set up without particularly involving the military (Krige and Pestre, 1988; see also Pestre, 1989), but there is no doubt that the military did not disapprove of its existence. Wartime experience therefore marked the first steps of megascience by facilitating the initial decisions on facilities.

At this time, the two types of decision making noted in the previous period were combined. Scientists became scientific entrepreneurs and tried to attract a varied coalition of allies to their projects: scientists, of course, but also politicians, the military, engineers, technicians, and industry. Because substantial funding was available, there were many competitors, all trying to obtain their own machine and seizing opportunities as they arose. At the same time, every project became too large for the ordinary resources of one laboratory, and it became necessary to rely on exceptional government funding. Here, the two trends intersected: on the one hand, the model in which the researcher or laboratory takes initiatives and set up networks; on the other, the one based upon support by governments or public authorities.

A few examples can serve to illustrate the decision making methods used during this period. In the United States, the cases of the Berkeley and Brookhaven accelerators are significant. At Berkeley, Lawrence's laboratory naturally capitalised on its wartime work and had virtually no difficulty in obtaining from the Department of Energy (DOE) the funding necessary to build a new machine. Brookhaven's experience was fairly similar. It is worth noting the kind of partners involved in the decision. The focal point was the laboratory itself, which cashed in on its wartime efforts. The proposed machine was therefore the property of the laboratory, which became the sole user and designed it specifically to meet its own needs. It used conventional techniques, although this did not stand in the way of general technical developments, since the important thing for the various laboratories and groups was to be able to work quickly to produce new results. From the standpoint of the decision-makers, it was simply a matter of going along with a recognised laboratory and counting on results some time in the future.

Decisions in countries with fewer resources than the United States lack this relative clarity. In Europe, the early days of CERN were characterised by a process of association among countries, which foreshadowed later models of big science development (Pestre, 1988 and 1989). However, two French decisions give a fairly good illustration of developments at that time. They concern the construction of the Mélusine nuclear reactor in Grenoble and of the linear accelerator at Orsay. For the former, Louis Néel's laboratory in Grenoble was the beneficiary. Because its work was focused on magnetism, the laboratory wanted a neutron diffraction facility and therefore needed a reactor. Néel, a renowned physicist with good political connections, pressed the public authorities to grant the necessary funding and stressed his laboratory's contribution to rebuilding French science. Despite the reticence of the CEA (*Commissariat à l'énergie atomique*), the French government agency responsible for nuclear energy, he obtained his reactor in

1955 after the United States offered, during the Atoms for Peace conference, to supply small experimental reactors. Néel was awarded the reactor after suggesting that he could perhaps obtain a small reactor from the United States. The decision-making model is therefore not unlike the American one: a laboratory mobilises its political and military allies – Néel maintained excellent relations, for example, with the French navy – to obtain an instrument expected to advance its own research programme, an instrument, in fact, whose full range of use Néel had not envisaged (Pestre, 1990; Jacq, 1991). All in all, although French resources were less abundant than those of the United States, both episodes involved events used by the promoters of the instrument as catalysts to promote decision making.

The Orsay linear accelerator illustrates a process that is somewhat different although similar in structure. The decision can be understood only in the context of the expansion of CERN. Certain French physicists protested against the flight of national funds to a European institution. The government, which was then caught up in the affair of the European Defence Community, attempted to devise a *modus vivendi* for the building of national accelerators. Yves Rocard and the laboratory of the *École normale supérieure* seized the opportunity and relied on the main French builder of accelerators, the *Compagnie générale de télégraphie sans fil*, to obtain a decision in their favour.

These few examples indicate how decisions were taken during this period. To begin with, the decision-making process could still take place at national level, where competition with the achievements of other countries played a decisive role. The decision-making process usually focused on one group or laboratory which requested an instrument for its own needs, without necessarily introducing any arguments beyond scientific development and better results. The scientists involved were implicitly convinced, and managed to convince their interlocutors, that science would continue to expand fruitfully, and that it was therefore necessary to increase the capacity of facilities.

Coalitions sought out political, military and industrial allies. For the politicians, this was part of the broad contract between science and politics entered into after the war. Against this background, competition for funding among projects did not take the form of the trait-for-trait comparison made for the Bellevue electromagnet. The basic model was that of the individual entrepreneur, together with massive support from public authorities.

Competitive approach and agency approach: the 1960s and 1970s

While it is not always possible to assume regular historical evolution, the turning points in modes of decision making are relatively easy to identify. The most obvious sign is probably the article of Weinberg (1961), which expressed his fears about the significant development of big science and which named big science and identified it as a separate category in scientific practice. This was a moment of quite profound change in the practice of big science. The era of the solitary builders was coming to an end for several reasons. To begin with, the economic situation was perhaps less rosy and new areas deserving support had been discovered. Many countries were giving huge numbers of contracts for industrial development, for example in the field of electronics. Also, the increasing size of the instruments planned made it less and less desirable that they should be used by a single group, however skilled. At the same time, the medium-sized countries, possibly inspired by the CERN model, increasingly looked to co-operative ventures to lighten the financial burden on their budgets. Finally, the contract between science and politics was losing some of its strength, and the providers of funds increasingly wanted to play an active role in determining priorities and choices.

These factors had a number of effects on methods of decision making. First of all, it was increasingly difficult for any one group to obtain the funds it needed for its projects easily. In the United States, as regards high energy physics, the 1960s saw the establishment of committees such as the Ramsey Committee, charged with reviewing the various projects, classifying them, and allocating priorities, while also making recommendations. Specific procedures were set up so that expert committees would review proposals. This was a partial return to the model used for choosing the large electromagnet. The various teams proposed their scientific and technical approaches and competed for the same resources. The Ramsey Committee then classified all proposed projects.

The result of this procedure was as expected: the 200 GeV accelerator project of the prestigious Berkeley group, seen as a safe choice, was ranked first. However, decision making was no longer as simple as it had been in the past. Many physicists protested against the decision, criticising the design of the project as too expensive and conservative. In sum, during this transition phase, several approaches were in evidence: the State's wish to control, but also the struggle against established monopolies, the reappearance of a hierarchical model, but also the idea of shared facilities. Thus appeared the notion of a national laboratory that could accommodate physicists from laboratories throughout the country. Finally, Berkeley lost the 200 GeV project to a national laboratory, which was to become the Fermi National Accelerator Laboratory or Fermilab (Westfall, 1989; Hoddeson, 1983).

The changes in the 1960s included two other new aspects: first an emphasis on bilateral or multilateral co-operative arrangements; and second, the emergence of powerful agencies responsible for particular fields. The first stemmed naturally from the desire to share costs. The possibility of attracting foreign partners became an important factor in a decision-making process. The Franco-German institute for the high flux reactor (ILL) in Grenoble originated in such an approach, with the help of arguments in favour of Franco-German co-operation.

The emergence and the strengthening of the role of national and international agencies with responsibilities in particular fields also significantly modified the decision-making processes. It is revealing, for example, that it was at the end of the 1960s that space agencies were established in the United States and Europe. From then on, they channelled the decision-making processes. CERN is also a good example of an agency that centralises a particular community's decisions.

A CERN decision of the 1960s can be used to show the nature of the processes. In high energy physics, the years 1956-59 saw intense discussions about future accelerator facilities. This coincided with the completion of the new strong focus proton synchrotrons (PS) based on work done in the early 1950s (Hermann et al., 1990).

A conference on this subject was organised at CERN in 1956. It produced three possible new avenues: one was to use an annular plasma for guiding the protons, the second was to obtain much higher intensities by adopting a different arrangement of the magnetic poles and a fixed field (the Fixed Field Alternating Gradient – FFAG), and the third, the possibility of achieving collisions between clouds of particles. Accelerated particles had hitherto been fired at fixed targets; the use of two intersecting beams, although technically and physically more delicate, would make it possible to increase substantially the energy of the collisions. This last project was known as the Intersecting Storage Ring (ISR). Over and above these three original solutions, there was a final alternative: the construction of an even larger machine (*i.e.* of higher energy but not of higher intensity) and of the same type as the conventional PS, a ''monster'', as it was called by the scientists of the time, with energy around 300 GeV, or ten times the energy of the CERN PS.

Discussions began in 1959-60. At the outset, emphasis was placed on the need for an original machine with very high intensities rather than higher energies. The need to extend the field of research was clear, but the community was reticent about the prospect of an enormous machine. While simply increasing the energy inspired fears, producing higher quality beams by increasing the intensity held out the prospect of better physics. As a result, a project which partially combined the FFAG and the principle of collision, with a view to constructing storage rings, was looked on favourably. A first change of orientation occurred as early as 1960. There were several reasons for this. It had been thought that energy and intensity could not be increased together, but when the CERN Proton Synchrotron (PS) was commissioned, it appeared that not only did the machine operate very satisfactorily, it also provided beams of outstanding intensity. It was therefore possible to hope that a large machine would not only cross a new energy barrier but also provide significant intensities.

At the same time, physicists had begun to envisage the kind of physics they could do at 300-1 000 GeV, and this opened the way to the large machine. Until that time, they had been occupied with the physics achievable with the PS and with using the results it provided, and they had hardly had time to get used to the idea of a new and even larger machine. On that issue, the engineers had clearly moved ahead of the experimentalists, since by 1958-59 they were already considering the future machines. The important role played by engineers and builders will be returned to again and again. Finally, the entire community of closely involved users became increasingly convinced that a machine of higher energy would be the best solution. Nonetheless, debate continued and was concentrated on two options: a large machine or an original approach, the ISR. In fact, the engineers did everything they could to keep the ISR project alive, despite a clear decision on the part of the experimental physicists.

Within CERN itself, there were at least three different interest groups. The first consisted of the physicists using the facilities. Having surmounted their initial reticence, they quickly became supporters of the high energy machine that would produce the beams they needed for experiments and extend their current know-how. A second group formed around those who could be called the ''builders''. These were the engineers and scientists who had just built the PS. They found themselves with little to do and looked very favourably on all attempts to find a successor to the PS quickly. To them, a large machine such as a 300 GeV accelerator enjoyed no priority; they found this ''big machine'' approach simplistic and technically unattractive, while the intersecting rings

(ISR) seemed much more interesting. Finally, there was the senior group which now had political control of the organisation, people such as Perrin, Amaldi and Cockcroft. They saw the large machine as the ultimate "monster". They intuitively mistrusted the increase in the size of machines. Having weighed the alternatives, they were more sensitive to the originality of the ISR.

Once the physicists declared themselves hostile to the ISR project, it seemed destined to die. Experimental physicists increased the pressure to choose a high energy machine. News from the United States brought additional arguments. In 1962, the Ramsey Commission, charged with determining American priorities for future accelerators, had opted for the 200 GeV machine proposed by the Berkeley laboratory.

In the space of a few months, proponents of the ISR project appeared reduced to silence, and at the end of 1962, there seemed little doubt that the new instrument would be a high energy machine. However – and this cannot be stressed too much – these setbacks did not discourage the builders, who continued their studies on the ISR on the principle that it was a bad thing to burn their bridges too soon, as they might still serve. The CERN accelerator division kept in its files the designs for building the ISR.

By then, discussions had gone on for over three years, and everyone began to feel the need for a fairly quick decision. To be sure, there was no particular urgency except as it was perceived by those involved, who considered that the time for a decision had come. Simply by passing, time creates irreversibilities by forcing decisions. The movement was accelerated by the appearance of a French project for a national machine.

The ISR project then officially reappeared on the scene. First of all, it was a fairly inexpensive project, and especially one that could be implemented quite quickly. It also had another advantage under the circumstances at that time: it would ensure that the CERN laboratories would remain in Geneva, as the necessary rings did not require too large an area, unlike a very large machine. This issue, which had initially received little attention, played its part in the changes in attitudes. The ISR also offered another significant advantage, that it could be built rapidly, in any case more quickly than a large machine. In view of the urgency, this was an advantage not to be disregarded.

Early in 1963, the management began preparing a project for submission to the CERN Council. After a great deal of tergiversation, a hybrid proposal was worked out. Although everyone agreed that in absolute terms the ideal machine would be a 300 GeV PS, an intermediate proposal combining the two projects (large machine and ISR) was submitted. It is likely that some were counting on the possibility that in the worst case, if funds were scarce, the ISR could be launched to start the process moving. It was therefore decided to add the ISR, specified as a subsidiary project, and to combine the fates of the two projects. The proposed option, therefore, became a complex consisting of a large machine together with intersecting collision rings. After lengthy discussions, the Council, sensitive to the lower cost and innovative aspect of the ISR, decided to separate the two projects and to give priority to the ISR. After a final attempt to resist, the physicists resigned themselves to this decision.

The ISR decision shows just how far the method of dealing with proposals had changed. From then on, choosing a project also involved organising the widest possible discussion among the different communities concerned. However, this discussion took place within an agency or organisation responsible for the whole field.

The objective was to produce a consensus on orientations within the agency. This being so, it was essential to have the various groups represented within the organisation: the conflict between "physicists" and "builders" was central to the decision making mechanism, the former stressing safety and continuity, the latter innovation. Their confrontation was affected by more subtle divisions between "experimentalists" and "theoreticians", and between "seniors" and "juniors". The big facilities now involved such a variety of personnel that allowance had to be made for these various nuances. Similarly, in terms of character and concerns, the members of the physics "establishment" stood opposed to the younger staff, and this was very clear in the choice of the ISR.

Finally, and more generally, an animated discussion within CERN, based on the different concerns and objectives of "engineers" and "scientists", was essential. The presence of a "technical" lobby, much stronger than in the United States, forced a continuing debate about the boundaries of the project and constant reconsideration of the alternatives. The gradual working out of a consensus, in a very particular direction thanks to a *modus vivendi* established between builders and physicists, made it possible to obtain approval from the politicians for an approach which the latter then proceeded to modify, but which remained strongly inspired by the spirit of CERN.

These various examples highlight certain lessons about the decision making practices of the period. They are characterised first of all by a broadening of the decision making framework. A single group was no longer able to obtain an instrument for its own purposes: the decision process had to involve other partners, to compare scientific and technical approaches, and to ensure access for all partners. Also, expert committees exercised greater control and, within disciplines, used a more or less formalised system to classify the various projects. At the same time, the public authorities set up – or delegated their powers to – new structures, the agencies which acquired a decisive role in managing the decisions. In doing so, they developed their own approach, since every megascience programme offered an opportunity to increase the agency's responsibilities.

At the same time, certain bodies, whose role it was to mediate, appeared. CERN can clearly be set in an intermediary position between the political outlook of governments and the preferences of the scientific communities. Also, the set of arguments advanced in the decision-making process encouraged a broadening of the national framework. In sum, the period was marked by the emergence of a new model, more sensitive to international alliances, more attentive to the importance of technical developments, and which ultimately involved, partly on the basis of a selection-competition model, greater participation by the public decision-makers, who might delegate their powers to major semi-public structures. Henceforth, to gain a favourable decision, it became important either to fit into one of these major structures, or to recruit influential technical and industrial allies.

Towards new procedures?

It is of course very difficult to establish a strict timetable for decision making. Models proceed at their own pace, depending on the country and the discipline. Thus, the

European countries, owing to their size, have tended to lead the United States in broadening the framework for implementing projects. However, towards the end of the 1970s, some decisions on facilities were still being taken on a strictly national or even regional basis. One such case was the Varennes tokamak built near Montreal (Gingra and Trepanier, 1993).

This project began with a proposal by Quebec scientists to design and implement a programme on fusion, which they submitted to the federal government. However, as they wished to attract broader membership, they were careful to present their project within a federal framework. The only problem, quickly noted by the other laboratories and universities, was that the proposal involved only Quebec partners. To solve it, the Quebec scientists, while retaining guidance over the project, brought in scientists from other Canadian provinces. The promoters then prepared a report on the actions to be taken and submitted it in 1974. They recommended establishing a research programme on fusion and specified a number of options, but did not give a preference to either of the two main approaches, inertial containment or magnetic containment.

When their proposal was received, Industry Canada was considering the subject of fusion from a different angle. The oil crisis was an prominent factor in the discussion. In view of the importance of the subject, the ministry's advisory council therefore converted the initial project into a federal instead of a provincial project, one which was to draw on the skills of the National Research Council of Canada (NRC). This body, a committed partisan of inertial fusion, obtained from the committee a recommendation in favour of this approach. From that moment, the government's priority was to develop inertial fusion. However, the oil crisis had also led to the establishment of a council specialising in reviewing research into energy problems, and it refused to endorse the NRC proposals.

To clear the way, the NRC went back to the original promoters of the project who, in turn, stressed the need to widen the project to include magnetic containment. They went on to develop a specific "niche" strategy and recommended research into the effects of impurities and micro-turbulence in tokamaks. In that way, they justified building a small tokamak which, although it could not compare with large machines of this type, nevertheless was valuable for reaching objectives in this particular field of research.

The project then underwent two successive modifications to meet the requests of different committees; in particular, it had to be revised to satisfy demands for co-operation with industry. The Quebec group then gained backing from a number of firms in the electrical industry. It should also be noted that the choice of magnetic fusion was a well-chosen strategic decision: although Canadian skills in inertial fusion were fairly well distributed, the Quebec group was virtually the only powerful scientific team using the magnetic approach.

The final twist came when, faced with the federal authorities' hesitation to provide funds, the Quebec group, which had initially promoted a "provincial" project, argued that this was discrimination against Quebec and finally, in 1981, obtained a ministerial decision that the tokamak should be built in Varennes. In the meantime, there were parliamentary discussions during which the arguments made were somewhat modified because, as the government hesitated, the press and a number of interest groups began to insist on the need for a Canadian fusion programme, with its potential for economic and industrial spinoffs.

The Varennes tokamak decision process shows the limitations of any full rationalisation of that process. It shows a number of characteristic features, such as the need for continuous modification of the project in order to achieve the best possible compromise between the different partners. However, there was also a continuing shift from a federal outlook, with the construction of a tokamak of modest power, and a more international option, involving participation in other programmes. In this case, no particular primacy was accorded to a transnational programme, since the project's framework appeared to be determined by continuous negotiations about the boundaries of the proposed scientific work. Not only overall political priorities, such as the search for energy sources, but also the specific type of scientific research proposed were part of this delicate process. Finally, it should be noted that the many organisations involved, the diversity of the procedures, and the few constraints placed on the formulation of proposals led to a flexible and easily managed decision-making process. There is another case involving fusion – this time in the United States (Bromberg, 1982) – which illustrates a much more controlled process, because it was in the hands of the Atomic Energy Commission's Controlled Thermonuclear Research Division, which has stricter rules for reviewing proposals.

Despite the apparent historical contingency of the process, a number of structural factors are apparent. These include the decisive role of the procedures followed, the need gradually to form a coalition of partners, the concern for a precise match between the scientific programme and the scope of the machine, and, finally, the always underlying discussion about limitation and extension of the project (national, federal, international). Every organisation or group involved showed heightened sensitivity to the different parameters governing the development of projects. The Canadian case is interesting in that it took place at a time of transition. One can still see at work the idea of triumphant megascience, which favours large facilities, and the political and industrial manoeuvring to obtain a decision in favour of a technical alternative. It also shows the limitations of this formula and illustrates the processes of negotiation that are necessary to produce a robust programme.

In the 1980s, although all patterns still contained contingency elements, although there was still oscillation between a specifically national policy and international involvement, although the agency approaches persisted, new ideas on decision making in big science were nevertheless emerging. The tighter financial climate and perhaps especially a questioning of the future of big science (as regards industrialisation, the sharing out of the work, and concentration on certain fields) brought to the fore new priorities, such as integrating decision making into a framework of joint development, examining projects on a longer time scale, emphasising the communities of users, and the need to introduce various design teams at an early stage.

Hence, big science may be seen to have entered a new phase in which the problem became how to manage and benefit from the proliferating decision-making processes (illustrated by the Canadian example). This is clearly revealed by the emphasis on broader co-operative efforts and the review of projects at different stages of development, as for the VLT (Very Large Telescope), ESRF (European Synchrotron Radiation Facility) or major programmes such as ODP (the Ocean Drilling Program), WCRP (the World Climate Research Program) or IGBP (the International Geosphere-Biosphere Project).

In this connection, the cancelled SSC project represents the failure of a conventional model of big science in which inertia alone would make a project succeed. In its case, neither the money already spent nor the agreement in principle already obtained could prevent the project from being halted. The project's ambitions were probably out of all proportion with the partners, the preparatory work, and considerations about its utilisation that should have been involved. In the terminology used at CERN in the 1960s, "monsters" strike fear again.

The introduction of distributed megascience programmes is even more pointedly raising issues of approaches to co-ordination and of factors to be considered when reviewing decisions. It is partly responsible for the need to reconsider the question of decision making methods.

To sum up, the coupling of the models of the individual entrepreneur and of regulation through procedures of public competition is bringing forth a new framework for megascience, in which discussions involve not only the scientific programme, long neglected owing to a generalised faith in the productiveness of science, but also the economic and industrial background, national perspectives, and international co-operation. Certain disciplines began to follow this new road some time ago (OECD, 1993*a*), but more and more are taking it.

4.   Major trends in decision-making processes

This section and the next present two viewpoints on methods of decision making. A broad outline of the characteristics of current decision making will be followed by a more detailed examination of the arguments and the "sociological mechanics" involved, in an attempt to define a few essential factors for the attention of decision-makers.

As already shown, decision making has evolved considerably over time. A brief sketch of current megascience decisions covers five themes. To begin with, the decision-making process is marked by the necessary internationalisation of projects, with a number of consequences. More significantly, decision-making modes have come to be the context in which megascience, more than any other form of science, essentially receives its characteristics. Moreover, review procedures are now being applied which, because they are not uniform, place constraints on projects and affect their ultimate shape. In this sense, review procedures also regulate decision-making modes. The greater role of decision-making modes and of megascience explains the renewed interest of communities usually at the edge of such undertakings on the one hand, and, on the other, the rigorous formulation of projects. This clearly marks a new stage in the progress of megascience since the Second World War.

The impact of internationalisation

Megascience projects increasingly require international co-operation, either structurally or financially. Distributed large-scale programmes, where the extent of the task and the need to make measurements at a large number of points around the world necessarily imply intergovernmental agreements and uniformity within a large structure, are a case in point. More generally, the expansion of megascience has placed new emphasis on the sharing of responsibilities and costs within international structures.

There are many possible forms of co-operation. The main ones are:

- participation of various countries in an agency such as CERN, to which they contribute in proportion to their resources;
- the creation of specific companies to manage facilities jointly owned by several countries, such as ESRF or ILL;
- specific co-operation agreements among countries, or representative agencies, as for a space astronomy mission;
- an agreement to establish a world-wide project signed by all interested countries, as for the International Thermonuclear Experimental Reactor (ITER) fusion project;
- the creation of new collaborative structures, as for the large-scale climate and ocean exploration programmes.

Here, the topic of interest is the mechanisms that make it possible to work out such structures and to come to a decision about them. One could argue, rightly, that the scientific communities have a long history of international relations. By definition, of course, science is based on trading and sharing information. However, apart from the fact that the practice of international exchanges is not as old as it might seem, there is a significant difference between pure scientific exchange – the communication of results, or even the sharing of experimental techniques, however delicate this might be – and the pooling of manpower and resources to complete a joint project.

A prerequisite for any international effort is the discussion of common projects by the scientific communities involved.[1] Future agreement on priorities presupposes setting up a joint structure for planning and then putting the activities in the field or discipline concerned into perspective. It is by making inventories of existing installations and projects and the prospects they offer that scientists from the different countries can determine what avenues appear most promising. As an example, the European high energy physics community set up an advisory body, the European Committee for Future Accelerators (ECFA), whose task it is to consider future projects and the state of the discipline. A feature of megascience decision making is the proliferation of such intermediaries, charged with bringing the scientific communities together and encouraging them to discuss their priorities.

Internationalisation has placed two further constraints on decision making. While it is essential that research groups hold foresight/planning meetings to pool ideas and projects, they cannot prejudge how the orientations they choose will fit into specific national policies. In other words, the process must involve the political authorities and the responsible agencies at a very early stage, if obstacles are to be avoided. Further, discussions in preliminary meetings can lead to proposals for which a country's scientists estimate their potential financial contribution, without agreement from the relevant authorities, who do not necessarily have funds available.

Thus, preliminary agreements can have important consequences either because they subject national budgets to new constraints or because the withdrawal of potential partners can destabilise them. In developing international projects, care must be taken to strike a balance between scientific and financial decisions and to limit the irreversibilities potentially created by certain projects. These constraints are particularly significant owing to the large number of partners and the complex interrelationships to be managed. This is why certain countries have set up specific procedures for reviewing international proposals which involve both scientists and administrators. Moreover, in some cases, proposals of this type come under a separate budget line, and this makes it easier to assess availabilities and the extent of the commitments that can be made.

Owing to internationalisation, decision making no longer proceeds in a linear way from a general project outline through to the submission of the financial decision to the responsible authorities; it is much more interactive, with scientific, technical and financial opportunities discussed and assessed together. Hence, the process involves gradually adjusting scientific priorities and primary fields of interest as well as refining the supporting arguments and financial procedures.

This also explains why such discussions take a long time and why the agreements reached are so fragile. Full consensus cannot be reached over a few weeks, and many steps must be taken before reaching a consensus to which all the partners can subscribe. Furthermore, neglect of a single link in the chain of responsible bodies is sometimes enough to cause an unexpected refusal and block the whole operation.

These difficulties are rather well illustrated by the European High Performance Laser Facility (ELF) project (ELF, 1990). A small group of researchers had tried to promote construction of a laser of about 100 kiloJoules, costing FF 1 billion to FF 2 billion. For this purpose, they assembled a number of European partners so as to share the total capital cost among the maximum number of countries and to be able to fund the annual cost from ordinary budgets. As it turned out, the decision-making process, in which only cost sharing had initially been envisaged, foundered on various technical, financial, geographical, and political issues. The French and British partners held different views about the best type of laser. The scientific programme suffered from an attempt to superimpose various national interests. Because the question of where the instrument was to be located had not been dealt with at the outset, this also raised financial and political questions. How should an instrument not on national territory be financed, and what co-operative procedure should be adopted? Worse still, the French side had neglected to have the project reviewed and approved by the Council on Very Large Facilities which normally approves projects of this type. In this case, international co-operation proved excessively burdensome, as the proposed instrument would have had to meet more demands that it could handle (see Latour, 1992, for a similar analysis of the difficulty of bringing together the ideas of various partners).

The decision-making process runs the risk of superimposing various demands, without adopting, as a general principle, the need to revise and adapt the project over time; in that case it may create a monster rather than a true project.

There are differences between the two types of megascience in terms of the project organisation defined in the decision-making process. Projects of the distributed type introduce additional constraints. It is not sufficient simply to discuss scientific priorities, as it is also necessary to address issues such as what information is to be collected, questions of calibration, procedures for linking the different laboratories, and how data are to be processed. Whether the objective is to share an overall task (the Human Genome Programme) or to co-ordinate information collected around the world, standardised and interchangeable data are required, and this issue must also be discussed in the decision-making process. There would otherwise be the risk of initiating the collection of a mass of data which could not be exploited owing to a lack of compatibility between the research programmes of the different partners.

As regards the fixed-site programmes linked to a large instrument, there are problems of a different order. The site clearly raises a very special problem, since the host country will be likely to procure the greatest scientific benefit, to say nothing of the economic and industrial advantages.[2] The other partners must therefore devise a scheme that will enable them to benefit from the installations both in terms of the involvement of their teams and of the definition of the research programme. This is already important in European projects, where distances are reasonable, but becomes crucial in global projects. Thus, when countries of medium size evaluate a project in the decision-making process, they must consider travel, the free movement of research teams, and facilities for training in the use of the instrument. All these factors may well affect the decision-making process at international level.

Finally, and more broadly, the internationalisation of decision making raises the question of relationships among countries and their respective policies. Any decision concerning megascience inevitably has an impact on national science policy. The issue just mentioned may be used as an example. Participating in an international installation such as a synchrotron radiation machine may mean that a country needs its own national facilities, or at any rate access to others nearby, for training researchers so that they can benefit fully from the more sophisticated system. Similarly, the fact that megascience projects are often entrusted to national agencies, which of course have other obligations, can create complications if budgets are revised or the situation of agencies changes. This happened in the case of the Varennes tokamak, where the involvement of the NRC contributed, unexpectedly, to redirecting the project to magnetic fusion (Gingras and Trepanier, 1993).

In a different context, CERN now delegates the manufacture of detectors to be installed on the accelerators to member country national agencies, thereby adding a substantial burden to their budgets, a burden which stems from an overall decision about the project that will require many adjustments on the part of the participating partners. In particular, if one of the agencies finds itself in difficulty, its own policy may seriously suffer or its participation may be jeopardised.

The sheer size of the projects concerned often means that negotiations have to take place at government level and that the decision then has to be approved by the legislative branch. In some countries, the parliament receives overall budgets for approval, but in other cases – notably in the United States – the Congressional budget review mechanism can threaten a project by refusing the necessary funds. The SSC offers an example.

The widening of decision making to an international scale has two effects: on the one hand, it increases the number of obstacles, since, as a rule, the support of national parliaments will be required; on the other hand, the existence of a balanced agreement, supported by a whole series of governments and the relevant communities, can be a valuable argument for a favourable decision. In the case of the SSC, the search for partners to contribute to funding the machine did not take account of the importance of international constraints. If the project proposed is already largely determined, attracting other countries is not an easy matter.

At this stage, the decision for and realisation of an international megascience project require countries able to enter into stable agreements over a relatively long period. Making a commitment to a project of a certain scale presupposes that a partner is prepared to see the implementation and operations through to the end. Some co-operative ventures have been unilaterally abandoned by a partner, either suddenly or when a contract came up for renewal, thus threatening the whole structure. The decision-making process is therefore the place to test the intentions and reliability of the various partners. In the longer term, the introduction of independent management procedures for large projects could be one answer to the problem of trust between countries. The international-isation of megascience offers every country a variety of possible agreements and may lead to changes in alliances. In moving onto the international stage, megascience exposes itself to greater uncertainty.

Finally, when the decision is being taken, a last point must be discussed: that of the most appropriate legal structure for the project. Generally speaking, beyond the extensive and complex preliminary work, megascience decision-making processes involve a search for the most flexible co-ordinating structure, one which not only allows the project to function in a stable way but also to be revised as necessary. It is the exploratory work undertaken during the decision-making process which more or less tacitly guarantees the stability of the whole, because it helps to clarify each partner's position and to integrate all of them into a cohesive body in which the scientific and financial responsibilities are shared.

To sum up, internationalisation has placed serious constraints on megascience deci-sion making. Every government urges its scientists to form alliances. This contributes significantly to the complexity of the decision-making process, during which it is appro-priate to ensure that not only financial but also scientific, technical and industrial respon-sibilities are suitably shared. A particular constraint linked to internationalisation con-cerns the balance between national policy and the decision to engage in co-operation. Here, the decision-making processes are particularly sensitive to the issues of resources for training, data utilisation, and the practical realisation of the facilities. As things stand, internationalisation also seems to have an adverse effect, because it produces greater uncertainty. In view of the costs that uncertainty entails, governments might well use decision making as a means of co-ordination to install confidence and stability.

Two opposing tendencies should be stressed. On the one hand, internationalisation implies complex decision making. On the other, it is not just a question of cost sharing, it is also a question of defending scientific dynamism and promoting innovation through broad scientific co-operation.

Decision-making processes as a means of co-ordination

When it began, the OECD Megascience Forum noted that megascience, almost by definition, involved specific decision-making modes. Examination of a number of cases and consideration of the definition of megascience suggest that the proposition should be partly turned around. If megascience is aptly named, one could argue that, logically, it is because of the proliferation and complexity of the modes of decision making. It is possible to establish a direct link between the decision-making mode and the nature of the instrument that emerges. Further, examining the decision-making modes teaches much about the future of the facilities, their evolution, their conversion, and their possible or future difficulties.

A characteristic of decision making for major facilities is that the instrument and the decision-making process are worked out together. Sociological research into technology has shown that the design phase of the technological object is crucial, and that the process involves social, political and technical considerations (Callon, 1987; Latour, 1993).

It is at this stage that the various components of the technological object come together: these components are not only the necessary techniques but also the groups of users, builders, and theorists. In one sense, each group takes its place in what becomes a co-ordinating structure. Without a doubt, a machine as complex as the CERN's planned LHC (Large Hadron Collider) incorporates theoretical physicists' expectations as regards the top quark, experimentalists' ideas on the most suitable methods of detection and the techniques for processing the signal, engineers' skills as regards magnets and microwave tubes, the support of the electronics industry, political ideas about European co-operation, the desire to maintain the status of high energy physics in the countries concerned, and the technical specialties of certain national agencies – all these elements contribute to the project.

While the establishment of megascience programmes meets a need clearly expressed by the scientific communities, usually a concern for increasingly detailed exploration of matter or the Universe, it also corresponds fairly broadly to scientific organisational practice. In this context, three aspects of decision making can be seen as a means of co-ordination.

To begin with, decision making must address the management of duration and the timetable. In evaluating projects or behaviour, economists have shown the importance of time as a parameter which can be used to reassess a particular option on the basis of its realisation in the near or more distant future. Decision making in megascience usually extends over very long periods, even up to fifteen years. It is somewhat paradoxical to bring together science, an activity subject to uncertainty and urgency and where great energy is deployed day after day, and undertakings that involve the planning of activities over some 20 years.

In this sense, it is in the decision-making process that foresight activities and temporal priorities are managed. Discussions of the different options and the task of devising and refining projects should make it possible gradually to forge a joint timetable which provides all participants with a schedule of activities and the programming of the essential elements of their scientific work for the years to come. Harmonising schedules is central to advancing the process. With the involvement of increasing numbers of partners and the relative lack of duplication of installations, the length of the decision-making process is tending gradually to lengthen. This is the inevitable effect of the preliminary work that must be accomplished by countries, various bodies, and scientists.

A second point, one that will not be belaboured here, is that the decision-making period has also become – in a manner characteristic of megascience – the period during which a consensus is built. By comparison with other types of decision making, for example in the political sphere or even scientific decision making of some 30 years ago, decision making is no longer primarily a forum for confrontation where one camp seeks to wrest approval from a provider of funds in order to carry out its projects. The situation has become much more complex. It is now not only a matter of the technical and financial magnitude of the facilities to be built, but of the management of actual priorities and scientific communities.

A basic and more or less accepted principle of science has long been that experimental results should be reproducible; this was acceptable since virtually anyone could reproduce a particular laboratory set-up and produce similar results. With the development of megascience, however, it becomes necessary to try to resolve beforehand, and differently, the problem of reproducing experiments. Since the proposed instrument or programme will be unique, the reliability of the proposed facility must be based on the negotiated and virtually unanimous support of the communities concerned. As often happens, this epistemological question is also a political one, and governments cannot be certain that the research to be undertaken is relevant until it has been settled (this point will be returned to in Section 7).

This has two important consequences. First of all, the decision-making process can guarantee a democratic management of the choice of directions within communities that is made democratically by bringing the various viewpoints together around joint projects that are discussed, conceived, reviewed, and modified in order to incorporate many viewpoints. The aim is not to superimpose different, even divergent concepts, but to use them to define a form in which they can be expressed, for example by proposing a number of experimental sites, by linking complementary techniques, and by suggesting various methods for examining and interpreting data.

The second consequence is the substantial growth in the number of questions to be tackled and resolved. For example, in a classic decision-making process for procuring a small machine for a laboratory, it was conceivably enough merely to outline the scientific programme and make a few recommendations for accommodating users, leaving the remaining problems to the initiative of the team concerned. In megascience, the problem takes on a whole new appearance. The many items to be specified and dealt with, and their interconnections, transform the decision-making process into an enormous undertaking with a large number of sub-routines, all of which have to be dealt with in parallel, thus complicating the discussions.

Indeed, one of the decisive changes as regards facilities is the increasing involvement of scientific communities and the possibility they have to renew continuously the discussion of these questions. Clearly, this is not true for all scientists: it is fairly obvious that the life sciences, even when they become users of major facilities (*e.g.* synchrotron radiation machines), have not yet acquired the reflexes of communities such as astronomers, particle physicists or, perhaps in the near future, oceanographers, who see large facilities as a integral part of their scientific work.

In sum, the large megascience instruments or projects and the decisions that bring them into existence create a particular form of co-ordination of the scientists, politicians, and economists concerned. The decision-making processes establish a whole series of relationships among the various partners and regulate the various projects. Expectations and actual programmes are redefined around the axis defined by the projects and their future realisation. In this sense, megascience, through the decision-making process, emerges as an instrument of science policy which contributes to organising the scientific arena. Efforts are made jointly, and schedules are set within large bodies set up to deal with megascience. In the final analysis, therefore, megascience resembles a hybrid organisation formulated as decision-making proceeds.

With the need to bring together an increasing number of actors, the decision-making processes tend to become more complicated. Negotiations cannot be limited to bilateral exchanges: gradually other scientific groups and the political and economic authorities take an interest in such projects. It is partly to respond to these ramifications that committees or specific bodies charged with monitoring and formulating the main lines of policy have emerged in the communities that are most advanced in this process. The European Committee for Future Accelerators (ECFA) has already been mentioned; there are also the foresight/planning seminars of the CNES (*Centre national des études spatiales*) or the INSU (*Institut national des sciences de l'Univers*) in France, and nuclear physics recently began similar debates with the NuPECC committee. The Pinkau and Mayer-Leibnitz committees have done similar work in Germany. Further examples are unnecessary.

This proliferation and this need for co-ordination are the conditions for effective operation, or more exactly for a form of operation that has dominated in recent decades. In a more historical perspective, certain disciplines and scientific fields have developed in the direction of bigger and bigger groups, which can enrol many forces to serve one or several objectives. It is clear that these forces, if well co-ordinated, can produce considerable synergies. Therein lies the originality of these forms of megascience.

The nature of this development model is worthy of some attention. It should be remembered that it remains highly specific to physics, which gave it birth. It has gradually spread from nuclear physics to other fields: synchrotron radiation, neutron physics, and soon, lasers. Astronomy, another community which already had a fairly strong tradition of large instruments and co-operation, has also joined the movement, all the more willingly as the emergence of space astronomy was already urging it in this direction. However, even today, this model does not apply to all science, and many disciplines are very hostile to it, either because they consider that they have no need for such approaches, or because they consider them dangerous.

At this point, the effects of the choice of big science, if choice it can be called, appear clearer. The need to focus resources that are increasingly more numerous and more diverse, and to establish the most durable consensus possible, creates a number of irreversibilities. It restricts the area of what is possible and the number of alternative paths. It would seem that this is the price to pay – the necessary thermodynamic compensation – that, after artificially creating enormous entropy and then trying to control it, one can no longer allow undertakings of this type to proliferate. Finally, these few remarks draw attention to the pressing need for an analytical approach to monitoring the decision process.

With the advent of megascience, decision making has acquired a decisive role in the elaboration of scientific practice. The need to co-ordinate an increasing number of actors means that the decision-making process serves as a way to co-ordinate the various technical, political, scientific and economic aspects. Only the attainment of an active consensus among all the actors can assure that this form of science will not drift towards uncontrollable projects. This consensus is not static, it is the impetus for reformulating the needs and the interests of all concerned. Decisions in big science may thus be considered fairly good examples of democratic consultation processes. This aspect should be reinforced and supported through political supervision: it is essential to ensure that all actors have been consulted and all possibilities explored.

Procedures instrumental in decision making

The inherent complexity of decision-making processes in megascience means that fairly tight control must be maintained. Procedures can take several forms and affect a number of points in the process. In any event, their introduction plays an important part in guiding certain phases of decision making.

The role of committees

First, there is the importance of the various foresight/forward planning seminars conducted to plan future activities. These often furnish the occasion for formulating and refining future projects in a discipline or scientific field. They are usually attended by a fairly large number of scientists who contribute their ideas, proposals, or recommendations concerning the projects they consider to be most promising for the coming years. Being aired in seminars of this kind or similar gatherings can be essential to a project. Indeed, when a project receives approval and closer study in such a body, this indicates its scientific maturity and constitutes an invitation to provide the resources necessary for a more detailed review. After this first stage, an idea selected or considered noteworthy may attract a small group of scientists, possibly supported by an agency, and a start may be made on proposing it to the various authorities for gathering the necessary support.[3]

This initial aspect of the procedures leads naturally to giving precedence to the scientific ideas that are judged to be the most mature and most promising. It can therefore lead to a fairly special method of selecting projects, one that emphasises the continuity of well-established programmes in the various communities. Conversely, it also guarantees maximum investment on the part of potential users and thus positive spinoff from the programme. For example, in the case of a space programme for astronomical exploration, predetermining priority tasks in this way makes it possible to guard against disgruntlement on the part of researchers who could only partially study the results obtained.

However, an aspect which calls for careful attention is the emergence of new ideas and the preservation of diversity. Scientific and technical systems often tend to drift towards the most stable positions and to cluster around those that appear most profitable, thereby occasionally neglecting to broaden the field of their investigations (Callon, 1993). The function of the foresight/forward planning seminars should be to push original ideas to the most advanced stage possible.

The committees charged with more formal reviews and classification of megascience projects at a later stage have a different task. These bodies may have variable links with the scientific communities and decision making bodies. The specialist committees whose task is to give their views on a given discipline should be considered separately. This type of committee remains close to the scientific field in question, formalises and endorses the main lines of projects, and helps clarify the discussion in the communities, without however rendering a final verdict. Its role in the decision-making process is therefore that of a catalyst.

These committees have become commonplace and are often essential to the smooth working of the decision-making processes. An intermediate forum for discussion, with a purely deliberative role, they also ensure some co-ordination. Nuclear physics, for example, which had always maintained a much more individualistic style, has changed its attitude. A lack of co-ordination and agreement in defining a list of priorities is now regarded as a weak point when facing political authorities. The nuclear physicists have learned the lesson taught by their colleagues in high energy physics and have set up a Nuclear Physics European Collaboration Committee (NuPECC) under the auspices of the European Science Foundation (ESF). It should play a role similar to that of ECFA and help nuclear physics to bounce back.

Other committees, charged with endorsing or rejecting certain projects, have a more rigorous task. They usually find themselves faced with a model involving explicit competition rather than a search for consensus. A number of solutions, all mutually exclusive or requiring altogether too many resources, are submitted to the committee which decides in favour of one of them. It has often been observed that this type of vertical arbitration tends to favour the safest solution, or even the most conservative one from the technical standpoint, thereby benefiting the best established groups and those with an already substantial scientific and technological capital. In this sense, these top-down procedures inevitably produce distortions in the choices they promote.

Most countries, even if they have no committees specialising in megascience problems, have nevertheless set up bodies charged with evaluating scientific programmes and assessing the different proposals. These committees develop their own concerns, as in the case of the Varennes tokamak. Their evaluation criteria combine judgement of the scientific validity of projects with integration of the projects in the more general orientations of science policy. This explains why the formulation of projects includes many possibilities for and means of adapting the projects to different assessment systems. Thus, in the case of the tokamak, the project was modified to become a national, a federal, and then a regional project. This means that the boundaries of a project can continuously be renegotiated along lines that correspond to the procedures and explicit motivations of the committees to which the project is submitted. From this standpoint, the existence of general review bodies significantly affects the decision-making process by highlighting the weak spots and strong points of projects.

How projects sell themselves[4]

The nature of the decision-making process is such that it forces megascience projects to take up a number of economic, political and scientific challenges. Thus, review procedures strongly influence the whole tone and practice of selling a project. A fusion physics project will give greater emphasis to the issue of cheap energy production when the review body is likely to concentrate on this type of selling point because of its own mandate. In a different review frame, it might prefer to stress the relative harmlessness of the process for the environment.

The purpose here is not to point out rhetorical ploys, but to show how certain expectations, more or less explicit, modify the arguments advanced and thus the general outline of projects. Indeed, to satisfy certain demands, the promoters of a project may be led to modify their technical priorities, change the laboratories with which they are associated, and so on. In the case of the Varennes tokamak, the insistence on industrial development reoriented the project towards greater ties to industry. It is through these successive changes in the links between actors and motives that the project is gradually formed.

It is difficult to find any sharp boundary between purely factual and more rhetorical arguments. In many cases, links will be created as the promoters do their work. Thus, for a synchrotron radiation facility, the energy promoters expend to obtain a machine which they justify by its many potential users is closely correlated with the effort they make to mobilise users, whose mobilisation subsequently confirms their predictions. In this situation, control is exercised by the strength of the bonds linking the interests of the different partners. It is of course possible to try to include certain other groups, but the effort will only succeed to the extent that the project meets the priorities and targets these groups have already set for themselves.

The rhetoric of arguments also plays a strong heuristic role in defining the projects and the scientific challenges. A characteristic feature of rhetoric is the juggling of concepts which are related or differentiated according to the needs of the argument. It thus encourages two basic activities: generalisation and reformulation. These are not important simply from a stylistic or opportunist standpoint. They reflect the nature of the decision-making processes. If projects are to succeed, they must be capable of attracting many allies and of satisfying them in one way or another. The objectives must therefore be general but able to be adapted to the situation of each or to be translated in their terms

(Latour, 1990 and 1992). To accomplish this goal, the project promoters must, like Penelope, constantly redo their work – weaving, unravelling, and patiently reweaving the fabric. Only a patient approach of this kind will enable them to withstand endless screening by the committees charged with testing the coherence of these proposals and the strength of the proposed associations. Big science puts discussion – continuing debate about the projects – at the heart of the process. Projects may go on for several years before finding their final shape, or, more precisely, the form of association appropriate to those involved. As the project evolves, rhetoric is essential, because it shows scientists how to make their "creature" credible by moulding and remodelling it. Thus, rhetoric, which can lead to new associations, appears praiseworthy, and the interplay of associations makes it possible to test the more or less valid openings offered by a project and thus ensure its future success.

The part played by rules

More generally, it is important to stress the leading role played by procedures and formal or tacit rules in the conduct of projects and decision making. The procedures for reviewing proposals contribute to shaping and moulding the projects. The case of ELF has already been mentioned. The general form of the project finally submitted largely stemmed from the various procedural constraints: attracting maximum support and sharing out expenditures very carefully in order to avoid having to turn to special funding.

Review by special committees helps define what constitutes a good project with respect to the committee's standards. This goes far beyond a simple list of standard criteria, and in concrete terms means that the project must be shaped to meet certain requirements. The tacit or explicit rules are many: the fairly systematic rejection of purely national projects, the need for cross-financing, for demonstrating the existence of a number of users willing to operate the instrument early on, among others. All these aspects are also linked to the internationalisation characteristic of megascience.

A study of decisions concerning an accelerator in Japan provides a good example of the constraints involved (Hoddeson, 1983). The need to go before many committees in turn, the vote of the community of physicists, and the procedure restricting the total budget assigned to a project of Monbusho were, in this case, all decisive in the gradual modification of the shape of the project. Funding channelled through a different ministry would probably have been greater, but other compromises would have had to be made. The same kind of process existed in France during the discussions about the large national accelerator at the end of the 1960s. According to the various priorities of the French Plan, the possibilities multiplied: a purely national project, a Franco-German one, further use of an old machine, but also the possibility of a Franco-German institute in Grenoble (ILL) around another kind of instrument. Each new machine attempted to satisfy the various rules governing the choice.

Proposal review at CERN is also a good example. In the case of a machine such as the LEP (Large Electron-Positron Ring) or even the LHC (Large Hadron Collider), CERN's accelerator division considers various possible approaches, and the ECFA foresight committee makes a first ranking. Then the experimentalists and technicians begin to classify the possibilities. In the second stage, effort is focused on attracting the maximum individual or collective support for a given project within the community. Once a quorum is reached, the project tends to become that of all the physicists concerned. It then continues its progress to the Scientific Council and the Council of Governments. In this case, the procedures effectively encourage defining the instrument in two successive stages: broad approval for a particular model, followed by endorsement and settlement of the financial arrangements. Such tacit rules broadly explain the general shape of projects.

The establishment of structures for reviewing projects, the existence of rules and procedures, whether formal or informal, are all part of the decision-making process. They facilitate the job of the decision makers by reducing the amount of arbitration. However, they also tend to impose stereotypes, as projects have to conform to a certain model. Of course, the requirements vary from one scientific area to another, but a degree of uniformity has emerged. It would be valuable to have an ethnographical study of committees and procedural rules, something which has not yet been done.

Among the problems frequently mentioned by the actors, the issue of how to distribute the financing of projects and which budget line is involved take an important place. A specific problem involves whether or not there is a separate budgetary envelope for financing the project. Where such a budgetary envelope does exist, the proponents know how likely their project is to succeed and what modifications they will have to make. When a certain annual sum is allocated, even within a certain range, either for funding new projects or for operating older facilities, and when a further distinction is made between funding available for international undertakings and national credits, the projects can be oriented or altered in response to the various incentives. On the other hand, when funding is scattered among several agencies, this can be harmful. Projects managers may be obliged to present, without concern for true coherence, as many *ad hoc* proposals as there are potential funding bodies, in order to satisfy each of them.

On the whole, therefore, procedures mould the projects, which must undergo many reviews, to a considerable extent. The principal instruments are, on the one hand, how the proposals are reviewed and the type of committees involved, and, on the other, the implicit and explicit rules that govern the development of the project. These rules can often lead to a fairly uniform presentation of projects. At the same time, the criteria they introduce constitute the standards to which the promoters must conform. However, they also indicate what margins for negotiation and recasting the teams can use as they adapt their reasons as best they can to the need for a convincing set of arguments. The procedures, or lack of procedures, serve as regulatory tools: they clearly give direction to the decision-making processes.

Attempts to extend the model

Historically, megascience has been tied to the development first of nuclear and then of particle physics at large accelerators. It rapidly took hold in astronomy, because of telescopes but also space missions. Since, megascience has more or less directly affected an increasing number of fields. One could mention its extension to traditionally "smaller" physics and to chemistry, which use synchrotron radiation machines and neutron reactors, to biology, with the programme on the human genome, to climatology, with the programmes of observation of the Earth's climate, and to oceanography.

There is no doubt that certain disciplines originally saw entering the domain of megascience as a way to obtain more abundant funding and to ensure continuity in their research. However, this motivation, if it existed, fades in the face of the need for specific facilities and the choice of a particular scientific organisation. A particularly good illustration is provided by the large co-ordinated programmes for exploring the seas and for climate research. Underlying these programmes is the idea that to achieve a new order of magnitude in the exploration of the Universe, a megascience approach involving large co-ordinated structures offers the greatest return on investment. It also seems to offer the best way to organise the scientific work in the years to come.

The case of biology is perhaps more problematical (Heilbron and Kevles, 1988). The programme of research on the human genome is certainly an attempt to concentrate scientific resources and to transfer the techniques of megascience to biology. It should be noted, however, that it constitutes an accelerated programme in a specific field, but that it is impossible to say whether it really defines a new approach for modern biology. In any event, co-ordination of a large number of laboratories and the massive investment in the programme indicate a move towards developments similar to those found in physics and astronomy.

The attraction of these forms of organisation is such that there have been instances of disciplines quite remote from physics calling for similar initiatives, arguing the need for expensive and co-ordinated instrument programmes in order to give a decisive impulse to their research (Kars et al., 1992).

This "success" of megascience and of the model implicitly underlying it raises the problem of how to manage priorities, and also that of maintaining a balance between different fields of science. From this point of view, decision making about a megascience project also pronounces a verdict on the most harmonious development of a discipline, and one that is reasonable in comparison with others.

Thus, the decision-making processes appear marked by three characteristic features:
- the growth in the number of countries involved in programmes;
- the co-ordination of the various actors involved, as a guarantee that the choices made will be relevant;
- the effect of procedures and implicit standards on the discussions.

Besides these three factors, there is also, partly owing to internationalisation, greater political involvement at a different point. The implicit contract between science and government has weakened to the point where science no longer enjoys a kind of "extra-territorial" privilege but must confront other social and economic priorities. Here the decision-making process has become the place where the interest groups that form can assure the political authorities that the undertakings envisaged are pertinent. To shape these groups, politicians can use procedures, but also earlier intervention in the discussions. More generally, these various developments have definitively transformed decision making into a process involving a large number of feedback loops.

5. The elements of decision making

Objectives and limitations

The foregoing discussion has identified a few major features of the decision-making processes, stressed their essential role, and shown the substantial influence they have on the shape of projects. This part of the analysis will involve a somewhat different exercise, the specification of the arguments that help crystallise decisions through an exploration of the social and scientific machinery. Which opinions and interpretations matter in decision-making? How are decision-making modes structured, and what are the consequences to be expected from particular patterns?

A semi-analytical method will be used to try to identify the main categories involved in the decision-making process. This will make it possible to specify some of the mechanisms and central points. However, it will not be possible to reduce all decision making to a linear pattern of similar form. In every case, the flexibility of situations, the multiplicity of the sets of arguments and their applications, and the diversity of partners create inevitable contingencies. Thus, every decision has surprises that are difficult to account for. In order to paint a broader picture, however, a generalisation is made on the basis of a number of cases. Finally, attention will be directed to some important criteria, this time from a normative point of view.

Decision-making parameters and arguments

Strict separation of the criteria on which decisions are based from the practices that designate the essential partners or the most promising themes is sometimes difficult. It is therefore simpler to review them in turn, trying merely to move from the criteria that are apparently most ''objective'' or conventional to those that arise from particular patterns.

The scientific programme and its development

It is has already been indicated that decision-making processes in megascience required upstream procurement of a fairly broad agreement on the part of the scientific community or groups concerned with a programme. This is achieved as much through foresight/forward planning seminars, which select the most promising ideas, as through the more formal bodies that define a plan for the future of a particular discipline.

One of the essential criteria for judging a megascience project is therefore the scientific objectives it proposes. What information will be gleaned from a new programme or a new instrument? For a long time, this question was not central to the discussions. All the actors had sufficient confidence in science to consider that any initiative, once guaranteed by scientists at a sufficiently high level, would provide its share of results. Nature was generous and the yields of science were bound to increase.

Building up a programme of scientific exploration whose excellence is acknowledged by a fairly large community is a prerequisite for developing a megascience project. It is impossible to overstress the need for communities to achieve a strong consensus on their priorities in the matter and to marshal solid sets of arguments. This will make the difference when they have to defend their projects in an increasingly stringent financial situation and face many potential competitors from other disciplines. There will be little hesitation between two projects if one receives unanimous support from the scientists concerned while the other is marked by hesitation over the choices to be made.

Another issue can then be raised to distinguish between projects. It involves assessing the marginal return on scientific investment or, in other words, determining how much value added the construction of a new installation brings to the programme of a discipline. This makes it possible to establish a gradient of scientific programmes extending from programmes of continuity to those that represent a break with former practice. In the former case, it is a matter of pursuing and perfecting the work of a discipline by adding another stone to an already well-established structure. In the second case, the instrument is supposed to open a path to new prospects and raise new questions.

The planned accelerators for particle physics research typically fall into the former category. The instruments are seen by the decision makers – and by many scientists in other disciplines – as machines devised to extend or even perfect the already well-defined theoretical and experimental framework of high energy physics. A revealing sign of this view is found in the virtual unanimity about the results to be obtained: the principal expected results are the demonstration of the top quark or the Higgs boson. In the extreme, some people may see the undertaking as a verification of theories that are already well confirmed.

Of course this characterisation is not as simple as it may appear, since the status of the scientific programme is always negotiable. Thus, when CERN attempts to broaden its perspectives by research into the early history of the Universe, when it forms links with other groups, such as astronomers working on neutrino detection, it is attempting to shift its project on the above-mentioned gradient to give it new prospects.

Quite apart from question of cost, US reticence about the SSC project was also related to concern about the scientific returns from the programme. The project in itself had the necessary scientific qualities, but it was not clear where it would lead. In some sense, what was feared was an adventure similar to the large Bellevue electromagnet, an excellent machine without much future.

Several programmes can illustrate the other end of the gradient. The recent attempts to detect gravitational waves represent a scientific programme with high dynamic potential (such as Virgo, 1989). Indeed, the proposed instruments intend not only to demonstrate a phenomenon that has not yet been observed but also to open a new window of astrophysical observation on the Universe, which promises a fairly rich harvest of new data. The same applies to space missions charged with exploring as yet unknown aspects of the radiation spectrum, which are assumed to be very promising, as was the case when infrared images were being sought. Similarly, the large co-ordinated research programmes on climate intend to combine and exploit information on a so far unattempted world-wide scale, and thereby open up a large number of possibilities.

Hence the question of the nature of the scientific programme does not come down essentially to the question of novelty. By definition, any scientific undertaking of quality – and all those mentioned are certainly that – will have to provide new data and explore virgin territory. What matters, instead, is the perception of the relation between the potential investment and the return and the assessment that can be made of the dynamism of the field and the marginal gains that it makes possible.

It is striking to note that high energy physicists have used this criterion for their colleagues in nuclear physics. The latter defend the need to explore atomic and nuclear interactions using energies of the order of a GeV. There is no doubt that particle physics, in its forced march to high energies, has not explored all aspects of nuclear physics, so that the accelerators in this range continue to be productive and provide new information. Yet, while they do not question that it provides new information, high energy specialists doubt the potential and true import of this research (see the discussion by Detraz, 1992).

It is therefore necessary, given current budgetary difficulties, for all scientific programmes to position themselves at a relatively well balanced point on the above-mentioned gradient. Attempts will be made much more systematically than before to eliminate programmes that are considered weakly dynamic or show a diminishing return. This explains why certain disciplines are making constant attempts to broaden their competencies. During the decision-making process in particular, the actors will be urged to increase the number of associations in order to strengthen the scientific potential of the instrument. For example, research on gravitational waves is mobilising physicists as well as astronomers and astrophysicists.

This aspect is accompanied by another criterion, which is the expansion of the communities concerned. A scientific programme can also be judged in terms of the number of scientists involved. Will a particular programme merely ensure continuity and keep the teams working or will it, as far as budgets permit, lead to diversification or extension? Thus, through the medium of the scientific programme, the problem of the future of the communities involved and their possible transformation is addressed.

At the other end of the gradient, a scientific programme well anchored within an established discipline over time is reassuring. It offers the certainty of the stable exploitation of results and avoids disappointment. Its function is to ensure continued scientific development.

The complexity of decision-making modes will lead to preferring a good balance. Scientific investment must ensure a strong dynamism while relying on stable scientific forces. This is one of the consequences of the difficulty of managing the entropy of decision-making processes. One measure that can be used is related to the nature and volume of the scientific operations; a scientific programme is more or less flexible, with a greater or lesser capacity to accommodate separate research modules.

One may ask to what extent a project can incorporate relatively diverse users and objectives. A synchrotron radiation machine and the programmes for ocean exploration or climate research are certainly well placed in this respect. On the other hand, certain narrowly focused instruments, by definition of low modularity, are limited to a specific objective and to a specific type of results. To some extent, this is the situation of the large accelerators, although a combination of various scientific prospects can be envisaged, whatever the programme.

Attempts should nevertheless be made during the decision-making process to favour modular programmes with a high level of association and diversification. This criterion overlaps that concerning the dynamics of information around the project.

In sum, the definition of a scientific programme recognised as valid by the entire community is a prerequisite that nearly all projects now satisfy. This unanimity is built up through the foresight/forward planning seminars, meetings of scientific committees, and exchanges among scientists. The main criteria concern the dynamics of the instrument or programme proposed and its modularity. As regards the former, the political authorities' growing concern for the best return on investment tends to benefit projects offering the broadest prospects for development. Conversely, there is a fear that a project which is too narrowly focused will gradually stagnate. Similarly, increasing the modularity of the programme makes it possible for the scientific groups involved to develop satisfactorily. Thus, the growing complexity of the phases of the decision-making process, particularly as regards political approval and scientific choice, results in a move away from the traditional support for disciplines firmly grounded in continuity. The case of the SSC in the United States is in part an example. It is by demonstrating its superiority in these areas that a project can obtain the most support from the political decision makers (ministries and legislatures) and the scientific authorities.

Promised spinoffs and economic contribution

This is now one of the compulsory waypoints in most presentations. However, it is important to specify the different types of project spinoff. The most obvious concerns the new resources it provides to the scientific community or communities involved. A science policy, usually conceived and applied at national level, attempts to provide researchers with the tools necessary for maintaining a good level of skills as compared to those of their colleagues abroad. Hence, the approval of a project will take into account the improvements made to the working conditions of the scientific group concerned, its marginal contribution as compared to existing resources, and the need to provide all the communities with the resources they need to work. In this context, a project which would represent only an additional input to a given group, without a marked impact, will tend to be rejected in favour of decisions to go ahead on facilities judged more urgent. In fact, although interdisciplinary rankings are never explicitly made, the comparative status of the different communities is a parameter which can always be exploited in the debate.

Evaluation of spinoffs takes place at a more detailed level of regulation than the evaluation of the scientific programme. Once the question of the greater or lesser impact of the development of a given scientific field has been dealt with, an attempt is made to evaluate the need for new inputs. Thus, for high energy physics, once the support for this field of research has been taken into account, once the smaller and smaller number of new accelerators has been taken into account, the impact and spinoff from building a new machine will appear considerable. The same is not true, to the same extent, for a particular space mission.

The second aspect of spinoffs concerns the developments expected from the scientific results to be obtained. A distinction should be made between immediate application and marginal results. In the first case, it is a question of elements destined to advance practical understanding and which can be applied immediately. The programmes in biology or on the climate are two good examples.

The explicit objective in the case of biology is the treatment of genetic diseases and an improved understanding of the human organism which will ultimately permit better health care. One need only consider how public opinion has rallied around the collection of funds for aiding genetic research to comprehend the weight of such arguments. To this is added another more important aspect, the consequences of such research for immediate industrial applications, such as the patenting of genetic sequences that make it possible to achieve a specific result. The industrial stakes are high and undoubtedly carry considerable weight in the decision-making process.

Fairly similar arguments can be made for the programmes of ocean exploration or climate research. For example, access to the seabed is providing a great deal of information on the wealth and resources it contains. In the case of climate observations, the spinoffs more immediately concern the environment, the control of industrial processes, and the preservation of natural resources, all of which have become essential issues as an environment policy gains ground in many countries.

Other megascience projects cannot claim such immediate applications. It should be emphasized that the study of spinoffs excludes the more general problem of the advancement of knowledge and concentrates on the practical justifications for the project. Certain disciplines may show, or suggest, how their research will ultimately have substantial consequences. High energy physics is a case in point.[5] Arguing from the unexpected repercussions of nuclear physics, physicists always defend, to a greater or lesser degree, the idea of future practical discoveries which are essential for economic development. For example, an article by C. Rubbia, the former general director of CERN, suggested embarking upon the search for new sources of energy (*Le Monde*, 27 November 1993). However, the influence these declarations have on decision-makers varies, depending upon the circumstances. In particular, the effect of certain distant promises, or those that are continually deferred, will gradually weaken.

More peripherally, projects may produce spinoffs in terms of technical or economic development by stimulating basic technological research and the development of new types of machine or instrument. While such arguments were never used in the 1960s and 1970s, CERN has employed this economic and technical justification since a first study of 1977 (Schmied, 1977; then Bianchi-Streit *et al.*, 1985; see also Cohendet and Lebeau, 1987). There is no doubt that, in a number of cases, being involved in certain megascience projects has perhaps played a more important role than direct investment in certain areas of research, whether concerned with power tubes, magnets or advanced miniaturised electronics.

Another side of this question is the impact projects have on economic activity. This is partly related to the installation of facilities in a particular country but, increasingly, to the rule of ''fair return'', according to which each country is entitled to expect benefits for its industry. The expected economic return is then more a preliminary in international discussion than a veritable argument.

With the current budgetary restrictions and the growing impact of political decisions, the old tacit agreement between science, technology, and economic development has come under careful scrutiny. Countries now wish to have a clear and long-term view of the practical contributions of megascience projects. They make a distinction between immediate spinoffs, as in biology, and longer-term ones. Orders placed with industry and the marginal improvement of certain kinds of know-how offer short-term economic arguments. However, where these motivations meet, the long-term development of certain industries is now evaluated. It is no accident that space remains a privileged field, given what the aviation industry owes to the technologies that space research makes it possible to master. Another sign of this is the gradual emergence of inertial guidance systems, and their development in the United States, which reflects a very similar approach to technological choices (MacKenzie, 1990; more generally, on the development of space research in astronomy, for example, see Smith, 1990). Thus the decision-making process increasingly leads to a focus on certain fields linked to the technologies that are considered most promising.

As things stand, arguments for direct spinoffs carry a good deal of weight early in the process but only affect the small number of disciplines that can claim immediate spinoffs. However, peripheral spinoffs come into play much later in the formalisation and elaboration of projects and provide a means of attracting important actors such as financial managers and removing obstacles when financial schemes are being set up. During this stage, increasing weight is given to the development of specific industrial technologies as compared with marginal contributions. However, there is still the risk of focusing projects on a few individual technologies, the source of long-term fossilisation (on this point, see the analysis in Section 7).

The role of competition and alternative prospects

Competition has long played a decisive role in decision-making processes as way to receive final approval if perchance a threatening competitor should appear. With the internationalisation of projects and decisions, its role has been reduced, although there are a few exceptions. Thus, some of the discussions about the LHC at CERN and the SSC in the United States showed signs of competition. The progress made by one of the projects was sometimes a powerful motivation for building the other. Conversely, the abandonment of the SSC will certainly have an effect on the LHC project, which will have to be reshaped to take account of this decision.

Direct competition between countries, within a given discipline, has been replaced by two somewhat different phenomena: on the one hand, discussion between disciplines, and, on the other, discussion of the various possible options for achieving an objective of the development of a scientific discipline.

The first of these features is increasingly clear, as certain scientists argue against equivalent projects they consider too expensive and of lesser interest. This suggests that consideration should be given to the role of interdisciplinary programme planning in decision-making processes. A programme will have a better chance in the decision-making process if it appears as one of the rare possibilities for scientific development. This more or less implies initiating a project at the optimal moment, so that it does not meet too strong opposition from competitors. It will then also benefit from the time factor, as its realisation will appear particularly urgent in a well-devised timetable.

In other words, proposing a project too long in advance does have advantages, such as the possibility of achieving a fuller consensus on how to carry it out and of assembling more allies, but it also presents some difficulties. The project risks being put off *sine die*, owing to a lack of perceived urgency. It is therefore necessary to make a clear distinction between the exploratory, forward-looking phase and the launch of the project as a public undertaking.

A second point plays an important role in decision-making processes: the alternatives offered within a given project or among several projects. Generally speaking, when several projects compete for the same resources, this generates confusion and slows the emergence of a stable solution. This goes back to the definition of priorities by the scientific community. If the latter is divided over a number of solutions which are fairly clearly opposed, the projects will have little chance to succeed and the result may even be an unsatisfactory compromise solution (Hoddeson, 1983). Initial clarification is a preliminary step in the decision-making process; however, focusing on a single project that is difficult to modify and does not include options leads to an often prejudicial inflexibility. The case of the 300 GeV and the ISR rings at CERN (see Section 3) illustrates the value of complementary and possibly separable projects which allow the political authorities and the public agencies to make choices and define priorities. The two projects offered two coherent approaches to the question of accelerators. By offering a project with a modular structure, the chances of approval augment, as the different partners can adjust the options on the basis of the various priorities. Also, for a project such as climate study, it is possible to include a variety of separate options which can help lead to a satisfactory conclusion to the decision process. It is therefore important to reduce initial diversity of projects while preserving a great deal of internal flexibility.

The traditional pattern, in which a project threatened by external competition won support more easily, is in decline. Competition from the LHC was not sufficient to promote the SSC which suffered from other weaknesses. Similarly, too many projects in a particular field will make decision makers cautious and tend to postpone the decision. Yet, caution is necessary: a frequent result of hasty compromises is solutions that are particularly unsatisfactory. On the other hand, as soon as this danger has been recognised, it is preferable to incorporate a number of congruent viewpoints in a given undertaking, so as to increase the project's chances and to encourage fruitful innovations.

Integration in an overall science policy

Megascience projects are often quite autonomous, as they concern scientific fields that are fairly strongly institutionalised and self-contained. Decisions were long taken within the discipline itself, but this practice is increasingly yielding ground to a combined evaluation of the merits of a project and of its repercussions on science policy. This type of judgement can only be rendered in a national framework, and it is at this level that the links between national decisions and the planning of projects in a broader geographical framework, made necessary by the internationalisation of megascience, are formed (see OECD, 1991).

The first issue is the scientific priorities determined at national level. It is in the interest of a project to align its characteristics with national orientations. Schematically, these can be of four kinds:

- the definition of general priorities, such as the environment or technological development;
- the preservation of national scientific communities and their facilities;
- the priority given to co-operation;
- the development of scientific diversity.

Each of these aspects must be specifically considered in terms of the decision-making process. A project cannot artificially link itself to a field considered to have priority without relying on very weak arguments. The only projects to benefit will be those closely related to current priorities (environment, health, etc.), if they also satisfy the other criteria for stable megascience projects.

At a second stage, other projects may attempt to show how they contribute to these priorities. Thus, fusion research may well point to its potential for economic development, or even its future contribution to reducing pollution. Statements by high energy physicists about the control of the innermost processes of matter give glimpses of similar arguments.

The way in which priorities are determined also plays a part. Governments, like parliaments, rely on scientific advisory bodies. Hence, a discipline or subject that is particularly well represented within these bodies will have its work promoted. This naturally goes along with the reputation of and the recognition granted to the most outstanding elements in these communities. At this stage is to be found the conventional process of scientific recognition and the hierarchy of disciplines which act over the long term. For the decision-makers concerned to implement public policy, this means assessing the relative weight of the disciplines on the basis of their dynamism so as not to give preference systematically to a field that is temporarily at the top of the pyramid.

This being said, current trends show fairly clearly that judgements are not only made on the basis of a simple criterion of scientific prestige. The continuation of programmes such as the Space Station, fiercely criticised by many scientists of all persuasions, shows that the choice of scientific directions is now bound up with a very broad range of other national and international priorities.

The second point concerns the development of national communities. In absolute terms, they would naturally prefer to have the installations they need for their work situated in their own country, but this is no longer possible for many types of research. However, a number of strategies are possible. It is possible to stress a national approach, as in the case of the Varennes tokamak, so long as the emphasis is placed on a particular aspect of the research programme. In theory, as regards the growth of fusion research, it may seem a waste of time to build a small machine that would merely reproduce on a smaller scale the results obtained elsewhere. In fact, once emphasis is placed on a particular aspect that can be investigated with this type of installation, there is a good chance of garnering support from the public authorities. This support is, after all, based primarily on the preliminary reports and national expert committees. The latter may consider that attempts to keep specialist expertise within the country are fully justified.

In fact, a scientific field's chances of developing megascience projects rises when each of the national communities concerned has adopted a co-operative approach. If refractory elements remain, they will often win out in national review processes and narrower projects will receive preference. For fixed-site projects, this also implies paying particular attention to the question of operating and sharing the installations. Mechanisms set up to ensure an equitable association of the different partners will lend their weight to projects oriented towards co-operation. In this case, the obstacle is the delicate problem of choice of site which, if badly handled, can seriously impede the decision-making process.[6]

More generally, a megascience project will have to envisage establishing an inventory of existing installations in the country. Only if there is concentrated demand for an installation, and only if that demand is integrated into a general development scheme for the field concerned will agreement be obtained in the medium term.

However, governments, particularly in medium-sized countries, are increasingly placing megascience in an international context from the outset. This applies to Finland, the Netherlands, Sweden, and others which have identified a budgetary envelope for this area. In these cases, a project will be looked upon more favourably if it can show true and well-developed partnerships between groups and institutions in different countries. However, watch will be kept for any artificial grouping of risks and budgetary requirements that would merely arrange for sharing expenditure, without true co-operation. Although such a formula may initially benefit a project, the inherent contradictions are likely to hinder it considerably as the process moves on – as the ELF demonstrated.

In most countries, support for innovation now occupies an important place in science policy. This involves not only developing basic technological research but also sustaining the diversity of skills in science. *A priori,* a megascience project does not fit readily into such priorities. In addition, the issue of allocating funds between big instruments and smaller ones for laboratories, which often complain of shortages, resurfaces from time to time (Jouffrey and Nauciel, 1988). Therefore, preference will be given in megascience programmes to an approach which gives priority to the development of new technologies and also provides for harmonious sharing of the use of facilities. Here, isolated disciplines which support a project of internal expansion will experience greater difficulties. One obvious exception is biology and the Human Genome Programme. In this instance, a single scientific field has mobilised resources in order to concentrate on certain techniques and obtained the support of all. This calls for two remarks. The priority given to the exploration of the genome stems in part from the expectation of immediate applications. Second, in the longer term, this concentration on a single activity, which uses biological research as a means to an end, is likely to raise problems very similar to those of other fields of science.

The internationalisation of megascience raises the delicate problem of the link between national policy and the development of new projects. As far as possible, each project places itself within the general framework of national concerns and thus acquires additional support. However, two aspects receive special attention: a direct contribution to a national priority such as health or environment and preserving the development of national communities. A project well situated in these two respects but perhaps less well situated in terms of other criteria mentioned earlier, will tend to succeed in the absence of a balanced joint review of the various priorities which involves the relevant authorities and other disciplines. This underlines the need for a study of all projects in the light of science policy in order to establish clear priorities, free from special interests (the influence of a specific group of scientists, for instance).

Community of users

The broadening of megascience, in terms both of internationalisation and the size of installations, means that it is no longer possible for a given group to acquire an instrument only for its own purposes. In the "users' facilities" model (*e.g.* synchrotron radiation machines), emphasis is now placed on the need to mobilise the widest possible communities of users and to increase the number of partnerships.

This factor has a dual relationship with the decision-making process. First, the process offers the opportunity to establish user groups, to bring interested scientists together, and to have them contribute to formulating the project. Second, the existence of these groups is an important factor in obtaining the agreement of the public authorities.

Of course, there are still situations where supply creates demand, particularly when the public agencies support their own programmes in the hope that ultimately they will recruit enough users. However, the difficulties encountered, for example, in the decision about and operation of the first Landsat satellite clearly illustrate the importance of identifying users beforehand (Mack, 1989). In particular, the large amounts of data collected and the often superficial processing they receive suggest that further consideration should be given to how much output should be required of scientific communities. At what point, for instance, does it become more advantageous to launch new programmes although old ones have not been fully exploited?

In this process, the actors in projects intend to determine far more carefully and precisely the numbers of potential users and their centres of interest. This leads to refining considerably the technical apparatus to be employed. The users associated with the project cannot play a passive role. It is not enough to invoke a vast potential public in order to gain a positive decision: intermediaries, in the form of spokesmen for these groups, must make their voices heard. With this in view, the establishment of consortia from universities and laboratories or of mixed private-public groups can be encouraged. This can prove decisive, since each user group will add local political and economic support and thus additional weight to the project.

Therefore, introducing procedures to stimulate users to group together and organise is important. In the case of the ESRF synchrotron radiation machine, for example, providing beam lines to established small groups, who can use these somewhat less sophisticated facilities to prepare themselves for working on the more advanced lines, gives considerable added value to the project.

More generally, early consideration of how teams should be formed and how results are ultimately to be exploited makes it possible to include a growing number of users in a project and thus ensure that the facilities are fully used. This concern the modularity and the flexibility of the facilities, which allows them to be adapted to meet users' needs.

Examining the relationship between the required investment and the number of potential users becomes an important waypoint in the decision-making processes, insofar as it relieves the public authorities of the fear that a large scientific operations will furnish no real breakthroughs. At the same time, the constituency for a project will increase the more it is supported by groups at local and national levels.

Cost and budgetary constraints

Contrary perhaps to certain expectations, the financial parameter, whatever its over-all importance, rarely plays the main role in decision-making processes. On the other hand, reviews of relative figures are increasingly important, whether budgets are com-pared to number of researchers, cost of the experiment, per centage of national budgets, proportion of R&D expenditure, or relative share compared with that of other countries. It can be concluded that projects are seen as better justified if they achieve a sufficiently balanced sharing of costs and if the resources allocated by a given country are in an acceptable ratio to earlier expenditure in a particular discipline, or comparable with similar data for other countries. One should of course not neglect the impact, in absolute terms, of the amount to be raised, which can create difficulties within the framework of certain countries' ordinary budget.

Until recently, using cost in decision-making processes was in part a skilful presen-tation of operations. When the time came to choose between the ISR and the 300 GeV, CERN had to submit several financial options. It examined two options: a 150 GeV machine and a 300 GeV machine, and established a comparative table of costs. The presentation gave the impression that it was more advantageous to adopt the second option, which nonetheless cost substantially more. It adroitly compared the two solutions, year by year, showing the differential expenditure; since the second option concerned a different number of years, the conclusion was obvious (Hermann *et al.*, 1990; on these questions see also Pestre, 1988). Ultimately, of course, comparing reasoned schedules of expenditure may prove relevant, since they indicate the specific rate of progress of the discipline. Compared with annual national budgets, it gives a comparative view of project costs over the long term. Yet, the rules for presenting expenditure still need further refinement.

When CERN obtained approval for the LEP by assuring that it could be completed within its ordinary budget, it proposed a solution which convinced funding bodies and politicians. However, despite considerable savings, the budgetary envelope was in fact insufficient, and CERN was obliged to borrow, thereby putting a significant strain on its budget.

This raises the issue of cost sharing. One of the major recommendations in preparing for decisions involves reducing the specific cost to each partner by arranging for expendi-ture to be shared among an increasing number of countries. If this suggestion is adopted, the project's chances are strengthened, since it combines the benefits of reduced cost and of international co-operation, both of which are regarded as desirable. There remain the questions of the real efficacy of this step and of a concerted review of expenditure, as well as that of the association mechanism and of the budgeting of funding. If there is no stable agreement between the partners, it will perhaps be better to abandon an apparently attractive solution whose long-term consequences, in terms of delays, hence additional costs, for example, are unclear.

Proposal reviews quite deliberately place emphasis on all attempts to make precise estimates of costs and the extent of expenditure. In particular, any preparatory work that simulates or evaluates technologies and the hazards involved helps stabilise projects.

This new priority is reflected in the recent vote against the SSC project. Although the total cost of the project alarmed the Congress, the startling rise in the figures – from $4.4 billion to over $11 billion in the space of five years – may have had even greater impact. The need for projects to guard against this tendency will be discussed below when monitoring procedures are considered.

Two final aspects remain to be dealt with. First, how does the proposed cost stand with respect to international standards? This is a delicate exercise in that there is rarely an exact duplicate of the project, but the existence of even an approximate term of comparison may seriously impede a project if the comparison is in its disfavour. This is what may have happened for the 200 GeV machine proposed by Berkeley, and it is also underlies the criticisms of those who reproach CERN with high construction costs (Irvine and Martin, 1984; Martin and Irvine, 1984 a and 1984b). Yet the exercise should be used with caution: CERN's careful definition of the technical aspects of its facilities was to be decisive in the conversion to moving target colliders which caused so many problems at Fermilab.

As for the second aspect, the evaluation of past results, in terms both of carrying out projects and of the results provided by the programmes, now plays a significant role in the decision-making process. The process thus involves foresight/forward planning of the scientific programme as well as an evaluation of past achievements. The latter is a difficult exercise not always reflected in the work of those who do it. By focusing on the speed at which certain results were obtained, and on the direct costs, there is a danger of paralysing scientific innovation by eliminating groups that contribute to the overall development of the scientific field (Collins, 1985; see also a discussion of these questions in Ducrocq et al., 1992).

A further question concerns the possibility of transferring funds. The fairly fanciful reasoning according to which funds might "mentally" be assigned from large facilities to small installations should be dismissed. This would almost certainly be ineffective. In the past, financial negotiations have rarely used such an approach. However, if another facility of comparable size and funding does exist, there is a temptation to move the funds from one to the other. This has become commonplace. The political decision makers reason, albeit theoretically, in terms of large masses and often consider it difficult to be involved simultaneously in two undertakings of high cost, particularly if cost overruns are to be feared.

Care should also be paid to balancing the different categories of expenditure: capital, operation, and staff. Since permanent scientific groups are available, it is possible to try to reduce investment costs significantly by hoping to spread certain studies over a longer period, using ordinary credits for this purpose; this carries some risk but does make it possible to negotiate a delicate budgetary situation. This goes hand in hand with numerous preliminary trials for testing certain aspects of the project. Any later imbalance among these three categories may suggest that the design of the project should be revised. Hence, any systematic underestimation of investment will perhaps make completing the machine a risky and finally more costly business. This observation applies to fixed-site megascience but can be extended in a somewhat different form to distributed programmes. For these, an exacting review will look closely into the costs of co-ordination, such as centralising and harmonising data and data-processing resources, which will fairly systematically be sacrificed.

The cost of facilities intervenes in the decision-making processes in two different ways. To begin with, it should be placed in an approach to planning which would smooth out expenditure peaks and contingencies. The more a discipline shows a need for investment at a particular time, the more favourable the result it is likely to obtain. Hence, a detailed breakdown of investments will be useful. Cost sharing is clearly favourable to a project, but it does raise the fear of creating monsters that ultimately cost as much because they are unmanageable. Therefore, project promoters should attempt to demonstrate the effectiveness of the management procedures. Also, the cost of megascience projects causes concern at certain times and can, through the effects of amplification, increase public deficits. A guarantee of stringent control of expenditure has thus become essential. This requires a whole body of preparatory work and technical and industrial studies as the decision process proceeds. All these reasons should encourage promoters to propose facilities that can respond flexibly to needs and to the availability of funding.

Project evolution, balanced planning, and continuity

Every megascience project opens up more or less clear prospects for the future of the scientific fields involved. They include the ease with which the instrument is operated, its evolution over time, its potential for modification, its integration into the smooth development of a discipline, and its prospects for conversion.

The first point is related to the question of modularity and flexibility. The more the project has built-in potential for change or technical modification, the more easily it will gain support, insofar as it allows for responding to an irreversibility which can be very costly for expensive projects. This factor applies particularly to large, fixed-site facilities.

For large-scale distributed programmes, such as those dealing with the human genome or Earth observation, the problem is of a different order. By definition, these efforts represent a substantial investment and sudden growth for the fields concerned. One may ask how these disciplines will succeed in managing the changes and spread this substantial augmentation over a long period? The review of a project will be facilitated if it fits well into the regular advancement of the relevant discipline and does not require great concentrated efforts. In the background, there is always the embarrassing question of conversion: following a massive investment, how will the discipline manage its growth? Will it not eventually seek further investment? The project must therefore provide prospects for evolution.

Also, this time upstream in the decision-making process, the negotiations about a project may include a discussion of the resources that already exist in a particular field.

The closure or conversion of certain machines may appear as an important prerequisite for supporting the decision. The process is risky, however, when an instrument or a programme is abandoned without any assurance that a counterpart can be found.

Overall, it appears that projects based upon strict continuity, although they are reassuring and may be based on results already obtained, do raise questions as to scientific yield and the dynamism they are likely to generate. The evolution of the programme is therefore closely related to the definition of the scientific programme in order to favour programmes that mobilise much scientific effort, are likely to engender growth in the long term, and for which facilities can be converted relatively easily.

Endorsement of a megascience project presupposes on the one hand a precise assessment of the way in which the project will evolve, particularly the investment it may require at a later stage. On the other, it must be integrated into the resource planning of a discipline over a period of several years. When there are budgetary constraints in cases where there is no joint review of resources, there is a risk of troubles that ultimately will halt the project. The SSC is only one example. Finally, the project should incorporate longer-term considerations of the evolution of the communities concerned.

Status of technology and industrial alliances

Virtually by definition, a megascience project necessitates technologies that are complex and delicate and whose implementation is fraught with uncertainties. It is therefore necessary to mobilise the teams of engineers and industrialists that are essential to satisfactory progress. While it is difficult to avoid completely the inevitable contingencies in this type of development, both scientists and decision makers are increasingly sensitive to the need to reduce them through careful preliminary missions or technological development. The misfortunes of the Space Telescope, for example, show very clearly that the slightest error can lead to considerable additional cost (Smith, 1990).

It is possible, in fact, to distinguish two contradictory ambitions: first, a search for relative technical stability and, second, a penchant for innovative technical solutions. Where competencies are otherwise equivalent, an open decision-making process will tend to prefer approaches involving the use of original technical systems, whereas a vertical review procedure is likely to classify projects and place greater emphasis on safety and conventional solutions.

Bringing innovative aspects to the fore therefore often implies having fairly advanced teams of engineers and co-operating closely with industry. Here, it is no longer possible simply to subcontract the construction of the project to industry on the basis of specifications. The close relations formed with industry, although they appear at first quite alien to fundamental research, are an essential asset in the decision-making process.

Moreover, in order to gain additional support, industrialists may knock on the doors of decision makers other than those with whom scientists are normally in contact. The traditional division between science and technology must yield to a broader vision in which the two sides are complementary. In many recent megascience decisions, the backing of industry in the field has given added assurances in the decision-making process.

110

If a megascience project is to proceed satisfactorily, it will often require mobilising complex technologies, with all the risks that this implies. To reduce these risks, emphasis should be placed on a series of preparatory trials for full-scale testing of the reliability of the solutions adopted. This also means making the decision-making process the scene where the different concerns – scientific, industrial and technical – come together. The more a project can demonstrate its competence in this respect, the more support it will receive. Since long-term economic spinoffs are also a matter of concern to governments, this phase also allows them to hear the views of industry on the know-how they are acquiring and thus refine their views on the project.

The role of procedures

The role of procedures, which are in a sense a means of regulating decisions by modelling the different phases of the processes, has already been stressed (Section 4). Suffice it to recall the essential role of foresight/forward planning seminars and committees, the influence of review committees and their rules of procedure, and the need for projects to comply with a fairly strict model for presenting information.

The role of the actors and co-ordination

One of the essential aspects of decision-making processes is co-ordination between the different actors. As decision-making modes have become more cumbersome, more and more diverse actors have become involved. The importance of user communities and of prior agreement among scientists in a particular field has been emphasised. Beyond this elementary stage, many other parameters intervene.

It is therefore worth examining the links that may be set up between different groups and that give a project a particular form. In the case of the Varennes tokamak, for example, the initial concentration of Quebec actors gave the project a strong regional flavour. More generally, as a project proceeds, the involvement of new actors may have to be negotiated. In the case of high energy physics and nuclear physics, the representatives of the latter field would like to be able to manage the decision-making processes within their own discipline. In fact, however, their colleagues intervene to check the allocation of significant resources to a field about which they feel they have a say. It is at this stage that the rights of each of the actors to be associated, or not, in the decision-making process are negotiated.

The large number of actors involved can cause reversals or abrupt modifications of the project, which lead to profound and substantial changes. Thus, the definition of a megascience project also includes the progressive incorporation of the different parties concerned, with their roles and their place in the hierarchy, so that each can be included in the process without difficulty or fundamental reopening of the question.

The negotiation process described for the Canadian tokamak was characterised by extreme mobility, potential appropriation by many actors, and great latitude in the definition of the main orientations; this created a relatively confused situation in which all priorities could be renegotiated in turn or simultaneously (Gingras and Trepanier, 1993).

The decision-making process for the ISR and the 300 GeV machine at CERN illustrates a different pattern, with the roles of the parties concerned better defined by the discussion about the machine. The roles of engineers and technicians, theoreticians and experimentalists, politicians and funders were kept separate. To some extent, this helped speed up the process.

It is worth considering briefly the main actors and the times at which they enter the decision-making process, the influence they bring to bear and the constraints this implies, along with the promoters of the project and the spokesmen for the community of potential users. The means of co-ordination and the incentives necessary to preserve the unity of these two groups have already been emphasised.

During the initial phase of the project, the various councils, committees, or commissions charged with determining priorities figure among the most influential advisers. However, their role is limited to the early phases of the process and to the setting in motion of the projects judged most promising. Depending on the procedures adopted for reviewing the proposals and the stage at which they are submitted, the opinions of the committees may differ. However, as a general rule, they tend to favour the most innovative projects which, marginally, promise the most results. This stage of the process may be confined to a scientific network and precede any formal announcement.

Depending on the nature of the project, the decision-making process then may involve one or more scientific agencies which support and possibly manage its completion. Their role is considerable. On the one hand, they often possess substantial funding, and they also develop their own programmes for which they try to obtain endorsement. It is therefore possible to call on them either to contribute to preparing the project, or because they will necessarily be the source of national support, or to ensure that they do not stand in the way. Alternatively, the project may emerge from and develop within one of these agencies, which will play a role through virtually the entire decision-making process. They may have a decisive influence on the success or failure of a project, because of the weight they carry, but also because of the international collaborative network that they have at their disposal. They are therefore listened to by political decision makers. In particular, agencies such as CERN or ESA, which are relatively autonomous, can manage, largely in house, decisions on the projects of communities they support.

The constraints affecting the decision then concern the need to reconcile and bring together different tendencies within the agency. The co-ordination procedures introduced often involve a sectoral division in which the chosen pattern should allow each partner to obtain maximum benefit. This agency approach usually favours projects that are located relatively high on the gradient that extends from continuity to new departures and have a high technical innovativeness coefficient.

As the project develops, the more the intervention of technical and industrial partners seems likely. In particular, the introduction into the process of industrialists who can guarantee the technical feasibility and, above all, the importance of the project for their own development and for technical progress, can also help convince ministries and technical committees.

At this stage, the process is very advanced and all the actors formerly located on the margins of the project begin to make a more significant contribution. To begin with, the scientific committees charged with advising the governments begin to review the projects more precisely; their role is to give the green light. However, more broadly, all the responsible ministries involved review the proposals and in particular transfer information to the financial authorities who give their views on the project's substance. The importance of this aspect of the process will be discussed below.

Among the other partners whose voice is important at this stage should be mentioned certain members of the scientific communities (Nobel prizewinners, recognised leading scientists, directors of agencies, and so on) whose endorsement may prove crucial. At the same time, for international projects, diplomats begin to work at a more general level to prepare the way for an agreement among the various countries.

National parliaments and political authorities also intervene to review the projects submitted and pay particular attention to the impact of scientific programmes on other budgetary priorities. In particular, in countries such as the United States, where the Congress must finally approve the funding of each project, legislators want complete assurance that the projects will evolve satisfactorily, owing, for example, to cost control or the reliability of the scientific associations that have been formed.

At the parliamentary review stage, scientists' arguments have often been reproached with being too esoteric. The remedy lies in refining scientific views and associating parliamentarians earlier in the decision process. If a detailed picture of the disciplines and their future development is presented along with the constraints imposed on research groups by the means at their disposal for their work, the support of decision-makers will be easier to obtain.

Finally, and this is a phenomenon that may become more frequent, public opinion can intervene in the debate, or more exactly be solicited by the various parties concerned through press campaigns, public debates, or lobbying by certain groups. Although the mechanisms of megascience still do not involve the public at large, projects of this type are publicised more and more often. A television broadcast may thus focus on major public programmes to show what could have been done with the same amount of money.

At this point, the main actors in the process are in place, and each develops a special kind of competence. This brief review gives at least a general idea of the different forces that have to be mobilised to obtain a decision and of the leeway available for them to interact at different stages of the process.

On the whole, the decision-making process should favour association and discussion among many actors. A convenient method of assessing a project is to examine how and how carefully it has embarked on the laborious process of co-ordination. There is in particular an increasingly strong interaction between the processes of scientific and of political review. The definition of priorities by the two areas increasingly converges, because of the association of the various actors, a guarantee of project stability.

Among the important actors in the decision-making process, a finance ministry or its equivalent plays an important part in weighing projects. Faced with an often large number of competing technical ministries or government agencies, it holds, in the last resort, the keys to the funds, except where it is the parliament that has the final word. By its very nature, it is less sensitive than the other agencies involved to purely scientific arguments and much more sensitive to comparative approaches.

In the context of a budgetary climate in which reducing costs is the order of the day, it reasons more in terms of spending priorities than in terms of an evaluation of the intrinsic worth of projects. From its standpoint, a number of decisive parameters enter: the ratio between the proposed investment and the number of scientific communities involved, the expected economic and technical spinoffs, the support from industry, the future possibilities offered by the project and the costs likely to be involved, and finally its links with some of the public agencies that propose the projects and whose budgetary credits have been drawn down to a greater or lesser extent.

In the absolute, there is little chance that a project will retain attention on its scientific merit alone; only the coalition of allies it has formed and a carefully argued comparison with similar situations will help the project obtain a favourable decision. Another option is of course for the project to be set into the framework of a more general political priority, such as the space sector in recent years. The financial authorities are more easily convinced when they have to regard the projects as having a priority that is independent of strictly budgetary considerations. Gaining such recognition requires lengthy efforts to work out the scientific programmes and disseminate them to parliamentarians and the political authorities.

For the discussions with the finance ministries, the negotiations will have to be conducted by a strong team representing all three aspects of the projects: scientific, technical, and industrial. The ministry – which faces demands from all sides – will react more favourably if they are presented with a coherent argument that combines these three points of view.

One of the items most debated is the amount of funds to be assigned to the project in question. The financial authorities do their utmost to reduce expenditure and spread it out over time. A possible area for negotiation is therefore the possibility of adjustments to the project and its constituent modules, and the ability to identify partial solutions that remain scientifically valid. These aspects may have been determined quite comprehensively during earlier stages of the process, for example when designers, users and builders were negotiating the details of the scientific and technical project.

In reviewing the project, the financial authorities use an approach different from the one used for scientific approval. They place greater value on the comparative aspects and will also seek to define a stable form of long-term financial review. Finally, they wish to have a clear financial analysis that can be adjusted to meet the different objectives.

The time factor is rarely considered in decision-making processes, yet it will necessarily play an essential role. All the actors propose specific timetables which structure time and make it seem to pass more or less quickly. In the case of the ISR decision, the competition factor, but also the realisation of the time that had passed since consideration of the future machine had begun, helped crystallise the decision.

There is no "best time" for a decision, nor any average gestation period. However, it is possible to arrange deadlines in such a way that the different partners perceive them as necessary. In particular, given the international negotiations frequently involved in megascience processes, the existence of deadlines will be seen as a means of channelling and catalysing decisions. A given community can specify a schedule for carrying out projects. If factors such as the closure of a number of installations, the existence of viable scientific projects, and a large number of researchers looking for funds are all placed in the balance, this will make a decision more urgent. In such a case, the project can be set in a scheduling framework where each deadline will appear very necessary.

The passage of time also gradually introduces a series of irreversibilities, even when no precise decision has been taken or rather when a series of micro-decisions, or the lack of decisions, gradually reduces the range of possibilities. For example, a co-operative approach involving several countries may be jeopardised simply because negotiations advance slowly and one actor invests resources in another project. An industrialist may lose interest or national priorities may change significantly. Certain analysts have suggested a decision-making model in which the principal actors are carried along by the inertia of the initial momentum and adopt, without making any real choices, certain directions for which none really accepts responsibility (Schilling, 1961; Wohlstetter, 1962). The establishment of a schedule and a precise list of meetings can help guard against irreversibility, just as regular review by a monitoring committee can favour final adoption of the project.

At a deeper level, the choices of association between different partners at every step in the decision-making process – however harmless they may seem – markedly affect the rest of the sequence. To give an extreme example, the preliminary work on the LHC which led to the idea of re-using the LEP tunnel set boundaries that make it very difficult to go back, either to modify or improve the project, or to abandon it.

This implies that all the actors involved must pay careful attention to problems of time and particularly to the use of the urgency factor as a way of resolving controversies. Once it becomes public, the stages in the decision-making process run the risk of stretching out, thereby tending to make the project obsolete before it is launched. In the same vein, the annual nature of budgetary procedures and the need to allocate preliminary funding, for example, may give rise to phases of acceleration or stagnation, thereby forcing a project to move at a pace which is not necessarily that of the actors or of the rate of progress of technical research. Phase discrepancies of this kind can lead to setbacks.

The combination of review procedures and a relative absence of formalised decision-making procedures helps increase the role played by time and irreversibilities, thereby favouring more immediate solutions without always allowing for in-depth study. While turning back is not impossible, it may be very costly.

Structure of processes and lessons to be learned

This fairly long exploration of decision-making processes has highlighted a number of points. To begin with, certain arguments that structure decision-making modes are widely used. The scientific programme, the expected spinoffs, and the general equilibrium of the programme are features which have to be negotiated, but which mark the project and have considerable influence on the final decision.

The need to think of the project as a vast co-ordinating structure in which the different arguments mentioned above assign a virtually necessary role to the different partners has been emphasised. From this vantage point, it is possible to identify a sequence of stages.

In the first phase, scientists, users, agencies, and possibly industry consider what should become of existing installations and programmes. These consultations generate a few main ideas with not only scientific but also technical and political aspects. The discussions include the type of research to be conducted, the necessary technical solutions, and the work of operating the installations or exploiting the data collected. This initial exchange on orientations is essential and should in fact provide enough substance to sustain the decision-making process that follows. Any project which limits its options at the outset and attempts to preserve this situation unchanged increasingly exposes itself to later frustrations.

In the second phase, these various parameters are taken up again and reshaped, with the involvement of expert committees and agency or ministry programmes, and this leads to renegotiating the boundaries of the different projects. At this stage, the breadth of the scientific programme and the strength of the links among users, builders, and operators are all tested; here also, the technical support or specialist departments of agencies charged with implementing the project intervene.

Identifying a second phase does not imply that the process is linear but simply that other partners are brought in who help to give a new direction and to abandon or supplement the original directions. Questions that typically help reshape the project concern, for example, the techniques to be used, how the various experimental zones planned are to be fitted out, what the most fruitful method of exploiting the data would be, how to achieve equitable financing, and what repercussions the project would have on national policies.

Finally, in a third phase, as the decision crystallises, there is a further broadening which mobilises all the necessary partners, and in which the scientist-funder and management-industry links are more closely interwoven. During this final stage, the coherence and strength of the links established during the earlier phases are essential. Can the programme promise dynamic and fruitful scientific results? Does in fit within the framework of a balanced development of national and international resources? Is it a matter of urgency for the different communities involved?

This overview calls for three further remarks. The process takes place under conditions of great uncertainty, and apparently banal decisions can introduce considerable irreversibility. The actors work their way through the process by using procedures whose induced effects are rarely neutral, whether they concern the choice of the committees reviewing the proposals, the schedules, or even the way the proposals are formulated. At every step, the actors must therefore reinterpret the general context in which they find themselves. This context, which gives the frame of reference for priorities, is not set in stone but can be reconsidered in various lights, even if it is sometimes impossible to escape from the prevailing view.

Thus, when the construction of a 300 GeV machine is seen as building a scientific monster, the actors must once again defend their scientific practice against the resurgence of a preference for small science. Through a long effort of reasoning, they can reverse the process by creating other arguments. Every project carries with it a scenario with some leeway for adaptation that must be recognised. Here, an attempt has been made to identify the strong points of decision making methods and the arguments which most obviously structure how events are understood, in other words the interpretative matrix used to evaluate projects.

The second point is related to irreversibility. During this kind of complex process, every decision exerts considerable influence by moving the project in a direction where it becomes less and less flexible. Maintaining flexibility is clearly done at a cost which is sometimes fairly hard to bear, but the skilful arrangement of technical, financial, sociological, and political alternatives is the best guarantee of a successful decision. Conversely, it means that the promoters must pay constant attention to the process of translating and redefining the project, particularly as regards the criteria defined in the previous section. Over all this hangs the question of the most effective calendar for the project.

Third, building a decision also involves working out a consensus among the "collectives" involved. Bringing these forces together requires strong links and not simply conditional alliances. In other words, the project cannot consist of superimposed and disparate forces engaged in a temporary coalition; it must reorganise decisively the practices of each. This is the essential criterion for success and for the emergence of a new "collective". If certain actors, for example, hesitate between choosing an international project and a fallback national project with more limited objectives, this means that the project has not yet succeeded in incorporating their expectations and interests to the point where it represents the only acceptable option. This applies, for example, to the construction of synchrotron radiation machines or neutron sources.

Using the criteria and parameters listed above, it is possible to outline a detailed table of the salient points in a decision making process. In particular, the precise implications of certain choices and the distortions that certain options introduce will be noted. Generally speaking, a project will have greater chances of succeeding and of gaining support if it begins by determining a scientific programme that is sufficiently open, consensual, and likely to engender dynamic scientific progress. This last should not be confused with the amount of new information the project provides. If the decision makers have long been more sensitive to projects that manifest continuity than to those more on the margins of the field, it should be recognised that this will lead in the long run to stagnation and to massive projects that are veritable monsters with little viability.

As has often been noted, megascience sees itself as international, and there is no point in reiterating the priority given *a priori* to international projects. The issue is how to use this priority to best advantage. It faces certain prejudices on the part of national communities and authentic problems of co-ordination. Establishing sensible structures and taking account of all the operating parameters will give international projects a stronger base. They will thus avoid the pitfalls of excessively flexible associations. Because these can be broken when circumstances demand and thus cause serious financial or technical difficulties, they can be much more costly and unproductive in the long run.

Two other essential factors consist in taking the users into account and carefully preparing the project. In view of budgetary reductions and the crisis situation in science, a project should bring in as many potential users as can be reasonably included, in order to increase the scientific and financial return. This stage involves the incorporation of the different communities and the search for representative spokesmen. In part, this will favour modular and flexible facilities that can accommodate the largest number of teams. A tendency to be feared in this respect is that the partners will enter into an artificial association in order to obtain funds from their respective authorities, without having harmonised their programmes in the framework of the project.

Budget preparation involves two aspects: the actual working out of the budget and adoption of the necessary measures for ensuring that schedules and costs are respected. The first item covers the need to share expenditure among various partners, a necessary corollary of internationalisation. In addition, it emphasises the benefits of long-term planning and of a specific budget line. The second item covers all the preliminary work for defining the facility. It would be wrong not to fund the studies that can make it possible to avoid certain irreversible errors. Control of expenditure depends heavily on preliminary work with the support of industry and technologists, in addition to a stable agreement between the different partners.

These two aspects are essential to the approval of programmes by the executive and parliamentary authorities. In particular, they should replace the "agency" approaches, the costs and risks of which have been underscored.

Megascience projects are increasingly asked to develop an in-depth justification in terms of spinoffs. This leads to giving preference not simply to economic return or to minor and specific industrial developments, but to the longer-term accumulation of industrial know-how. This tendency can be seen in the systematic support accorded to space activities. Similarly, a project such as research into the human genome garners support from all quarters. The danger, of course, is an excessive focus on certain fields of science and a lessening of the diversity of scientific and technological development.

Complementary parameters are competition and national policy. All projects must now seek to establish links with the science policy of the different partners. Essentially, this relates to the issue of a balanced development of national communities. With this assurance, the project will attract members more easily.

The growing involvement of politicians – and this is an increasingly sore spot in decision making – now leads to sudden reversals in arrangements that were apparently well assured. The case of the American SSC shows that the irreversibility implied by the commitment of funds no longer suffices to protect a project. Unless varied support has been mobilised from the outset, unless a small number of major orientations have been formed into a coherent edifice, the project inevitably courts failure. The SSC has been much criticised for the esoteric nature of the research proposed. The fundamental point is more related to the failure to clarify the stakes to the Congress and to an insufficiently negotiated development of a discipline. This draws attention to the need to build feedback loops into the decision-making process and to keep open options that make it possible not only to combat irreversibility but also to have wider margins of manœuvre in negotiations among partners.

The preceding discussion has reviewed the phases and main parameters of the decision-making process. The final section will attempt to provide a clearer structure; here, it is partly hidden here by the analytical approach used. It is nonetheless worth recalling the main parameters identified thus far:

- scientific programme;
- need for the broadest possible associations at the international level;
- community of users;
- preliminary work, especially technical aspects;
- justification of project spinoff;
- maintenance of feedback loops throughout the decision-making processes;
- presentation of a comprehensive set of arguments, early involvement of public decision-makers;
- taking account of irreversibilities;
- long-term planning for the different communities;
- determination of a common budgetary envelope for projects;
- establishment of balanced funding;
- project modularity and flexibility;
- allowance for future developments of projects and communities;
- integration into national policies;
- introduction of control and management procedures;

It is in the decision-making processes that megascience projects are decisively formulated. Many characteristic features that will turn up in projects at a later stage have their origin in this period. Some of the central points around which discussions are based have been highlighted. For each of these, various options are available, and the foregoing has summarised their consequences and drawn attention to the possible risks.

6. Monitoring decision making

For a megascience project, the tasks of the promoters and decision makers do not end when a decision is formally adopted. Once the project has been confirmed, and without considering its operation, there are the problems of overseeing construction, managing expenditure, budgetary monitoring, and the development of the necessary technologies.

Many of these points will already have come up in the decision making process to which the shape of the project owes a great deal. The tools, procedures, and approaches used vary enormously, perhaps even more than in the decision process itself. According to the country, projects, disciplines, and megascience in general are treated more or less thoroughly, individually, and easily.

Implementation structures

Roughly speaking there are four types of partner:
- the body charged with building the installation or setting up the project's structures:
- the body or structure that will be in charge of managing the project over the long term (it may be the same as the preceding one);
- the body that holds and manages the funds assigned to the project;
- the body responsible for the undertaking, when it is not the same as the preceding one.

In view of the marked international character of megascience, for each of the last three types, a national opposite number will take over some of the tasks. This presentation therefore deliberately stresses the strongly international aspects; how these questions apply to important national projects will be discussed below.

Fixed-site international projects

There are a number of possible ways of implementing an international project.

The simplest concerns projects that are decided and carried through by an agency with virtually exclusive responsibility for research programmes in the field concerned. For example the space agencies, whether European, American, Russian, or Japanese, but also organisations such as CERN, which manages research projects in high energy physics. In general, this type of project has advanced within the agency concerned, while attracting the various competencies it requires. Once the project has been approved at Council level (CERN) or voted into the agency programme (NASA), these bodies are allocated the necessary funds and the responsibility for the project. Clearly this does not prejudge the structures the agency may set up to help it in this task. CERN is undoubtedly the most obvious case, as its technical departments have the capability for implementing the project directly. These departments take charge of the implementation under the responsibility of agency management and work with the scientists who have promoted the project. In the case of a space experiment, close liaison is established between the team responsible for the experiment and the laboratories and industries charged with building the instrumentation, if the two are not the same.

The various national participations complicate the structure somewhat. Thus, in the European Space Agency (ESA), a group of countries is usually involved in a project.

Each is represented by its own space agency, if it has one, or by the national committee responsible for co-ordinating such research. Implementation then requires dividing the necessary work among the different partners. This division is defined during the decision-making process, when a particular country is given the task of building the detector, another the camera, and so on. ESA then receives the funds from the different countries and redistributes them to the different subcontracting bodies.

It is easy to see that this process is relatively complex, with financial arrangements that are never simple to manage. Again in the space sector, budgetary discussions may in fact cover three areas: the allocation by the countries of resources necessary for the international agency, the allocation by the agency of funds to national agencies, and overall budgetary discussions between an agency and the public authority responsible for it. Uncertainties may arise in this process at any time. Indeed, although the funds set aside for this type of operation are theoretically designated for a given agency, they are in fact managed globally, so that various tasks are mingled.

One simplifying measure is for the relevant national agency actually to transfer the necessary funds to the international agency after receiving the allocations designated for the latter, which then reassigns them to the national agency. Whatever formula is adopted, confusion is always possible and can lead to delays in executing programmes. There is a similar mechanism at CERN, where the accelerator is essentially built by the agency, while the detectors are divided among the national partners and thus come under the budgets of the national agencies. When the physical installation has been completed, it falls under the responsibility of the international agency and the results are divided among the various potential users.

For implementing European megascience, a model whereby the agency involves a certain number of countries is often preferred. This is one of the possible approaches to international co-operation and has the advantage of providing a stable structure for projects. In the long term, these agencies often manage priorities and realisations in the scientific field in question. Thus, CERN has become the prime mover in high energy physics. The model has also been extended to the field of astronomy, with the establishment of the ESO to monitor and operate the telescopes installed in Chile.

There are other ways of implementing projects, such as creating international companies to manage them, as in the case of ESRF, which manages the synchrotron radiation machine in Grenoble. The various countries are represented in a council where voting is governed by special provisions that vary from body to body. ESRF has a project team made up of staff from national bodies seconded for realising the machine. It is also responsible for project finances. In terms of national support, it receives help either from research management and operation bodies or from committees and councils responsible for allocating funds in the various countries. It should be remembered that this is a very specific situation, the construction of a single large fixed-site instrument. It concerns a single instrument and not several programmes spread over time.

A third means of monitoring and accomplishing a project involves "settling for" a memorandum of understanding between two or more partners. In this case, the implementation does not involve a specific structure but a flexible framework, within which each partner is more or less committed to supporting a joint project. This arrangement is preferred partly for its greater flexibility. It also takes account of the problem of setting up new structures, particularly if the parties concerned are already large agencies; there is, for example, the associations between ESA and NASA, or the bilateral partnerships between NASA and agencies of certain countries.

This approach does give rise to a number of difficulties of monitoring and management. To begin with, the division of responsibilities may prove delicate, particularly with respect to the realisation and harmonisation of technical tasks in the framework of a common plan. In practice, one of the partners often takes on the general management of the project, so that the other associates are no longer in control of the technical, industrial, and financial realisation. Also, while the agreement may be flexible, the commitments may well be weak, and a partner may drop out unilaterally in the event of budgetary problems, technical difficulties, or disagreement about scientific objectives. As a general rule, this type of arrangement often results from a laborious decision-making process in which the association of the various actors has not reached the degree of cohesion that would have been desirable.

There is a final formula, much rarer, in which governments themselves sign an international agreement that commits them to build a major installation. The main example of this is the ITER agreement for building a tokamak for fusion research. Associations of this kind raise different types of problem, in that they further increase the number of partners and levels at which implementation must be dealt with. The intergovernmental structure is superimposed on the national agencies responsible for nuclear energy, and in Europe, there is an additional level owing to the existence of a European structure which deals with the United States, Japan and Russia.

A number of remarks may already be made. An important condition for good project management over the longer term appears to be close relations between the team charged with carrying out the project and the organisation responsible for monitoring, or the establishment of close relations between them. If such ties are lacking or if co-ordination is too weak, there is the risk not only of delays in building the parts of the instrument, but also of cost overruns and a poor correspondence between the project plans and its technical realisation. This can occur particularly if the future managers of the project are kept apart from those responsible for the technical aspects.

The idea of entrusting the task of keeping track of the instrument to a consortium free of the administrative yoke is a good one but calls for considerable care. Efforts should be made to ensure that realisation of the project closely involves the promoters, the technical teams, and the future managers of the machine.

As regards the other partners, there will be a large number of interlocutors, a potential source of troublesome redundancy. With certain configurations, the increase in the number of groups charged with funding and keeping track of projects can have adverse effects, as in the case of financial and technical negotiations. The sometimes complex circuits in the allocation of resources between a national agency and a ministerial authority, to say nothing of the possible need for annual approval of funding by the parliament, occasionally contribute to clouding the issues.

Too often, collecting the resources necessary for satisfactory operation of the project means, for example, that responsibilities are spread thin among the many bodies responsible for funding, who hand the projects back and forth. Clarification of the implementation of projects apparently involves – and certain countries have set up such structures – combining, or at least harmonising, the financial authority and the national body responsible for project support.

This would make it possible to avoid two adverse effects: on the one hand, the ignorance of decision-makers about the projects of certain agencies which develop their programmes in their own way, and on the other, the destabilising effect on the same agencies of recommendations from their responsible authority to maintain their international commitments while applying a policy that restricts them to the national level.

To give two brief examples, the French Council on Very Large Facilities, which is charged with reviewing all projects in megascience or big science, has a co-ordinating role and therefore facilitates the allocation of budgets. It nevertheless has difficulty monitoring and controlling the budget of agencies such as the CNES.

In a different context, NASA in the United States may be obliged unilaterally to withdraw from certain operations because the way in which funding is allocated and the annual vote of the Congress force it to make choices within its own programme. Canada also draws attention to difficulties of implementation resulting from the sharing of responsibilities among a number of bodies, when their missions are not always clearly defined.

In other words, the disparity between different approaches – the policy approach at the level of the responsible authorities, the agency approach at the level of major research operators, and the implementation approach at the level of the body in charge of building the facility – often produces adverse effects and can handicap certain projects.

More generally, although flexibility is to be encouraged in megascience projects, it should not be to the detriment of closer integration of the partners and of the technical concepts that can be developed during the decision-making process. The memorandum of understanding is open to such a broad range of interpretation that it is better to seek more systematically a stronger type of co-ordination among the partners. This presupposes an overall view of funding that makes it possible to go beyond the framework of the different agencies and envisage commitments at national level. For NASA, again, it is only by identifying priority megascience programmes, regardless of the agency's own undertakings, that stable funding and real commitment can be assured. In the long run, an overall review should provide the agencies with the means of making a more certain commitment to co-operative projects.

This description has only considered co-operative ventures involving two or three partners. Once the framework is widened to encompass several agencies, or several representative bodies, the need for monitoring and overall review is even clearer. Often, preference is given to informal arrangements, or gentleman's agreements, for carrying out certain parts of projects; however, such arrangements totter when the first budgetary problems arise, creating many difficulties and threatening the continuity of projects. Co-ordination may thus be necessary at this level as well. The increased visibility resulting from making public the costs and budgets of megascience could help in this respect, without any need for complex bureaucracy.

All in all, for the implementation of international megascience projects, it appears useful to clarify a number of points. On the one hand, bringing together the instrument's construction and long-term management teams appears to create a favourable environment. It permits exchanges of view about the most appropriate options for the machine, but also the emergence of a concerted policy for the presentation and development of the project. It should not of course be forgotten that a project, even when partly launched, is not certain to be carried through. To ensure sufficient control and permit effective management, it is essential to have a team of managers covering the scientific, technical, and financial management aspects who are in a position to interact with the specialist committees, agencies, and public authorities in order to modify the project if required. A consortium established to handle construction but without direct responsibility for sound development of the project is not enough. The weaknesses revealed by the audits of the SSC project requested by the US Congress reflect in part the difficulties of setting up an integrated and coherent structure in this respect.

The involvement of a number of countries in a single project inevitably increases the number of authorities concerned. Merely setting up a centralised implementation structure that included the different partners would already make relationships easier. At national level, however, it remains possible to avoid scattering of responsibilities by appointing a single body to oversee the operations.

Finally, depending on the nature of the projects, the choice of the most suitable legal structure may vary. Nevertheless, setting up an *ad hoc* company or signing a specific agreement between countries often appear to guarantee a relative degree of stability.

Large-scale distributed international programmes

It is useful to consider this second type of megascience separately because it raises problems of a fairly different kind (Praderie, 1993). An international programme, such as climate research, does not call for building particularly large instruments, but it does demand extremely close co-ordination of the different partners, joint exploitation of data, and harmonisation of the means employed. These programmes include the International Geosphere-Biosphere Programme (IGBP), the World Climate Research Programme (WCRP) and somewhat different undertakings in the field of the environment (UNEP).

Participating countries generally meet these needs by delegating these tasks to their bodies with responsibilities for research in the relevant field. The different partners are brought together in flexible structures or bodies which supply temporary tactical support, such as ICSU (International Council of Scientific Unions).

It goes without saying that this option, although at present the only one for bringing the various countries together, raises the problem of regular funding. At the same time, the questions mentioned above concerning the link between the agencies' budget, national priorities, and particular programmes recur. Moreover, in this type of undertaking, the allocation of credits for implementing the co-ordination and for the circulation of data will rarely be a priority of the responsible organisations, who prefer to allocate their resources to their own teams or to bilateral partnerships. In such cases, it is difficult to determine the best form of organisation. Perhaps support for these programmes should first involve general discussion of priorities in these areas at national level and a search for the major lines of research.

The provision of the necessary resources presupposes in particular that the national organisations incorporate support for these co-ordinating activities into their own clearly identified priorities. Moreover, a team should be charged with setting up and guiding the network of laboratories that are to collect and exploit the data. As modest as this infrastructure is, it is essential to the satisfactory deployment of projects. If these aspects are not properly taken into account, there may well be some scepticism about the true effectiveness of the undertakings. Two kinds of work are involved. If, initially, a number of laboratories around the world wish to work together on these problems, their initiative would have the value of setting up networks of co-operation and trust. Control and monitoring would not require costly resources. The situation is entirely different if countries wish to become massively involved in the projects. In the implementation, the necessary input of individual initiative in setting up networks for circulating scientific information must not be confused with the amount of co-ordination involved in the proper allocation of resources. Such a programme cannot be a mere collection of the respective research programmes of national agencies.

National or multilateral facilities

Every country recognises that megascience makes international participation obligatory, but there are still a number of facilities that have been decided and built by countries individually or through bilateral collaboration, such as some small facilities designed for training and improving the competencies of scientific groups or for conducting very targeted research. The type of partners involved then varies, and the alliances sought at national level can be more diversified, involving several laboratories, universities, and funding bodies, as well as additional partners if the facility is open to other countries. The result is greater dispersion of the allocation of funds and technical monitoring. This can make these projects as difficult to manage or monitor as international ones. In particular, this creates a gap, which countries often deplore, between the funding and the implementing bodies, whether the latter is a university or an agency laboratory.

The coherence necessary for megascience presupposes effective co-operation at national level as well. On the one hand, a general inventory of other projects in progress is a prerequisite for ensuring that the use of funds is satisfactorily monitored and that the projects remain efficient. On the other hand, inciting the different organisations to submit their projects to review committees can prevent too much dispersion. In addition, owing to a laudable wish not to concentrate all national installations within the major agencies, the management of some machines is entrusted to universities or consortia. In these cases, very close links to a central public authority charged with supervising funding can be useful. Finally, megascience can also be a point where national and international priorities converge. The teams charged with national machines could be urged to maintain contact with their counterparts in other countries to share experience and ensure complementarity. There is a sign of this in the project for a synchrotron radiation machine envisaged in France to replace the one at Orsay. Partly designed by the laboratory housing the old machine, the project will establish consultation mechanisms at European level so as to fit optimally among the resources available in the field and perhaps especially to find additional financial partners (Soleil, 1991).

The problem of budgetary management

At the centre of all discussions on the implementation of megascience projects is the question of annual budgets. Most countries adhere to the principle of yearly allocations, which allows an annual review of the funds assigned to one project or another. When substantial funds are voted directly by the parliament, the situation becomes more crucial since it is possible for participation in a project to be suspended from one year to the next. Yet even in countries where an overall budget is voted, a budgetary reduction will also ultimately affect current projects, since the usual tendency is to distribute the reduction equally.

All countries recognise the need to examine funding over the long term and to programme it in the budget, but the procedures used vary considerably. In most cases, attention is drawn to the fact that megascience projects need overall support in the long term and a non-reducible budget envelope.

It is generally acknowledged that the lack of a comprehensive review of projects and their funding is a potential source of inefficiency and delay. The dispersal of projects among many agencies, the splitting up of funding, and compartmentalised budgetary monitoring all raise difficulties that are commensurate with the nature of the projects involved and often poorly resolved.

Countries have used three different instruments which, taken singly, risk being insufficient. First, certain countries are now proposing legislation on scientific planning over several years so that priorities on major projects are written into law and thus constitute a guarantee, if only a formal one. It is known that such legislation may undergo revision as new priorities or constraints emerge, and it is in no way equivalent to a definitive vote of funding. For projects already in progress, the irreversibility acquired is likely to mean that they will not be halted but simply delayed or revised. In this case, it would be necessary to take into account the comparative costs of execution now and execution later, and to see how the necessary funds could be disbursed at minimum cost. The problem of halting projects will be discussed below.

The second instrument is regular review of the planning of expenditure, its evolution, its breakdown by category, and the prospects of developing new projects. Certain countries either formally or informally use this type of review. Thus, France, the Netherlands, and Sweden identify the funds granted to megascience or big science facilities. The total amount so earmarked is substantially of the same order each year, and the various projects, while they do not all come under a common budgetary heading, are sufficiently grouped for an overall view to be possible.

A far-reaching review is conducted by the French Council for Very Large Facilities, which centralises data on big science and is therefore in a position to give an indication of the total amount of funding devoted to these programmes and the proportion of the national budget they represent. It is then a simpler matter to make the different budget authorities aware of the requirements and realities of megascience which, however extensive, utilises only 8 per cent of the allocation for civil R&D, excluding salaries, in France (Petiau, 1992; Ducrocq *et al.*, 1992). This makes it possible to monitor closely the growth of allocations and their distribution by discipline, thus to indicate indirectly that the expansion of megascience is under control.

This type of review has two other functions linked to planning and to overall balance. An important factor in monitoring megascience projects is the way in which credits are distributed among the three major categories of capital investment, operations, and staff. A reasonable balance among these three areas gives a good indication of the evolution and nature of the portfolio of megascience projects. Rapidly rising staff costs occur when a large number of often lengthy projects are undertaken; this is incompatible with the approval or execution of various other investments when the budget is growing slowly or diminishing.

In terms of longer-term management, the planning of expenditure and the detailed monitoring of projects, together with financial planning for new projects, make it possible to draw up an approximate schedule of expenditure, to smooth it over time, and, if a cost overrun is expected, to make those responsible aware of it well in advance. This management tool is more than a *pro forma* aspect of planning; it is an essential instrument for negotiating priorities and approaching the financial authorities which makes it much easier to carry out a megascience project. While a precise budgetary envelope is often identified at the same time, this does not imply that the distribution of the funds would fall under the authority of a single body. Such centralisation would go against current national practices, although the updating and grouping of funding for megascience would increase awareness of the amounts involved and allow every project to establish a longer-term plan.

The third aspect concerns the rigorous management of the allocated funds and the battle against cost overruns. Experience shows that most megascience projects exceed the original budgetary forecasts. There are two good reasons for this. One is the novelty of the instruments to be set up; this implies technological developments which can easily run into complications, so that construction costs are likely to fluctuate considerably. The second is what might kindly be called the natural optimism of the project promoters, which sometimes leads them to underestimate the required expenditure. This factor, where it still exists, can be countered in the decision-making process by encouraging very detailed technical studies and obtaining guarantees from the best teams of engineers and industrialists.

The objective would then be to bring out not the particularly low cost of a project but the search for technological approaches that are not only new but whose reliability has been tested. Beyond this, detailed monitoring of projects, with a frequent review of spending and of progress, is essential to fight against cost overruns. Germany has set up a specific procedure to meet these needs and to provide the teams responsible for implementation the support they need during this phase. It would be useful to give all project managers a series of tools to help them in this task. In the longer term, more reliable implementation of projects would also guarantee more stable funding.

The recent cancellation of the American SSC illustrates the importance of this task. The upward drift in project costs, over 100 per cent over a few years, led to justified concern on the part of the responsible authorities. Under such circumstances, a mega-science project can contribute to upsetting all budgetary projections and threaten other areas. It has already been stressed that such tendencies should also be opposed earlier, during the preparatory stage of decision making, but this illustrates the need for early alarm signals to stop the project from advancing before objectives and resources are reconsidered.

A problem that arises at an earlier stage concerns the distribution of budget management activities. Certain countries insist on a separation between the funding bodies and the institution that hosts a project, as well as on a large number of sources of finance; this occasionally leads to overlapping competencies and can result in inefficiency. This co-ordination and the setting up of procedures to ensure harmonisation of management still seem at a rudimentary stage and are areas for future consideration. In any event, an exhaustive list of sources of available funding and more systematic use of co-operation during the decision-making process should make it possible to combat these problems. Once a decision has been taken, it is dangerous to apply an *ad hoc* funding arrangement which focuses on short-term resource allocation and does not take account of the overall project. It would be strange, in particular, to bring in organisations which have been involved only marginally in decisions about the project or its preparation. This would inevitably lead to a waste of energy and money.

Budget preparation is an important part of the work involved in megascience. While megascience does not, as has been claimed, account for a substantial proportion of total budgets, it does raise special questions owing to the necessary concentration of resources in space and time. What is needed is relatively uniform programme planning over time so that unexpected factors will not lead to additional costs. One way might be to establish long-term programming with close control over increases in expenditure as a means of demonstrating strict management. More practically, centralised funding allocation and a concerted review would obviate the problem of wasted funds. Similarly, the institution of review structures that would systematically alert the authorities would avoid speculative expenditure. Finally, special assistance to project managers would allow them to supervise more effectively the allocation of expenditure. These remarks do not imply that the same procedure should be used in all countries. Local characteristics should be preserved; these are merely suggestions of general directions that are worth considering.

Technical implementation[7]

Like financial monitoring, this aspect concerns the decision-making process and the harmonisation of the technical teams. Among the risks involved are dispersed implementation, inadequate co-ordination in setting up facilities, and uncertainty about the availability of the proposed techniques.

Some of these aspects should have been settled during the decision-making process, but regular reviews of technical choices, of the harmonisation of teams, and of dialogue with future users are necessary. Countries usually focus on control at a higher level, through the allocation of funding, and give little attention to these issues. However, technical monitoring should play an essential part. Two particular points deserve emphasis:

- establishment of a scheme for realising the project and a schedule indicating the main technical meetings, to be submitted with the budgetary review;
- the care taken to co-ordinate the work and preserve the modular nature of the facility.

In fact, if a given approach is adopted too quickly, before all the necessary technologies have been fully explored, a problem may surface that jeopardises the entire structure and means incurring substantial costs to redesign the system. Exceeding original financial estimates often occurs when all the technical developments have not been taken into account. The most extreme case is probably that of the Space Telescope, whose costs have risen by several hundred million dollars owing to the repairs that had to be made to its optics. It is true that the reason is faulty construction of part of the facility, but this extreme example does illustrate the need to test all technical assumptions.

In the same vein, but more especially for large-scale distributed programmes, technical specifications for treating, transferring, and collecting data can raise formidable problems which should be submitted in good time to surveillance committees.

Project reorientations or shutdowns

Project monitoring also involves drastic changes in current operations. One form of review is the periodic review of a project's progress, its technical performance, and the funds committed. This type of monitoring is done in a somewhat unco-ordinated manner and often after the fact, for example when a report is required on progress in a particular scientific or technical field. Committees or groups of experts could be set up to conduct intermediate reviews of programmes. They could point out weaknesses and suggest which aspects deserve rethinking. To prevent projects from moving in an inappropriate direction, a moratorium might then be declared in order to explore alternative technical approaches or to reconsider the general design of the project.

Governments have become ever less hesitant to question projects already under way. Without returning at length to the cancellation of the SSC, one may note that it seems to reflect a trend. Megascience projects no longer have a privileged position, and the irreversibility attributable to money already spent only plays a moderate role. For the SSC, $1.7 billion had already been spent, and a further $1 billion will be needed to cover the cost of closing down the installations already built. Nevertheless, this is only a small share of the approximately $11 billion projected. The Congress thus decided between a substantial but fixed loss and constant increases in construction costs.

From now on, the monitoring of megascience projects will include a continuing evaluation of the costs of halting or systematically redefining projects for other purposes. The decision-making process no longer stops with the formal approval of the project; on the contrary, permanent feedback loops are set up so that the project can be reassessed in the light of the objectives achieved, the technical difficulties encountered, and the funds committed. This new situation should incite those responsible for projects to refine the boundaries of the project as much as possible during the decision-making process and also to prepare fallback positions, by means of modules that fit together but are sufficiently independent.

In sum, in the monitoring of decisions, inadequate links can be observed between three aspects: budgetary monitoring by the authorities or agencies involved, scientific monitoring by the scientific committees, and technical implementation. All countries try more or less to improve the links among these three often centrifugal forces. They do so largely because wherever megascience is not recognised or identified as a particular category of science, there is a tendency to use methods similar to those used in smaller scientific disciplines, which tolerate these centrifugal tendencies better.

In fact, while megascience does not represent as large a share of budgets as some suggest, the repercussions of inaccuracies in megascience are proportionally much more strongly felt and visible. This explains the prickly reactions to big science: the announcement of huge cost overruns inevitably gives rise to scepticism about the effectiveness of such machines. In themselves, these inaccuracies are not very different from those that occur in other laboratories, and probably from the sum of these, but the weight of irreversibility in big science makes such errors even more damaging. The co-ordination procedures already well established in the scientific megascience communities need to be extended downstream.

7. A scheme for decision making and its regulation: science as a public good

At the end of this analysis of decision-making methods, it may be useful to envisage, in more general terms, their place and their nature and to suggest an ideal standard model. Such considerations are necessarily preliminary, since any detailed review of historical cases, with their many contingencies, often destroys efforts to generalise or propose standards.

This exploration can usefully begin by an introduction to the model of science as a public good and its implications, which relies to a considerable degree on an insightful study by Callon (1993). Although megascience, for reasons that include its modes of decision making, represents a highly specific universe in which co-ordination and discussions among those concerned appear exemplary, it also tends to hasten the focusing of scientific activities on a small number of areas, sometimes to the detriment of diversity. As shall be seen, this is not a return to the debate between big and small science, but another view of scientific work.

Science as a public good

Economists define a public good in terms of four essential qualities. First, the good must possess some material characteristics and be capable of being treated as an object or as a set of techniques. Then come the three main characteristics of a public good: it is non-appropriable under normal conditions of circulation of information, it is non-rival under the same conditions, and it has lasting intrinsic characteristics.

Under normal conditions, non-appropriability means that neither an individual nor a group can make the good their own and deprive other members of the society of it. If a good, once its existence is known, is freely available to all, it is non-appropriable. The other side of the coin is revealed by considering the participation of private industrial firms in scientific research. What can be the value for them of contributing to the progress of general scientific knowledge if the fruit of their studies is immediately made public without their being able to profit from it? On a related issue, how can the development of science and of scientific research be encouraged if it is not easy to profit from the results? These are basic questions for public research policies, but in a broader sense they target problems of the ownership of knowledge, the system for protecting discoveries, and overall scientific development.

The non-rivalry of goods means that the use of a good by an individual or a group in no way hinders its simultaneous use by others. Hence, if information circulates normally, a non-rival good may be used by anyone without impeding its use by another. Finally, durability implies that the good is stable: its nature does not change, and no effort need be made to preserve its integrity and its characteristics.

It can easily be seen how these three aspects contribute *a priori* to defining a good in general use in a "collective" or a group, a good that is universal and whose characteristics, in terms of trade, set it apart when reasoning in strictly economic terms.

Starting from this definition, the economists consider that science is a public good, or a quasi-public good, in view of the fact that all the above criteria are not strictly met, particularly non-appropriability. Science is seen as a system producing statements that are stable and durable. Under normal conditions, they cannot belong to a particular individual, and – one only need consider the laws of physics – they can be used at the same time by two people, neither of whom interferes with their use by the other. It is important to examine this conception because it lies at the heart of all economic approaches to science and of the justification for its support.

The goal here is not be to deny science its public good character but to show why the economists' definition does not entirely correspond to reality and how it should be modified to take reality into account. To this end, following Callon's example (1993), this analysis will apply the recent results of the sociology of modern sciences.

The study of science through detailed monitoring of laboratory activities and scientific practice argues against the applicability of the first criterion in the economists' definition. Science appears in fact as highly appropriable. A scientific statement rarely circulates on its own without reference to the conditions under which it was produced and to everything that makes it possible to ensure its stability. In other words, the statement is attached to the instruments that made it possible, along with the practical and technical skills necessary for using the instruments, the implicit theoretical framework, and often the organisational background and division of labour involved.

It is difficult to imagine a statement about some particle or other in high energy physics, without any reference to the accelerator and detector involved. More broadly, it is also necessary to mention the algorithms used to process the observed events, the different competencies in electronics and control of the machine, the theoretical model that suggested such an observation, and, finally, the more general goals of particle physics as a discipline and the type of organisation involved (*e.g.* CERN).

When they took an interest in the reproduction of one laboratory's results by another, sociologists of science soon observed this feature of science. They soon found that a simple statement of a phenomenon, even with information about the experimental method, was generally insufficient for reproducing the scientific result. To master the latter requires much more detailed work, with an exchange of a great deal more information among the laboratories involved.

Moreover, and this is fundamental, some of this information stems from tacit know-how, from skills that have been acquired by the scientists and are not easily expressed through algorithms. In order to acquire these skills, it is necessary to go to one's colleagues, to work side by side with them, and to absorb their experimental culture. Such are the important conclusions reached by the British sociologists of science who, like the eminent scientist Polanyi, revive the role played by tacit know-how and embodied knowledge in scientific output. The best proof is found in the scientific controversies occasionally arising between two laboratories, for example with regard to the existence of a phenomenon. They illustrate the possible misunderstandings between two experimental approaches and are virtually impossible to resolve without visits and work in common.

All these factors show to what extent science is easily appropriated. Announcing a result commits to very little without the entire array of means that made its production possible. Further, to benefit from a statement means being able to handle it, master it, go beyond it, and reuse it, and this mastery requires, without a shadow of a doubt, acquired competencies. In other words, it is easy for a laboratory, even under normal conditions of circulation of information, to remain in control of its data even while gaining scientific acceptance. In fact, and this is another point demonstrated by the sociology of sciences, nobody can be held to the impossible: reporting tacit knowledge cannot be a basic objective of publication. Even if a publication lacks certain elements for exactly reproducing results, a laboratory will receive credit for its work since nobody will consider it appropriate to embark on highly expensive verifications that produce no scientific gain.

Seen in this light, a scientific group appropriates the results it produces. This also explains why, even though science appears to be a public good, laboratories of private firms increasingly develop advanced research while giving their researchers, particularly in the most advanced fields, relative freedom. They know that the instrumentation, working techniques, and skills acquired will remain theirs.

The second point concerns non-rivalry. Here the economic analysis, which resembles that of common sense, in fact applies an unsuitable category. It can be observed that, in itself, a scientific statement is of little use. It must be transmitted, used and integrated in a broader framework and reinterpreted in a specific perspective if it is to mean something. Thus, the idea of non-rivalry is correct, but it is tautological. Two people may simultaneously use a given statement without doing one another harm, but essentially because the statement, reproduced and used in another context, has changed. The two people are handling different and necessarily non-rival goods.

On the other hand, it is possible to imagine rivalry over a statement that is taken over by a certain group. For example, in order to use a statement, certain scientists may wish to give it concrete form by building a facility to test whether or not a phenomenon predicted by the statement exists. Assuming that competition for obtaining the resources needed for this facility is strong, it is clear that another group, which wishes to use the statement in a very different way and also require resources, would find its way blocked by the first group's option. The use it seeks to make of the statement rivals that of the first group. Since the scientific statement is of interest only to the extent that it circulates, mobilises scientists, and allows new developments – without which it is relegated to the museum of dead science or regarded as obsolete – the use of a statement may thus be exclusive and thereby calls the concept of non-rivalry into question.

Finally, there is the question of durability. Here again, the interpretation of this criterion depends upon the extent to which the focus is on scientific practice. In absolute terms, of course, one can argue for the preservation and identity of scientific statements. In practice, there are two shades of meaning. First, a scientific statement, as such, is not transmitted unchanged, but enriched by all the additions made by the various scientists who have handled, exchanged, or developed it. Can one really say that Newtonian mechanics remained stable from the seventeenth to the beginning of the twentieth century? Kuhn (1962) has shown how changes in the scientific paradigm invest concepts, such as mass, for example, with varying meanings.

There is more, and it is related to the idea of science policy. In practice, scientific statements remain alive only if they are maintained, sustained, circulated, and used. A moment's reflection shows that this calls for considerable effort. They must in fact be taught, and this implies teachers, manuals, and means. Further downstream, it also implies researchers, facilities, research centres, and institutions designed to encourage the dissemination of science and its development. The heritage of science, as of other fields, must remain alive and, consequently, be kept sufficiently lively. This is the task of public science policy. In brief, the criterion of the durability of science hardly seems more assured than the previous criteria.

As regards the conclusions to be drawn from these remarks, the first and most obvious is an observation: maintaining science as a public good requires considerable effort and the deployment of substantial resources. In fact the natural trend is what Callon (1993) calls "the privatisation of science", the transformation of scientific work into a private good.

As for the signs of this conversion, they can be found in the increasingly rapid convergence of scientific networks. In other words, science, instead of ramifying, is focusing more and more on certain areas, within which the study of certain aspects is pushed to the limit. The possibility of appropriation and the idea of increasing returns make it possible to explain this phenomenon. The notion is easy to understand. Benefits gained from massive commitment to a particular technological approach manifest increasing returns. This commitment leads to acquiring new competencies and training both through practice (learning by doing) and through contacts among a wide variety of partners. No comparison can be made between two technologies unless it takes into account the gains accumulated through massive investment in one of them or through the learning process (see, for instance, the case of the electrical versus the combustion engine).

The second reason concerns the extension of the network of users of a technique. To take the example of the telephone: when only two people are connected by the instrument, its value is slight; however, the value of the network increases more than proportionally with each new subscriber. This idea of increasing return and the notion of appropriability show what can be expected if scientific research evolves towards the private sector.

As regards appropriation, one can understand why the ever increasing development of embodied know-how allows laboratories to remain in control of a certain domain, define priorities, and obtain the greatest share of funding. This already applies to private laboratories, and a trend towards private science would extend the phenomenon beyond these simple boundaries.

The different groups concentrate their efforts, form increasingly close co-operative arrangements, and gradually find themselves "locked in", in the language of economists. In other words, they are trapped within a technical option or technological path from which it becomes impossible for them to escape. David (1986) described this phenomenon in his study of the introduction of the "QWERTY" keyboard for typewriters and showed how a non-optimal technical solution was able to impose itself. In science, the consequences are similar, with increasing emphasis placed on making skills more uniform, on collaboration, which brings groups together and makes them more alike, and on the choice of a small number of widely shared research objectives.

Seen from this standpoint, science does in fact become a private good with several shareholders. There is the phenomenon, already discussed, of the irreversibility of research paths, when the cost of turning back becomes so high that it is no longer possible to diversify. Similarly, when massive investments have been made in a particular technology, all the alternatives seem unattractive, and the options chosen will be maintained to the last moment.

It is nevertheless possible to conceive of science as a public good and to encourage its development as such, on condition that careful attention is paid to science as it is actually practised. Science is a public good insofar as it preserves the resources of innovation, development, diversity of knowledge, and flexibility. Even more, it becomes the source of such diversity and flexibility. The originality of science is therefore that it assures the future by maintaining a diversity of knowledge and skills.

The economic, political and structural mechanisms of science are tending to converge towards certain anchor points, but it is in the interests of scientific movement itself to produce flexibility and variety. To do so, it is important to encourage the proliferation of new "collectives", new associations, and departures from existing techniques and methods of thought. To avoid co-ordination based strictly on market forces and rules, it is necessary to encourage a dynamic of knowledge in which the irreversibility of certain paths is resisted by other projects at the margins or by the redirection of practices.

Of course diversity has a price – and a high one. The concentrations introduced by the market, on the basis of the idea of a private good, clearly aim at greater efficiency and a reduction in the loss of energy. As in any process, this reduction also has a price: it is the resultant irreversibility with, in the long term, the fossilisation of the chosen scientific options. The resources needed to ensure diversity and to protect science as a public good correspond, instead, to an enrichment of knowledge and of the "collectives" that produce it. Yet, the point is not to develop fundamental research indiscriminately, but to stimulate new and original developments which might produce, especially at the beginning, new associations, new collaborations, and new forms of scientific practice.

The overall cost of such a process explains why it can only be envisaged in the framework of concerted policies for scientific development taken at international level. An attempt will be made to show how this is possible in the field of megascience, which seems to offer a good example of the tensions involved.

More broadly, of course, this question raises important questions concerning intellectual property, patents, and the mechanisms required to combat scientific appropriation. As a simple example, an undertaking such as the Human Genome Programme is at the centre of all these discussions. The question is how to design the programme in such a way that it does not result in a situation where all the groups of biologists focus on a type of research because it is seen as the most profitable and because it makes it possible to establish the greatest number of links with various partners, to say nothing of the discovery of patentable gene sequences that can be used by industry – the epitome of the appropriation of fundamental knowledge.

In view of this thorny debate, should the appropriation of scientific knowledge be strictly controlled, by checking centrifugal initiatives? On the other hand, if the choice is made to support diversity, which is necessarily expensive, how is it to be funded? Is it conceivable to control access to certain technologies or branches of knowledge and to require payment for that access? It is clear that the question of science as a public good is at the centre of current thinking. Here, these questions will not be taken any further in a general way; a few consequences for megascience will be pointed out.

Megascience as a public good

The issue of science as a public good can be transposed to the decision-making mechanisms and hence to the choice of priorities in big science. Superficially, megascience may appear to exhibit some private market mechanisms. With the passage of time, the decision-making processes have tended to favour increasingly consensual decisions by the scientific communities, opening the way to a greater convergence of scientific networks.

Furthermore, the development of certain very powerful and well-established disciplines has suggested that a phenomenon of increasing returns would accompany increasingly high investment in certain facilities and in certain scientific directions. Thus, just as increasing returns and irreversibility force a reduction in the techniques used and a concentration on a small number of paths, there would presumably have been a similar development in certain scientific fields, that would, to some extent, have sustained themselves by their production of knowledge. In so doing, they would have neglected a number of other approaches, in line with the rivalry characteristic of private science. Finally, the truly industrial structure of megascience would have accelerated this process by requiring maximum return from the projects. At the same time, the accent placed on economic return from projects would have reinforced this trend by favouring the fields most likely to produce a large number of immediate applications.

This statement is only very partially justified; however, it does highlight, antithetically, the dominant features of megascience and the aspects to be accentuated in developing it. Decision-making processes in megascience, reviewed in the light of the above remarks, show, in fact, fairly different orientations. If convergence exists in megascience, it lies in ensuring proliferation and discussion among many groups.

In other words, there is no united front; on the contrary, the decision-making process leads to the elaboration of an instrument which includes the multiplicity of scientific and technical aspirations. It is in this sense that these processes can, in the final analysis, be described as democratic. The consensus reached in megascience is not a priority plucked from the air, but stems from the successive and co-ordinated introduction of a variety of elements in an attempt to integrate the most promising options, but also their perhaps more original counterparts.

Paradoxically, the evolution of megascience, as sketched in the historical review contained in Section 3, shows a movement which maintains quite well the variety and flexibility of the scientific approach. During the 1950s, many decisions were made using a model of imitation and competition, with certain small groups acquiring large machines for their own purposes. However strange it may seem, this lack of consensus, this existence of apparently singular cases, reflected in fact considerable standardisation and great uniformity of instrumental and theoretical models. The race towards accelerators of increasingly high energy based on conventional technical designs, during the 1960s, confirms this. Conversely, the virtual disappearance of these phenomena, one of the last of which may have been the American SSC, favours broadening of discussions and the independent development of groups of scientists and users who can now envisage machines or projects as malleable undertakings able to incorporated different concepts.

The logic of this development is then easier to understand. If there is concern to preserve science as a public good, then, taking into account the cost of doing so as well as the need for an appropriate institutional framework, megascience has a relatively favourable position thanks to its capacity to develop "collectives" and co-ordinate diverse ideas in a flexible way. Further, this concern also justifies the internationalisation of projects and a sharing of the costs of scientific diversity. Thus, beyond the immediate constraints of cost and technical complexity, megascience also represents a challenge in terms of balanced scientific development.

Another reason for criticising megascience, when regarding science as a public good, concerns the existence of self-sustaining processes of development and the undue power of certain disciplines. High energy physics, for example, has sometimes attempted promote the homogeneous development of its research at all costs.

As already noted, the competition between the LHC at CERN and the American SSC stemmed partly from this perverse process. Yet, even in this field, the value of preserving diversity and flexibility can be observed. High energy physics could ultimately suffer the consequences of excessive focus on certain objectives. Decision-makers and other scientists in fact see the dynamic potential of this field becoming exhausted.

Locking into such behaviour, if it is self-reinforcing and creates irreversibilities, also leads to a weakening of the field.

This has been well understood by the high energy physicists, who seem to have readjusted their priorities and now envisage a much more diversified future with machines and projects of different types. They are also initiating co-operation with other fields, such as astrophysics (in the area of neutrinos) in order to develop new centres of interest. Incidentally, this shows the need for the decision-makers to keep a careful watch on whether disciplines maintain criteria of openness, variety, and scientific dynamism, this last to be understood, as defined above, as the innovative and unexpected potential of a project.

Although the trend towards uniformity has often been observed in recent years, it is by no means general and is certainly not found in most disciplines. For example, astronomy has preserved the diversity of its means of exploration. Similarly, and perhaps contrary to appearances, the great diversity of space missions makes this field of megascience one of those in which complementarity and variety are relatively well protected. This is true even though certain projects may be jeopardised more easily than in other areas and certain missions may be cancelled in order to balance the field. This is unfortunate for potential users and can lead to financial losses, but on the other hand, it does indicate a relative flexibility.

One could cite many other examples from the new co-operative programmes on climate and oceanographic research. Only biology, in view of the orientations apparently adopted for the exploration of the human genome, has embarked on a programme excessively focused on one subject, with mobilisation of resources and techniques and a relative uniformity of the research pursued. It is not certain, however, that this orientation will be maintained. Finally, and more generally, it is striking to note that original projects such as those on gravitational waves, which represent possible new sources of dynamism, can emerge and be deployed.

In order to understand the position of megascience, the question of the nature of facilities and programmes must be studied. Through the negotiations of the decision-making process, and as a result of the increasingly heavy constraints on megascience, the idea of an instrument with modular design and shared use has come to be stressed. These two features clearly apply to all the sources of synchrotron radiation or neutron beams and to astronomical observatories. More broadly, megascience projects are now conceived as complex systems for co-ordinating and accommodating a variety of approaches, the extreme case being the large-scale distributed programmes that are based exclusively on this principle.

Thus, two often opposed aspects are reconciled: diversity and efficiency. At the same time, the emphasis placed on co-operation and on the variety of users has made it possible not to base all projects on a single uniform model. Hence, diversity is preserved in megascience through technical modularity and the notion of a shared instrument.

Finally, there are the relationships between megascience and economic spinoffs. This delicate matter calls for a number of remarks. The first concerns the greater or lesser appropriability of results. The price of diversity is, as has been pointed out, the one paid at international level to maintain science as a public good. The very basis of this approach lies in keeping science freely available, subject if necessary to appropriate control.

The move to an international scale should then be seen in a positive light and not as a backward step. Some actors are often heard to complain that, in international co-operation, they lose control of the techniques and of scientific advances. Owing to the way in which megascience is constructed, *de facto* sharing does occur, theoretically, during the decision-making process. Countries can no longer retain all the accumulated know-how for their own benefit. This illustrates two very important points in the preparation of megascience decisions. Satisfactory development of this type of scientific practice requires the results to be non-appropriable by a single partner for his own purposes, otherwise the approach no longer has any value; it is therefore rather vain to regret this apparent loss of control. Moreover, the production of new results and the development of scientific dynamism involves cross-fertilisation of skills and formation of new networks. By adhering to a narrow ideal of control, all the potential advantages of the process are lost; sharing the costs of diversification means that each must accept his positive and negative share.

Again as regards economic spinoffs, a justification based upon much shorter-term considerations has long been put forward. When a particular institution argued for the economic return from its project by stressing great advances in electronic material or specialised optics, it helped hasten the focus on a few key techniques, thereby pressing excessively for the technological development of certain approaches.

There is no better illustration of the effects of increasing return and appropriability. Once one has embarked on perfecting a particular type of product, one will always tend to take this approach further, with substantial gains, it is true. However, in the long term, the result is fossilisation of the industrial and technical fabric.

Instead, as regards industrial feedback, attention may be drawn to the new technologies, the new associations, the new approaches, and the new know-how that can be explored through a project. This concept of economic return seems more appropriate than simple reliance on a few particular techniques. For example, the improvements that accelerators make to techniques for tubes or magnets correspond to an accelerated convergence; they may work against other, more novel orientations.

These remarks lead to two other recommendations on economic spinoffs in the context of science as a public good. First, they call attention to the need for considerable vigilance against very short-term technical and economic considerations which will not permit effective development; and, second, they underscore the need to ensure the formation of mixed "collectives" that involve science, industry, and technology, out of which new orientations are bound to emerge.

It is now easier to understand why the methods of decision making have acquired, or are in the process of acquiring, the features described earlier, and also why it is important to encourage this trend. Megascience is one way to preserve scientific diversity and allow for diversified development of knowledge. It is in the decision-making processes that these linkages and this vocation can be tested and established. Indeed, if insufficient attention is paid to these aspects during the decision-making process, the effects on the subsequent course of a project may be unfortunate.

Returning to the three main points in the definition of a public good, one observes that each has a decisive influence on the future success of the facility or programme. First, the problem of non-rivalry should be resolved during decision making by integrating the different concepts of scientific exploration in a modular facility. This is essential if certain groups are not to be excluded from using the results. More significantly, resolving this issue avoids rapid sclerosis of the project envisaged, its paralysis, and its insufficient exploitation, and, at the same time, it keeps open several simultaneous avenues of investigation.

The question of the durability of scientific goods is related to maintaining scientific dynamism and therefore to the choice of projects with high potential whose predicted results offer significant possibilities for later developments. Finally, non-appropriability corresponds to shared access to the knowledge needed to open up new prospects. It also underscores, ethical considerations aside, the caution necessary in the Human Genome Programme which might harm biological research if it is pushed to the extreme.

Thus a review of science as a public good and the recognition of the importance of decision-making processes in megascience lead to a few recommendations which, although elementary, may be helpful in reviewing projects:

– It is necessary to encourage the association of as many scientific "collectives" as possible with the project. This proliferation contributes more to project quality than excessive selectivity. Contrary to expectations, the most profitable stand during the preparatory phase may not be strict selection but multiplication of links and alternatives.
– Such an approach means favouring emerging "collectives" while urging them to fit into the overall framework of co-ordination. This is a role both for the scientific communities and for the public authorities, who can test the variety and solidity of the links formed.
– Among the important criteria in project reviews, attention must be paid to the likely dynamism of the project, and to the extent to which it avoids increasing returns and the decline of diversity.
– To sustain non-rivalry, it is necessary to make projects more modular. This will assure them greater flexibility for future development. This point goes along with the attention paid to the community of potential users as a good indication of the openness of the project.
– During the realisation phases, it is necessary to support and to ensure close association among science, technology, and industry. This cross-fertilisation of competencies will ensure mutual enrichment of projects.
– To ensure renewal of the field concerned, it may be worthwhile retaining incentives for small megascience projects which involve the reorientation of certain fields or the emergence of new trends.
– The definition of science as a public priority implies discussion about its directions and its possibilities for diversification. It may be advantageous if the latter are submitted sufficiently early to parliamentary and government authorities for cross-cutting review.

8. Phases of the decision-making process and methodology rules

Megascience has recently been subjected to a number of reviews by economists, historians, and official bodies (Averch, 1993; OECD Megascience Forum, 1993*b*; Galison and Hevly, 1988). This section briefly presents the ideas developed about the choice of megascience projects and show how these are partly based on an erroneous view of science as a public good. Then, the decision-making process is broken down into three phases, and a few key points of each are underscored.

To study the issue of *ex ante* selection of megascience projects, it is useful to look at the underlying assumptions of an interesting study by Averch (1993). The first and most important involves regarding science as a public good in the conventional sense adopted by economists. This view leads to seeing megascience as a process which absorbs a substantial share of public funds, in an unjustified or at any rate poorly managed way. From this standpoint, it becomes necessary to devise rules for selecting projects and regulating their development. According to the classical economic principle of optimal allocation of resources, the respective merits of projects are to be evaluated by means of an extremely severe competition in which the most meritorious projects will progressively be selected. The consequence of this view is therefore a position of indisputable selection and a totally rigid decision-making process. The proposed options should be exclusive and the projects should be forced to compete.

However legitimately intended, this view seems to go against the interests of megascience as presented above. Reducing discussion to a fierce battle between competing options tends to develop too strong an irreversibility and to create artificial poles of focus, so that increasing returns, prestige, and more than usually *ad hoc* arguments will win out. This leads to the danger of a situation of artificial competition in which certain projects will be undertaken without taking into account the diversity of the field of science concerned. This is clearly very different from the negotiated and concerted allocation of a reasonable budget, programmed over time, within which the emergence of a variety of projects that bring together the broadest possible teams is encouraged.

Another proposition merits discussion. It involves reviewing projects on the basis of the ratio of the information yielded to the investment required. The curve of the amount of information obtained would be plotted as a function of the money invested, and projects that offer the highest yield of information would be favoured.

This criterion raises formidable problems. It more or less assumes, whatever tactics are used, that information from different disciplines is commensurate. The question is how information on the top quark, the exploration of the Universe in the far infrared wave length, and the detection of gravitational waves can be compared and evaluated, in terms of volume. It would be difficult to answer it.

To move on to the next step in the argument, it would also be necessary to plot the volume of information against the money spent. What types of consequences would such a criterion have on decisions? One may think that it would lead, willy-nilly, to a mechanism of increasing returns. In fact, a well-established discipline that has already been explored in great depth will be better able to demonstrate the large amount of expected, and unexpected, information that can be gained from its investigations. The more its theoretical and experimental results are developed, the more each increment will be likely to affect all other elements and provide, in the strict sense, a richer harvest of information. In this context, assigning a low information yield curve to the SSC, for example, does not stem from an analysis of the project in terms of information but from current opinion about the project.

On the contrary, it has been suggested here that a reliable criterion for evaluating a project would be the dynamism, rather than the volume, of the information flow it is likely to generate. In other words, it is not only a question of information yield but also of the possibilities offered by the project in terms of networks and diversity. A project like the SSC may have a high information yield without necessarily halting convergence of the scientific network, *i.e.* an exclusive focus on certain aspects. In fact, these are the very trends that threaten to convert science into a private good. Subscribing blindly to the idea of information yield as a criterion of choice is to move towards increasing returns, emphasising acquired positions, and eventually justifying the fossilisation of scientific networks.

On the basis of the above remarks and the analysis contained in Sections 4 and 5, it is possible to propose an ideal decision-making method, whose only virtue is to recapitulate certain methodological rules brought out during the analysis.

This ideal view of the decision-making process can be divided into three main phases:

- phase of proliferation;
- phase of association, extension of networks and consolidation of links;
- phase of convergence.

Phase of proliferation

This phase takes place essentially in the scientific communities, but it should be monitored and encouraged by the public authorities who will have identified the challenges involved. The main idea is to permit the greatest possible number of proposals to be suggested and to preserve the diversity of scientific research. At this stage, the decision making process has two sides, one the initiative of the scientists and the other the vigilance of the public authorities, responsible ministries, and agencies to ensure that all the conditions necessary for proper discussion are met. The following are a few essential steps and some criteria that should be recalled.

P1: Broadest possible association of scientists, discussion of all ideas, forward-looking consideration of disciplines, non-selectivity. From the outset, this stage has a strong international tone.

P2: Announcement by the authorities of a general scheme for allocation of funding, long-term programming, and a specific volume of funds for megascience projects.

P3: Provisional specification of the nature of the scientific programme, taking care to engage it in a dynamic of scientific expansion.

P4: Placing of these considerations in a more general framework of scientific pro-gramme planning. How are projects situated with respect to the development of megascience? Are they central to or on the margins of the fields concerned? Over what period will they develop? How can they be introduced into long-term programming without generating unwanted peaks?

P5: Consideration of the rate of progress in the field concerned. Will the project under consideration enable a number of scientific networks to be developed in the future? Or, on the contrary, does it represent a phase of concentration of a discipline, of increasing returns, or of locking into certain techniques? How would it be possible to broaden perspectives?

Phases P4 and P5 require interaction between science policy as a whole and the more specific orientations of scientists.

P6: Generation of the largest possible number of alternatives. The project envisaged should preserve the diversity of the scientific coalition, possess real flexibility, and have inventoried the largest possible number of realistic options in order to maintain them to an advanced stage of the decision-making process. There are three aspects here: the integration of many perspectives in the instrument or project, preference given to an instrument shared among users, preservation of several forms of technical solutions.

P7: Stress must be placed on internationalising contacts.

At the end of this phase, it should be possible to draw up specifications and a general statement of intent to which the scientific communities of all countries can subscribe. This statement should now be consolidated, confirmed, and gone into more deeply by the different partners, in close association with the responsible authorities and the advisory organisations and expert committees charged with the assessments.

Phase of association, extension, consolidation

The main idea in this phase is to establish the maximum number of firm links among scientists, technicians, funding bodies and industry. It is also the most practical time for determining the technical plan and the outlook for machine operation, funding, and support structures.

P8: Creation of a central team to co-ordinate and encourage contacts and to assist with the division of work. The team should have a balanced composition, with the scientists concerned, potential users, technicians and engineers, industrial repre-sentatives if necessary, and funding bodies.

P9: Determination of the modules of the facility and sharing responsibilities for evaluating the funding and technical effort required.

P10: Recruitment of the communities of users, determination of potential volumes, identification of consortia or of spokesmen for these users. The estimated volume should be an important parameter for assessing viability.

P11: Determination of a preliminary technical plan for the project, essentially based upon flexibility and therefore proposing a number of different construction options. This goes hand in hand with the simultaneous production of a financial scheme and an evaluation of the funding possibilities.

P12: In parallel with P11, encourage links with industry and carry out reduced-scale tests in order to explore the technical problems expected in construction.

P13: Consideration of the scientific and technical information, economic spinoffs, the way in which knowledge is to be appropriated by the different partners, and the scale of economic projections (short-term/long-term).

P14: Review by the committees of national experts, which should have a sufficiently wide range of members, so as to emphasize horizontal evaluation and reinforce the financial teams.

The principles needed for these evaluations include the following points already mentioned:

- gradually emerging dynamism of the field;
- community of users;
- true modularity of the facility;
- solidity of the links formed between the scientific communities;
- announced spinoffs;
- coherence of the technical plan;
- preparatory project work, particularly technical work;
- maintenance of feedback loops during decision-making processes;
- scientific programme;
- accounting for irreversibilities;
- long-term planning for the different communities;
- determination of a common budgetary envelope for projects;
- integration into national policies.

P15: On completion of this review, the national committees may either simply suggest that a project should be halted, if the conditions for assembling and developing networks do not appear to have been fulfilled, or, as is more likely, specify all the points that should be reviewed or completed. They may then set a new date and suggest that an international committee be appointed and meet to harmonise national positions in a more formal manner.

P16: Discussion of the project in the framework of national policy priorities, involvement of the political decision-makers directly concerned to examine what modifications are necessary to the project.

P17: Close involvement of the funding bodies sounded out during the joint preparation of the general plan.

P18: Further review by the committees of experts.

On completion of this phase, the project is relatively well advanced, with an agreement from the national communities, sufficiently solid collaborative networks, a technical plan with several options, and attention given to the methods of funding. A final point to be noted is the need to make room in this process for megascience projects of intermediate size which might benefit from special support because they contribute to diversifying the particular scientific field.

Phase of convergence

This phase sees the finalisation of the project, the definitive setting up of its host structures and the international agreement.

P19:   Submission of the project to an international committee with a definition of the procedures for co-ordination among national teams and between scientists and technicians. The committee comments on the project for the benefit of the central team and the national committees. As in the previous stages, it is worth ensuring that this committee includes all possible actors and is open to representatives of other disciplines.

P20:   Suggestion of a location for the project, if appropriate, and review of all necessary compensation, for further discussion with the national committees.

P21:   The committee's views should particularly include its assessment of the relation between the state of technical progress and the financing, of the modularity of the project, and of the coexistence of various research and development directions.

P22:   Proposal for a host structure and definition of responsibilities. The host structure may be an existing agency, a new company, or a specific international framework. Structures which do not really stimulate an association of partners should be avoided. If no other solution can be found, it is important to be particularly vigilant about the stability of the associations and each party's recognition of a priority for the project.

P23:   Return to the national committees, discussion of national priorities and how they fit with the international discussion, establishment of the financial scheme, desig- nation of technical and financial support at national level. If possible, these last two points should be handled together, otherwise one group will supervise both the allocation of resources and technical monitoring.

P24:   At this stage, before a next step, it is possible to review the project and halt its progress.

P25:   Summary presentation of main lines to national decision-makers and parliamentar- ians, determination of the margins of manœuvre for the final phases of negotiation.

P26:   Small-scale tests to examine the reliability of the project and consolidate the technical options.

P27:   Return to the international committee, final negotiations to decide on the legal form, the sharing of funding and responsibilities, the site, the limited number of technical solutions to be retained, and the methods to be used to monitor the project.

P28: National approval and conclusion of a firm agreement among all the countries. Extension or modification of the international committee and the central implementation team.

For the setting-up phase:

P29: Updating of the funds to be committed in line with the general plan, determination of a precise timetable.

P30: Start of technical construction. Monitoring of expenditure.

P31: Intermediate review by the technical committees. Meeting between financial authority and team responsible for construction. Possible adjustment of project modules in conjunction with the international committee.

P32: Continuation and completion of construction.

In conclusion, it is indispensable to draw attention to the "ideal-type" character, in Max Weber's sense, of this scheme. It defines an outline which can be adjusted in any number of ways. It obviously disregards the special features of particular scientific fields in order to highlight points that are very general but can serve as methodological rules. This study has tried to bring out the implications and assumptions of such an approach, particularly the tools and structures that would be needed to make use of such a scheme. In particular, the scheme assumes recognition and identification of megascience as a category as well as a careful inventory of this kind of operations in the different countries.

9. Conclusion

The decision-making processes in megascience are a decisive stage in the formulation of projects. This is where large "collectives" of scientific and technical actors are formed. The processes cannot be conceived as a linear series of decisions, but on the contrary as a series of feedback loops which render gradual adjustments to projects possible. From this standpoint, their function is to encourage discussion and the determination of scientific directions by the communities, but also by the political authorities.

Megascience is ultimately characterised as much by the complexity and extent of these methods of decision making as by the parameters of cost or the breadth of the techniques to be implemented. The decision-making processes are actually methods of co-ordinating scientific activities and groups. The extension of the model reflects the attraction of this form of regulating scientific activity. The internationalisation of megascience is also placing its mark on decision-making processes by making new procedures and a very special kind of vigilance necessary. The large number of countries involved in decisions introduces additional difficulties in the planning of projects and partly explains why decision making is taking appreciably longer.

The analysis of the structure of the processes has made it possible to determine the main points under discussion:

– definition of an extremely dynamic scientific programme;

- need to associate the largest possible number of international partners;
- community of users;
- preparatory project work, especially technical work;
- justification of project spinoffs;
- maintenance of feedback loops during decision-making processes;
- presentation of a comprehensive set of arguments and early involvement of public decision-makers;
- attention to irreversibilities;
- long-term programme planning for the different communities;
- determination of a common budgetary envelope for projects;
- establishment of balanced funding;
- modularity and flexibility of projects;
- attention to the future development of projects and communities;
- integration into national policies;
- introduction of monitoring and management procedures.

The attention paid to these different criteria will partly determine the success of a project as the decision-making process proceeds. They also highlight the adverse effects that need to be avoided (Section 5). The decision-making processes have a predominant role, in that they decisively model the nature of projects and their future development.

Aside from these different parameters, the importance of megascience as a public good has been emphasised, in the sense that it should make it possible to preserve the diversity and flexibility of scientific work. This option means favouring the emergence of new "collectives" and the cross-fertilisation of scientific and technical skills as the decision-making process proceeds. The public authorities should take care to encourage this faculty of association and not systematically favour short-term spinoffs and the convergence of scientific networks which, in the long term, are likely to lessen scientific dynamism.

This being said, the decision-making processes should rely on a balanced and long-term programme of investment. Such a programme presupposes that megascience is recognised as an essential element of national science policies. There is some reticence in certain quarters which fear a reduction in their prerogatives or a weakened instrument of industrial development. Here, instead, it is suggested that megascience is the ideal place to maintain diversity in science and should therefore encourage the sharing of scientific results. Thus, placing megascience under a separate heading appears to be an important waypoint in the determination of priorities. Beyond the few methodological rules suggested, attention has been drawn to the value of a concerted review of projects as they proceed in order to guard against potential slippages in the technical and financial implementation.

Subject to these precautions, megascience decision-making processes – beyond the natural diversity of local practices – can offer an ideal space for international co-operation, as the Megascience Forum has already shown.

Notes

1. See Chapter 1.
2. See Chapter 4.
3. See Chapter 7.
4. See also OECD (1995),"The Definition of a Mature and Complete Megascience Project Proposal", OCDE/GD(95)44, Paris.
5. See OECD (1995), *Particle Physics*, Chapter 3, Paris.
6. See Chapter 4.
7. See also OCDE/GD(95)44, *cf.* note 4 above.

References

AVERCH, H.A. (1993), "Criteria and Rules for Evaluating Competing R&D Megaprojects", *Science and Public Policy*, April, Vol. 20(2), pp. 105-13.

BIANCHI-STREIT, M., N. BLACKBURNE, R. BUDDE, H. REITZ, B. SAGNELL, H. SCHMIED and B. SCHORR (1985), *Utilité économique des contrats du CERN*, CERN, Geneva.

BROMBERG, J.L. (1982), "TFTR: The Anatomy of a Programme Decision", *Social Studies of Science*, Vol. 12, pp. 559-83.

BURCH, G. and G. TEGART (1992), "Big Science for Small Nations: Evaluating Options to Invest in Research Facilities", paper presented at the Conference on "Equipping Science for the Twenty-first Century", Amsterdam.

CALLON, M. (1987), "Society in the Making: The Study of Technology as a Tool of Sociological Analysis", in W. Bijker, T. Hughes, and T. Pinch, eds., *The Social Construction of Technological Systems: New Directions in the Sociology and History of Technology*, MIT Press, Cambridge, Massachusetts.

CALLON, M. (1993), "La privatisation de la science est-elle inéluctable?", paper presented at the University of Laval, 28 October.

COHENDET, P. and A. Lebeau (1987), *Choix stratégiques et grands programmes civils*, Economica, Paris.

COLLINS, H.M. (1985), "The Possibilities of Science Policy", *Social Studies of Science*, Vol. 15, pp. 554-58.

CONSEIL DES TRÈS GRANDS ÉQUIPEMENTS (1992), *Rapport du Conseil des TGE*, Ministère de la Recherche et de l'Espace, Paris.

DAVID, P. (1986), "Understanding the Economics of QWERTY: The Necessity of History", in W.N. Parker, ed., *Economic History and the Modern Economist*, Basil Blackwell, Oxford.

DETRAZ, C. (1992), "Où va la physique nucléaire?", *La Recherche*, Vol. 241, pp. 348-52.

DUCROCQ, P., F. JACQ and A.T. MOCILNIKAR (1992), "Grands équipements et science lourde : La place des grands instruments dans le développement scientifique", Ministère de la Recherche et l'Espace, Paris.

EDGE, D.O. and M.J. MULKAY (1976), *Astronomy Transformed: The Emergence of Radioastronomy in Britain*, Wiley Inter Science, London.

EUROPEAN HIGH PERFORMANCE LASER FACILITY (1990), "Scientific and Technical Working Group Report", Rutherford-Appleton Laboratory, Didcot.

GALISON, P. et B. HEVLY, eds. (1988), *Big Science: The Growth of Large-Scale Research*, Stanford University Press, Palo Alto, California.

GINGRAS, Y. and M. TRÉPANIER (1993), "Constructing a Tokamak: Political, Economic and Technical Factors as Constraints and Resources", *Social Studies of Science*, Vol. 22, pp. 5–36.

HEILBRON, J.L. and R.W. SEIDEL (1989), *Lawrence and His Laboratory, A History of the Lawrence Laboratory Berkeley*, Vol. 1, University of California Press, Berkeley, California.

HEILBRON, J.L. and D.J. KEVLES (1988), "Finding a Policy for Mapping and Sequencing the Human Genome: Lessons from the History of Particle Physics", *Minerva*, Vol. 26(3), pp. 299-314.

HERMANN, A. J. KRIGE, U. MERSITS and D. PESTRE (1987 et 1990), *History of CERN*, Volumes I and II, North Holland, Amsterdam.

HODDESON, L. (1983), "Establishing KEK in Japan and Fermilab in the US: Internationalism, Nationalism and High Energy Accelerators", *Social Studies of Science*, Vol. 13(1), pp. 1–48.

IRVINE, J. and B.R. MARTIN (1984), "Past Performance and Future Prospects: II. The Scientific Performance of CERN Accelerators", *Research Policy*, Vol. 13(5), pp. 247-84.

JACQ, F. (1991), "Un regard sur la science et l'industrie dans la France d'après-guerre", Centre de Sociologie de l'Innovation, Paris.

JOUFFREY, B. and M. NAUCIEL, eds. (1988), *Les équipements scientifiques mi-lourds*, Ministère de la Recherche et de la Technologie, Paris.

KARS, H., C.C. BAKELS and J.B.H. JANSEN (1992), "Science-based Archeology: Future Needs and Priorities for Facilities and Instrumentation", paper presented at the Conference on "Equipping Science for the Twenty-first Century", Amsterdam.

KEVLES, J. (1988), *Les physiciens*, Anthropos, Paris.

KRIGE, J. and D. PESTRE (1988), *Some Thoughts on the Early History of CERN*, in Galison and Hevly, *q.v.*

KUHN, T. (1962), *The Structure of Scientific Revolutions*, University of Chicago Press, Chicago.

LATOUR, B. (1990), *La science en action*, La Découverte, Paris (traduction de *Science in Action*, Harvard University Press, 1987).

LATOUR, B. (1992), *Aramis ou l'amour des techniques*, La Découverte, Paris.

LATOUR, B. (1993), *La clef de Berlin*, La Découverte, Paris.

MACKENZIE, D. (1990), *Inventing Accuracy: A Historical Sociology of Nuclear Missile Guidance Systems*, Cambridge University Press, Cambridge.

MACK, P. (1990), *Viewing the Earth: The Social Construction of the Landsat Satellite System*, MIT Press, Cambridge, Massachusetts.

MARTIN, B.R. and J. IRVINE (1984a), "CERN: Past Performance and Future Prospects: I. CERN's Position in World High-energy Physics", *Research Policy*, Vol. 13(4), pp. 183-210.

MARTIN, B.R. and J. IRVINE (1984b), "CERN: Past Performance and Future Prospects: III. CERN and the Future of World High-energy Physics", *Research Policy*, Vol. 13(6), pp. 311-42.

PRESIDENT'S COUNCIL OF ADVISORS ON SCIENCE AND TECHNOLOGY (1992), *Megaprojects in the Sciences*, Office of Science and Technology Policy, Washington, D.C.

OECD (1991), *Choosing Priorities in Science and Technology*, Paris.

OECD (1993a), *Astronomy, The Megascience Forum series*, Paris.

OECD (1993*b*), *Megascience and its Background*, The Megascience Forum series, Paris.

PAPON, P. (1983), *Pour une prospective de la science*, Seghers, Paris.

PESTRE, D. (1988), "Comment se prennent les décisions de très gros équipements dans les laboratoires de science lourde contemporains", *Revue de Synthèse*, Vol. 4(1), pp. 97-130.

PESTRE, D. (1989), "The Creation of CERN in the Early 50s: Chance or Necessity?", in M. de Maria, M. Grilli, and F. Sebastaniani, eds., *The Restructuring of Physical Sciences in Europe and the United States,* pp. 477-87, World Scientific, Singapore.

PESTRE, D. (1990), "Louis Néel, le magnétisme et Grenoble", *Cahiers pour l'Histoire du CNRS*, Vol. 8.

PETIAU, P. (1992), "Determining national priorities for future investment in capital-intensive research facilities: Lessons from the French *Conseil des Très Grands Équipements Scientifiques*, paper presented at the conference on "Equipping Science for the Twenty-first Century", Amsterdam.

PRADERIE, F. (1993), "International Co-operation in Big Science", in *Megascience and its Background*, OECD, Paris.

SCHILLING, W.R. (1961), "The H-Bomb Decision: How to Decide Without Actually Choosing", *Political Science Quarterly*, Vol. 76, pp. 24-46.

SCHMIED, H. (1977), *"Essai d'évaluation des effets économiques des conventions conclues entre le CERN et l'industrie"*, Thesis, Université Louis Pasteur, Strasbourg.

SHAPIN, S. and S. SCHAFFER (1985), *Leviathan and the Air Pump*, Princeton University Press, Princeton, New Jersey.

SHINN, T. (1993*a*), *The Giant Bellevue Electromagnet: Dynamics of Instrument Development*, seminar, CRHST, Cité des sciences, La Villette, Paris, forthcoming.

SHINN, T. (1993*b*), *The Giant Bellevue Electromagnet: The Birth of the Research Technology Community*, seminar, du CRHST, Cité des sciences, La Villette, Paris, forthcoming.

SMITH, R.W. (1990), *The Space Telescope: A Study of NASA: Science, Technology and Politics*, Cambridge University Press, Cambridge.

SMITH, R.W. (1993), "The History of Big Science" in *Megascience and its Background*, OECD, Paris.

SOLEIL (1991), "Source Optimisée de Lumière d'Énergie Intermédiaire", draft project, LURE, Orsay.

UHLHORN, C. (1992), "Setting Priorities for German Investment in Costly Fields of Science during the 1990s: Lessons from the BMFT Committee on Basic Research", paper presented at the conference on "Equipping Science for the Twenty-first Century", Amsterdam.

VIRGO (1989), "Proposal for the Construction of a Large Interferometric Detector of Gravitational Waves", CNRS and INFN, Paris.

WEINBERG, A. (1961), "Impact of Large-scale Research on the United States", *Science*, Vol. 134, pp. 161-4.

WESTFALL, C. (1989), "Fermilab: Founding the First US Truly National Laboratory", in F.A.J.L. James, ed., *The Development of the Laboratory: Essays on the Place of Experiment in Industrial Civilisation*, pp. 184-207, American Institute of Physics, New York.

WOHLSTETTER, R. (1962), *Pearl Harbor, Warning and Decision*, Stanford University Press, Palo Alto, California.

Chapter 3

INTERGOVERNMENTAL AND INTERNATIONAL CONSULTATIONS/AGREEMENTS AND LEGAL CO-OPERATION MECHANISMS IN MEGASCIENCE

EXPERIENCES, ASPECTS AND IDEAS

by

Josef Rembser
Director, German-American Academic Council, Bonn, Germany

Executive summary

Megascience projects/programmes require not only scientific ideas, but also sound organisation, management and finance. The most successful large-scale European programmes originated thanks to eminent scientists with well-established contacts in political and government circles. However, politicians and science policy decision makers alone cannot maintain "big science" activities by using a top-down approach, even though such an approach may provide the necessary impetus for implementing programmes dealing with broad societal issues. Politicians would be ill-advised to use "political activism" to manage science or to judge its importance and its merits solely on the basis of its present and foreseeable usefulness.

Successful preparation of an international megascience project/programme requires the involvement of experienced partners, well-organised delegations with a clear chairman, and representation of all government authorities and institutions that play a role in the proposed project/programme. Heads of delegations should have broad leeway to negotiate.

Because large projects/programmes extend over many years, they require reliable long-term commitments, especially when they have been developed in an international framework. Therefore, good working relationships need to be established between the sponsoring government administrations and their respective parliaments, whose commitment will provide the necessary political stability.

Obstacles to successful negotiations for large international projects and programmes arise mainly from potential partners' political positions, *i.e.* they may be inexperienced, overburdened, or unwilling to co-operate in a joint project/programme. Partnership implies making important decisions together, using agreed procedures and rules. Each potential and participating partner should respect well-defined ways of sharing responsibility and avoid imposing decisions based purely on its national political and economic aims. Co-operation on megascience projects should begin early in the planning stage, before important aspects of the project have been decided.

At a time when national budgets are constrained, the transfer of national funds, tied to automatic indexation, to international megascience projects is encountering growing resistance from national parliaments and governments. One solution to this problem is for participating countries to make contributions in the form of hardware and experienced personnel. It can best be used by involving potential partners in the planning from the outset. At the Hadron-Elektron-Ringbeschleuniger-Anlage (HERA) at DESY, Hamburg, for example, partners supplied hardware in the form of high-technology components. This has the advantage of giving partners an opportunity to test new technological developments and to prepare their industries for future markets. However, the host country should not receive all, or nearly all, of the high-tech hardware from abroad.

When megascience projects/programmes financed from a joint investment budget involve the supply of industrial hardware and services, a conflict of interest may arise. On the one hand, it is important to spend the project's budget efficiently, *i.e.* by awarding contracts to the lowest bid that meets all requirements. On the other hand, participating countries are likely to seek a return on their investment. Ways to deal with this issue include awarding industrial contracts on the basis of the level of member countries' financial contribution [European Space Agency (ESA) model] and delegating decisions about important industrial contracts to a special Industrial or Finance Committee, with representation from all participating countries, which evaluates bids considering both "fair return" to member countries and economic implications. This second model, used by the European Organisation for Nuclear Physics (CERN) and the Institut Max von Laue-Paul Langevin (ILL), may reveal industrial weaknesses and consequently incite governments to improve industrial competitiveness.

Hosting an international facility results in important economic returns, and it is therefore necessary that discussions among governments about the site of a facility be sound and sensible. Host states are now asked to provide additional compensation in view of expected benefits [*e.g.* Joint European Torus (JET), European Synchrotron Radiation Source (ESRF), European Transonic Windtunnel (ETW)], but the additional voluntary contributions from the host nation rarely completely satisfy the expectations of other participants. This issue therefore requires particular attention. Extra contributions from host states need not always be regulated by organisation statutes, and special contributions are sometimes voluntary. They may include supply of cheap electricity, low interest loans, or extra grants.

Participation in megascience projects is particularly difficult for smaller countries, but it provides them with an otherwise unavailable opportunity to develop scientific and technological activities in highly specialised, complex, and expensive research fields. The "one country--one vote" rule is common to most megascience organisations; it offers policy-making advantages to smaller countries. Relations between large and small countries need careful attention when establishing the statutes and rules during the negotiation stages; members' contributions are generally calculated as a share of gross national product (GNP), a practice that places the financial burden on the larger countries and may cause difficulties, particularly for those that do not spend a comparable share of GNP on R&D for national programmes. The ESRF, for example, has established special voting rules for the most important Council decisions, in light of the heavy financial burden shouldered by the larger member countries.

Countries that are still developing their R&D effort may receive special consideration, notably in the form of reduced contributions, when joining an international scientific organisation, as when Finland, Poland, and Hungary were accepted at CERN.

Existing international organisations, with their experienced staff and well-established organisational structures, can play an important role in the preparation and implementation of intergovernmental decisions on new large projects, especially where many partners with vested rights are involved. They can collect and analyse information, give advice during negotiations and discussions, and provide existing operating structures for new megascience activities. However, their role may be more limited when large investments are to be financed from national budgets, when the implications and consequences of siting are being considered, and when officials from a small number of countries are taking the initial, informal steps for a possible megaproject/programme.

In 1982, the G-7 heads of state addressed some of these difficulties by setting up a "Technology, Growth and Employment Working Group" (TGE) with one high official from each member country. Its mandate was to provide a stimulus to additional and improved international co-operation in science and technology. The TGE was aware that it was mainly a platform for the largest countries and therefore recommended a policy of openness in world-wide international co-operation.

In 1984 the London G-7 Summit prepared a "Report on the Environment" that surveyed current international collaboration in six key areas of environmental research and identified gaps in knowledge that might best be filled by further international co-operation. Many of its findings and suggestions have been applied in international S&T decisions and practices. Later, as new world-wide problems and challenges arose, the G-7 focused its attention on classic economic issues.

1. Introduction and general remarks

The ideas, positions, and conclusions presented here originate in the practice and experience of science communities and administrations in Western European countries. They thus reflect the author's experience in planning and realising projects for European large facilities, particularly in particle and solid state research, in geosciences, and thermonuclear fusion.

Three main types of megascience projects/programmes have developed:

i) large facilities for basic science;

ii) research on general challenges concerning planet Earth, nature, man, and society;

iii) the development of emerging industrial technologies.

Table 6 presents examples of past and present civil megascience projects/programmes. The Megascience Forum does not cover the development and assessment of emerging industrial technologies. However, it would be worthwhile to extend the Forum's work – in co-operation with other OECD and/or non-OECD institutions – to the applications-oriented sector of science and technology.

For a long time, megascience was identified with large facilities for basic science. Large programmes devoted to challenges concerning planet Earth, nature, man, and society later entered the realm of megascience.

Megascience projects/programmes need scientific inspiration as well as organisation, management and finance. Most successful projects in Europe originated with eminent scientists who were able to draw on contacts established with the political and governmental sectors and the respect and the high esteem they enjoyed within the relevant sectors of the science community and even the community as a whole. Politicians, government administrations and administrators could not have maintained successful big science activities by simply using a top-down approach.

Today, ideas, suggestions, and proposals for new megascience projects/programmes encounter difficulties. Public understanding and support for curiosity-driven research is diminishing, particularly for basic research using large equipment and facilities. Confronted with an overwhelming number of complex and often dramatic problems, society expects science and technology to play a "problem-solving" role. Society is less and less interested in simply deepening its knowledge of nature, man, and society; existing knowledge is often considered to be so extensive that further knowledge seems unnecessary, even unwanted. The short-term effects of science and technology on industrial competitiveness and productivity, on securing and increasing market shares of enterprises' products and services through innovation, on creating new jobs and employment opportunities and the quick pay-off, are today, more than ever, the main focus not only of private industry but also of public and political support for science and technology. However, politics would be poorly advised to manage science through political activism and to judge its importance and its merits solely on the basis of its present and foreseeable future usefulness.

For large instruments, scientists and engineers must join together from the beginning of the project. A large programme usually develops out of many specialised smaller projects located in different places and with a large number of research teams. Ideas for "joining forces" have to be discussed among scientists at international meetings and conferences, by national science organisations, and by participating administrations, in order to integrate dispersed activities in view of common aims and goals and in view of their scientific, social, and political significance.

It is difficult for science alone to realise large programmes. Scientists, by training, seek high-quality individual achievements, which they publish through lectures and articles. This is what generally counts for an academic career and for potential employers

154

Table 6. Past and present civil megascience projects/programmes

Relevant research fields/sectors	Institutional/organisational framework	
	Multinational organisations/institutes	Individual projects/programmes (examples)
1. Basic science with large facilities		
Particle physics and chemistry	CERN, JINR Dubna	DESY/HERA, (KAON), SLAC, CEBAF, TRISTAN, (SSC), LHC, etc.
Condensed matter	ILL, ESRF, High Magnetic Field Lab., Grenoble	ISIS, (ANS), ESS, etc.
Ground-based astronomy	ESO, "Club" of Canary Islands telescopes	GEMINI, VLT, VLA, etc.
Molecular biology/genome	EMBO/EMBL	HUGO
Geosciences		
– Oceans		ODP
– Earth crust		KTB
– Atmosphere		
Gravity		VIRGO, LIGO
Space science and technology	ESA	
– Atmospheric and space science		AMPTE, GIOTTO, ROSAT, etc.
– Manned space missions		Space station ALPHA, D1/D2 missions
Fusion		JET, ITER
2. Research on concerns/challenges for planet Earth, nature, man and society (see also geoscience and space science/technology)		
Oceans	IOC/WMO	GOOS
Atmosphere/climate	WMO, ICSU	WCRP, IGBP
Environment		
Arctic and Antarctic		GRIP
Health		WHO
3. Development and assessment of emerging industrial technologies		
Energy		OECD/IEA Implementing agreement projects
– Solar energy		
– Nuclear energy	EC DRAGON reactor and ORGEL reactor	D2/D3, LOFT, SEFOR experiments, EFBR
Aircraft	DNW Transonic windtunnel (ETW)	Concorde, Airbus, hypersonic plane

Note: In brackets, projects which have been cancelled.
Source: Author.

in industry and government. A top-down approach is therefore necessary to give impetus to large programmes dealing with broad societal issues.

2.   The role of government and government administration in megascience projects/programmes

Items to be addressed by a megascience project/programme

Realising a large project/programme in megascience requires a specific organisational, legal, and financial basis. Many issues have to be addressed, negotiated, and settled in the course of developing each project/programme. These include:
- the precise objectives, aims and content of a project/programme;
- the time schedule for its realisation, with the possible phases and/or milestones;
- the role and responsibilities of the participating institutes, institutions, organisations, and agencies;
- the most appropriate organisational and management structure for the project/programme;
- the status of the personnel employed in the organisation of the project/programme, their salaries, social conditions, and provisions for retirement;
- the expenditure/cost estimates for the development, construction and operational phase of a project/programme;
- the financing of expenditures/costs by the participating partners;
- the selection of a site for a large facility or the decision on leadership of a large programme;
- the taxation of project/programme expenditures, contributions, and financing;
- the involvement of funding institutions and/or governments for important decisions at the highest level;
- the procedures and criteria for industrial contracts for supplying hardware and services, with particular attention to contracts placed with enterprises in participating states;
- external relations and policies towards non-participating institutions/countries.

Some prerequisites for successful negotiations

Negotiating and clarifying these and other issues requires time and patience, thorough preparation, the involvement of experienced partners and persons. Delegations must be organised, and chairmanships must be clearly defined. Heads of delegations should have very broad leeway for negotiating, so that they do not have to engage in constant feedback and double-checking with their governments about every small modification or new circumstance that arises during discussions and negotiations with partners.

156

All government authorities and institutions with responsibility for a project/programme or some part of it should be represented in delegations in order to avoid doubts, objections, and resistance at home.

Role of parliaments

Particular attention has to be paid to the role of national parliaments in this respect. National parliaments have the power to make final decisions on public funding appropriations, and budgetary decisions are made annually. As large projects/programmes extend over many years, project/programme partners must be reliable if a megascience project/programme is to be managed efficiently and economically. Relations must therefore be established between the sponsoring government administrations and their respective parliaments. Without reliable and long-term commitments on the side of every partner's government and parliament from every partner, large projects/programmes cannot be developed in an international framework.

Each country has to choose for itself the members of its parliament who will participate in the consultation and negotiation process for large projects/programmes. Clearly, the division of power between the executive and the legislative branches of government has to be respected. Experience shows, however, that the assistance and co-operation of dedicated and responsible members of national parliaments, with responsibility for the science and technology sector and even for finance and budget, are of great advantage in realising scientific endeavours.

In western Europe, contacts between and with members of national parliaments, but also institutional and personal contacts with the European Parliament [the Parliament of the European Union (EU)] and official contacts with the Council of Europe, form a good foundation for consultations and deliberations on important scientific issues.

Begun in 1985 as a programme to instigate and support transnational, industrial, and technological co-operation among European enterprises in order to promote industrial innovation, EUREKA introduced in 1990 a Parliamentary EUREKA Conference as a way to involve its member States' parliaments in this initiative.

Should megascience projects/programmes not rely as well on organised international parliamentary interaction and support structures?

Political parameters and political environment

The preceding remarks about national parliaments and the participation of some of their members in consultations and negotiations for preparing and deciding on a large project/programme describe only one element of the political environment and framework conditions under which scientific and government partners operate for large projects/programmes.

It is important that partners involved in consultation and negotiation for large projects/programmes are aware, during the preparation and development phases, of how political and other parameters affect the way in which parties and delegations operate and debate.

Tactical considerations – the wish, even the necessity to hide one's own constraints, instructions, and tactical routes – may force a party to conceal some or all of its positions. Nevertheless, all partners involved should be made as aware as possible of national constraints and conditions. In the end, mystery-mongering tactics will not pay off.

Organisational approaches for megascience

A second dimension of this issue is the organisation of a large project/programme. Three main solutions have been adopted:
- realising it through a newly founded or an already existing multinational/international organisation/institute;
- realising it within an already existing national organisation/institute;
- creating an *ad hoc* organisation.

Multinational/international organisations and institutes are often chosen and established for scientific activities planned for a long, even open-ended duration. In this case, they often need their own qualified personnel (CERN, JINR Dubna, ILL, ESRF, ESO, EMBL, ESA, for example). In other cases, the project/programme will become an integral part of an already existing organisation/institution, founded for activities similar to those of the new large project/programme (IOC and WMO, for example).

A national organisation is mainly chosen as an institutional base for large undertakings when one country takes a strong lead in the realisation of the project/programme. This also means that a large part of the expenditures are covered by that organisation or its responsible government (examples are the HERA project at DESY, the Spallation Neutron Source ISIS in the Rutherford-Appleton Laboratory, or the Deep Continental Drilling Project KTB).

A specially set up, well-defined organisation is chosen in all cases where the project/programme will be realised within a fixed time period and when there is no intention to use the organisational umbrella for other purposes. This model is quite common in megascience because it offers great flexibility and avoids new heavy administrative structures and implications. Examples listed in Table 6 include GEMINI, VLA, HUGO, VIRGO, LIGO, AMPTE, ROSAT, JET, and ITER.

The "dense population" of international institutions, institutes and organisations, from world-wide UN organisations to specific, dedicated regional structures, which has developed in science as elsewhere during the last decades, militates against creating new institutions. This means realising new ideas in existing frameworks, thereby minimising obligations and burdens later, when the mission is terminated. Today, arguments in favour of new institutions should be very strong indeed.

The alternative to a new institution is a dedicated organisation. It is a particularly efficient solution and thus attractive when the partners are supported by their governments and have authorisation from their governments to act. The need for bureaucratic feedback and for obtaining the government's position and instructions for every detail would hamper flexibility in the organisation of the project.

Intellectual property rights

Examples of important items to be negotiated and clarified before a large project/ programme can be realised were mentioned above. An additional, substantial, and special item is the matter of intellectual property rights (IPR).

When dealing with fundamental research in basic science, with the development, construction, operation and scientific use of large facilities, and with public programmes, IPR regulations should, in principle, not be as strict as in technological, industry-related collaborations.

A closer analysis of the statutes of international scientific institutions, of multina-tional project/programme agreements, and of other forms of megascience activities would show in detail the practices that are based upon laws and/or unwritten rules that have proved their worth. In each project/programme, the issue of IPR has to be approached and solved. There have been no instances, to date, in which the IPR issue finally prevented the realisation of a qualified co-operative effort, although in special cases it may have needed time-consuming and cumbersome negotiation.

The more matters are settled in a spirit of true partnership – of mutual understanding and trust and based on clear rules and skilled negotiation – the less the issue of IPR will lower enthusiasm and optimism. Know-how gained in common projects should be com-mon property and placed equally at the disposal of all partners involved. Alternatively, each partner might have equal rights to the information obtained, but other partners should have well-defined and fair participation in possible benefits.

Issues of IPR in megascience should not be exaggerated, but they should be settled and clarified at the beginning of the undertaking in order to prevent unpleasant surprises and tensions.

Obstacles to successful co-operation

The main obstacles to successful consultations, negotiations, and agreements for large international projects and programmes are not legal or procedural ones. Nor are they financial. The main obstacles arise from the political positions of the partners, who are inexperienced, overburdened, or unwilling to co-operate in a joint megascience project/ programme.

Some, even the main, elements of a successful joint large undertaking are the willingness, preparedness, and ability of each potential and participating partner to operate on the basis of well-defined methods for sharing work and responsibility. Also, co-operation in a megascience project should begin early in the planning stage, not when important aspects have already been determined.

In an international project/programme of megascience, no member state or partici-pating country can dominate or make decisions according to its national and economic aims alone. World leadership and partnership participation in a megascience project/ programme are incompatible. Partnership implies that the important decisions are made together, using agreed procedures and rules. Sometimes decisions must be unanimous, but most are made by simple majority, for example on the site for a large facility, on the headquarters for a project lead team, on the appointment of directors and top-level management staff, and on external contracts for services and hardware supplied by industry.

The past decades offer many examples of how the natural and legal interests of nations and of their scientific communities and their political and industrial sectors have been harmonised with the interests of other countries and the needs of an international undertaking in megascience.

Decisions in megascience organisations

The following discussion deals with how decisions on three important items – annual budget, appointment of the director, and industrial contracts – are dealt with and taken in some megascience organisations (institutes and projects). Table 7 contains a (simplified) breakdown of the main regulations in the major European scientific organisations.

Contributions in cash and kind

The transfer of national budgetary funds to international megascience institutions and projects/programmes is meeting with growing objections from national parliaments, governments, scientific and technological groups, communities, and enterprises. The issue becomes particularly sensitive when resources for national science programmes or disciplines are on the same budgetary line as the international contribution, as member countries' contributions to the budget of an international body may withdraw these funds from the pool available in order to meet national demands. The automatic indexation that is often part of the budgetary planning for international organisations, institutes, projects, and programmes gives rise to further annoyance, particularly in times when national budgetary increases are significantly below the growth rate of the annual international megascience budget. In addition, returns on international funds available for industrial contracts to national enterprises might be lower than expected (and sometimes promised).

In the face of these problems, other solutions have been developed, particularly in Europe. A classic example is the so-called "HERA model". For the development and realisation of the Hadron Elektron Ringbeschleuniger Anlage (HERA), a "circular" electron/positron-proton collider at the DESY laboratory in Hamburg, other countries (Canada, France, Israel, Italy, United Kingdom, etc.) made contributions exclusively in the form of hardware components and experienced personnel. Thus, about 20 per cent of the HERA construction costs were covered by contributions in kind and in personnel from abroad.

Table 7. **Main regulations for important decisions in international megascience organisations**

	CERN ESO EMBL	ILL	ESRF
Annual budget	2/3 majority of all member states in the Council; each member state has one vote	Simple majority in the Steering Committee, including at least two votes each from French, British and German members	Qualified majority of the Council (qualified majority means: 2/3 majority of the capital and 50% or less dissenting votes from trustees)
Appointment of the Director		Unanimous votes from all trustees	
Industrial contracts	Decisions taken by a Finance Committee established by the Council	Decisions taken by an Industrial Committee with delegated power from the Steering Committee	Decisions on contracts between FF 3 and 30 million taken by a Purchasing Committee established by the Council. Contracts with a volume of FF 30 million and higher are decided upon by the Council. Council may make corrections in cases of extreme imbalances of contracts among member states.

Source: Author.

A similar model was to be used for the Canadian particle accelerator KAON in Vancouver and for the US Superconducting Super Collider (SSC) in Texas, two projects which were finally cancelled.

HERA's success in mobilising external contributions in kind depended on the fact that potential partners were included in planning from the very beginning of the undertaking. This was rather easy because the statutes of the DESY laboratory called for setting up a high-level scientific advisory board in the first years of its existence. Leading scientists and engineers from abroad were consulted and were thus able to influence new laboratory projects/programmes from the start. Participation of scientists from abroad was accompanied by government activities to develop and obtain partners for the new project from other countries.

Many governments are very interested in participating in a large project by supplying hardware in the form of high-technology components. This is particularly true for Russia, which can offer large capacity and remarkable experience in the manufacturing of heavy components and the supply of special materials. Basic research projects offer an opportunity to test new technological developments and to prepare industries for future markets. Obviously, however, the host country for a large facility with contributions in kind from foreign partners cannot receive all or nearly all of the high-tech hardware from abroad.

One of the most technologically advanced systems of the HERA facility is the set of more than 200 liquid helium-cooled, superconducting dipole magnets for the proton ring. Because of the long history of excellent German-Italian co-operation in high energy physics, the responsible Italian partner institution INFN (*Istituto Nazionale di Fisica Nucleare*) offered in 1984 to supply DESY with all dipole magnets, with financing from a special high-technology programme of the Italian government. This met, for obvious reasons, with severe objections from German industry and from the concerned ministry. As a result, the German and Italian governments negotiated a settlement, by which the industrial enterprises of both countries would supply half of the dipole magnets – a solution that is probably unique for a megascience project.

Industrial contracts

Whenever a joint investment budget is part of an international megascience project/ programme that is financed from member country contributions, and whenever this investment budget involves the supply of industrial hardware and services, the question of supplying these products and services from member countries' industries arises. There are two main, conflicting principles:

– The need to spend the budget of any project/programme in an economic and efficient way. This implies that all procurements have to be made on the basis of invited tenders, where contract awards are given to the lowest bid which meets all requirements.
– The intention, and to a great extent the need, to place industrial contracts with enterprises of the member nations according to their budgetary contributions.

There are various ways to escape the dilemma, such as:

– The statutes of a megascience organisation/programme oblige the organisation to contract industrial deliveries from each member country according to its budgetary or programme contributions. Generally, this is an expensive solution. It is advantageous for industries of member nations and avoids difficulties for participating governments with their partners from abroad, but it is rather disadvantageous for the taxpayer and goes against free competition. The European Space Agency (ESA) saw convincing arguments for choosing this alternative.
– A second approach is to delegate decisions about the more important industrial contracts (for example, those exceeding a certain sum) to a special Industry or Finance Committee, with representation from all countries participating in a project/programme/institution. The Committee makes decisions on the awarding of contracts after thorough evaluation and discussion of all bids. It considers aspects of industrial return to member states as well as the necessary economic implications. CERN and ILL offer examples of this approach.

The second model favours the most competitive industrial enterprises of member countries, regardless of their level of financial participation. It also reveals industrial weaknesses and serves to incite governments to improve the competitiveness of their industries.

Committees deciding on bids should seek solutions that do not systematically deny a member country's hopes of obtaining a contract. If a country always failed in such competitions, it would find it difficult to maintain enthusiasm about membership and partnership. In the case of the ESRF, the power of decision for larger procurements was delegated to the Finance Committee: a contract might be given to the "second or third best" bidder if the "first best" has already received more than its "fair return" in a defined time period.

Statistics on the distribution of industrial contracts among participating countries, which are published by international organisations such as CERN and ILL, ensure transparency and are a source of stimulation to international big science businesses.

Return to host countries[1]

Hosting the headquarters or large research teams of a megascience enterprise or providing the site for an international large facility naturally results in economic gains for the relevant region and country. Local and national industrial enterprises have an advantage over competitors from abroad, owing in particular to short distances for transport and to the availability of a skilled work force for whom no extra living costs have to be paid. The region hosting a megascience project attracts small specialised businesses which commit a large part or even all of their capacity to the megascience project. Staff members of the project, experienced in special technologies and well trained in management, might establish their own new ventures with the economic and technological backing of the project, thus contributing to the industrial infrastructure of the region.

Project staff spend most of their income in the region, creating a demand for additional high-quality municipal and social infrastructure (housing, for example) for themselves and their families. Discussions among governments about hosting and/or siting a megascience project must therefore be sound and sensible.

DESY statistics show that during the construction of the HERA facility in Hamburg, a substantial part of domestic industrial contracts for components (about one-third in equivalent German marks) were placed with firms in neighbouring regions. This does not include expenditures for buildings and conventional infrastructure, where local and regional firms participate even more.

In 1989, data on the actual benefits to the two CERN laboratory host countries, France and Switzerland, were collected on behalf of the CERN Council. They showed the remarkable returns the two countries enjoyed from purchases by the CERN laboratory and its visiting teams during the period studied (1984-88) (see Table 8). In addition to contracts for items purchased, the host countries receive income for other CERN expenses, in particular for services to the laboratory (electricity, water, gas, insurance, etc.). The figures in Table 8 must be viewed in the context of the additional costs borne by the host countries, owing to the presence of international personnel and their families and their demands and expectations regarding investments in infrastructure and administrative services. However, such additional expenditures are only a fraction of the returns gained.

Table 8.   **Purchases of the CERN laboratory and its visiting teams 1984-88 and contributions to CERN budget 1988 and 1992**

Member State	Purchases by CERN and visiting teams (1984-88)	Contribution to CERN budget (1988 and 1992)
	Million SF and percentage	
France	693 (34.1)	147/161 (18.7)/(16.9)
Switzerland	483 (23.8)	32/36 (4.1)/(3.8)
Twelve others	853 (42.1)	609/753 (77.2)/(79.3)

Source: CERN/FC 32 35/45/46, *Annual Report 1992.*

In the case of the European Space Agency, instead, there are also some special advantages to hosting the ESA headquarters and facilities. Owing to its different types of activities, the decentralisation of its research and service centres in several countries, and its statutes, the imbalances are more or less accepted. Its launch site in Kourou, French Guiana, might be an exception. According to its statutes, the general aim of the Agency's obligatory programme – as far as paid contracts with institutes and enterprises of the member states are concerned – is "to reach a coefficient of 1 for all returns to each member state". In each optional, *i.e.* non-obligatory programme – the majority of ESA programmes – a minimum return coefficient of 0.96 is at present guaranteed. Inequalities from the past are to be corrected. If a member country remains disadvantaged, it should be compensated by modifying the scale of contributions for certain programmes and periods. These mechanisms avoid granting special advantages or causing special disadvantages to any participant.

Special contributions from host countries[2]

It is the economic benefits that are particularly attractive to those who host megascience undertakings, especially those who offer the site for large ground-based experimental instruments.

One must therefore not be surprised that, as large international facilities and laboratories multiplied in western Europe, the idea emerged of asking host states for compensation in view of expected benefits:

- JET, the Joint European Torus, the nucleus of the EURATOM fusion programme, was constructed and is operated in Culham, United Kingdom. The Cu0lham site was chosen over a second proposal in an EU member State, Garching near Munich. According to the statutes, the United Kingdom, as the host country, had to make all necessary infrastructure investments to start the project (land, buildings, roads, power and water facilities). The United Kingdom covers an extra 10 per cent of the investment and operating costs of the project in addition to its normal share because it is part of the EU, whose budget covers 80 per cent of JET costs. (The final 10 per cent are contributed by the participating fusion laboratories of EURATOM and various countries, among which the United Kingdom is represented once again.)
- The ESRF, the European Synchrotron Radiation Facility, which operates in Grenoble, was set up in the beginning of the 1980s. The ESRF convention originally defined a special contribution from the host state, France – an additional 10 per cent (*i.e.* 34 per cent instead of 24 per cent) for the construction phase and an additional 2 per cent (*i.e.* 28.5 per cent instead of 26.5 per cent) for the operating phase.
- The European Transonic Windtunnel (ETW), an undertaking begun about the same time as the ESRF, took a somewhat similar approach. It was constructed and is now operating in Porz near Cologne. Germany, as the host state, pays 38 per cent of the investment cost. The contribution for construction from the other two major European partners, France and the United Kingdom, was 28 per cent and the Netherlands contributed 6 per cent. No extra host country payment was defined for the operational phase, because the operating costs are covered by income from individual users.

Extra contributions from a host country need not be regulated by organisation statutes. Sometimes, hosts voluntarily compensate for their economic advantages through special contributions, either in cash or in kind. Such special contributions might cover the supply of (cheap) electricity, particularly in the case of accelerator laboratories which consume a great deal of electrical power, special low interest loans, or extra grants. However, additional voluntary contributions designed to compensate for the economic and social advantages obtained from hosting an international organisation rarely completely satisfy the expectations of non-host nations.

Different procedures have been tried to decide on sites for megascience facilities, *e.g.* for CERN, ILL, JET, ESRF and ETW. They can perhaps be useful, at the end of this century, when a site is selected for ITER, the International Thermonuclear Experimental Reactor. They might help if, following the abandon of the SSC, a new global strategy evolves in high energy particle physics, with joint decisions made by partners in Europe, North America, and Japan for the construction and development of new large machines and their experimental use.

The number of participating countries

"Let us start the project alone, just our two countries", said a high government official several years ago, expressing his views and feelings about an emerging megascience project. "Other countries might join the undertaking later." Although this approach was not chosen, the official's frank opinion pointed up the complex process of preparing a large international project/programme, particularly in its start-up phase.

Small and large countries in megascience

Participation in megascience projects and programmes is particularly difficult for smaller countries, although such participation offers opportunities that would not otherwise exist. These opportunities include the possibility of developing scientific and technological activities in a highly specialised, complex, and expensive research field. They also offer highly qualified scientists and engineers the possibility to take scientific, technical, and managerial responsibilities in international institutions, to participate with their own national industrial enterprises in high-technology development, and to supply their own products and services, thus stimulating national industrial capacity and deriving economic advantages from technology transfer with the international activity.

The "one country--one vote" rule, which is common to most megascience organisations, offers policy-making advantages to smaller countries, particularly when they coordinate their interests and their actions.

The relations between larger and smaller countries as partners in a megascience project/programme, as well as their roles and interactions, need careful attention, particularly in the negotiation stage when statutes and rules are being established.

Large projects/programmes require substantial financing, particularly in the initial or subsequent investment phases, but also for operation. It is common practice to calculate members' contributions to the annual megascience budget as a share of GNP. The exchange rate influences the level of contributions paid in a defined national currency (such as US dollars or Swiss francs). High inflation rates nominally increase contributions.

This practice places a great financial burden on the larger countries. For CERN, for example, the four largest member countries – France, Germany, Italy, and the United Kingdom – contributed 71 per cent of the budget in 1992. Fourteen other countries contributed about 29 per cent. In the case of ESRF, the four countries mentioned above cover 84 per cent (55 per cent for France and Germany alone), and 16 per cent are covered by seven other countries.

Using past experience as a guide, the ESRF convention has modified the GNP-based share rule and the "one country-one vote" rule. Denmark, Finland, Norway and Sweden have established a consortium, NORDSYNC, as their representative partner and shareholder (4 per cent of shares) for ESRF. Because the financing is dominated by the four largest member countries, there are special rules for the voting procedures for the most important Council decisions (see Annex 1), for which no decision can be taken against the wishes of half of the members of the organisation (*i.e.* four out of eight member parties, as the four Scandinavian countries are represented by one member, NORD-SYNC). On the other hand, simple and two-thirds majorities are defined by the capital shares, so that France and Germany alone have a simple majority.

The ESRF statutes are an intelligent approach to respecting the heavy financial burden shouldered by larger member states of a megascience organisation. The rules mainly serve as a fallback when there is no consensus among all parties. However, consensus, understanding, tolerance, and a maximum effort to achieve consensus are the real and effective basis for operating multinational enterprises in science.

Charging member countries for their financial contribution to an international organisation on the basis of GNP assumes that they spend a more or less comparable share of GNP for R&D at home. By no means all European countries have reached this stage, as Table 9 shows for EU member countries. Contributions to international science based on GNP weigh far more heavily on the national R&D budgets of countries that spend only a relatively low share of GNP on R&D. In some sense, this creates a disequilibrium in national R&D budgets, which may produce objections from those areas of the national science landscape that are not involved in the relevant organisation. It would be worthwhile to give this issue more attention than it has received in the past.

When a country is still developing and increasing its national R&D efforts, it may receive special consideration, by comparison with fully developed R&D-intensive countries, when joining an international scientific organisation. Thus, the CERN Council decided that recent new member states of CERN such as Finland, Poland, and Hungary (like Portugal some years earlier), would contribute for several years at a rate below what would be required on the basis of GNP and exchange rates, thus smoothing the political path to full membership.

Advantages of larger countries in siting a megascience facility

Owing to their powerful scientific and economic potential and their ability to offer special contributions for investments and operating costs, larger countries are now in a far better position than smaller ones to host large scientific undertakings. This was not yet the case in the "early history" of scientific co-operation in Europe. When Geneva was chosen as the site for the newly founded European Centre for Nuclear Research by the CERN Council in 1952 (over three other sites, one near Paris, one in Copenhagen, and one in Arnheim), there was "a strong feeling among a majority of states that the laboratory should be located in a small country, for fear that a larger, more powerful host could take unfair (scientific) advantage of a facility of this type on its soil."[3] Additional arguments were based on questionnaires, but in the end a combination of technical, social, and political arguments, not unmixed with emotional influences, was decisive for the selection of Geneva.

Economic return to the host country was not an issue 40 years ago. Consequently, no special contributions by the host state, beyond those that existed for all international organisations in Geneva, were discussed or even demanded; at that time nobody could foresee CERN's later development, expansion, and economic weight. Today, a smaller

Table 9.　**R&D expenditures of EU member States as share of GNP (%)**
(1992 or earlier)
and comparison with Japan and the United States

	Total R&D (civil and military)		Total R&D financed by government	
	1990	1992	1990	1992
Belgium	1.69	–	0.47	–
Denmark	1.62	–	0.68	–
France	2.42	2.36	1.17	–
Germany	2.75	2.53	0.95	0.95
Greece	0.46	–	0.26	–
Ireland	0.91	1.11	0.27	0.26
Italy	1.30	1.38	0.67	0.66
Luxembourg				
Netherlands	2.02	–	0.91	–
Portugal	0.61	–	0.38	–
Spain	0.85	0.85	0.38	–
United Kingdom	2.19	2.12	0.77	0.75
Japan	2.08	2.99	0.55	–
United States	2.74	2.68	1.29	1.24

Source: Main Science and Technology Indicators, OECD, 1994.

country might not present the advantage that it evidently had in the case of CERN in 1952.

The role of existing international organisations

Preparing, structuring, and initiating intergovernmental decisions on large projects and programmes is a complex, colourful, and many-sided affair. Each new proposal is somewhat different from all of its predecessors. Tasks become still more difficult when many partners with vested rights are involved.

Nevertheless, existing international organisations can play an important role. They have experienced staff and well-established organisational structures. They can collect and analyse information, give advice for discussions and negotiations, and offer, where relevant, their operating schemes, structures, and programmes for a new megascience activity. Large international organisations, on the other hand, might have difficulties with the large investments to be financed from the national budgets of the project/programme participants and with the implications and consequences of decisions on sites.

International organisations with a large number of member countries and established rules for interaction might also find it difficult to act as an umbrella for the initial, often informal steps in a possible megascience project/programme taken by personalities from science (and government) from only a few countries.

The G-7 approach

A useful approach to overcoming these difficulties was taken by the G-7 heads of state in the 1980s.[4] At their Versailles Summit meeting in June 1982, they set up a "Technology, Growth, and Employment Working Group" (TGE Group), with one high official from each country. Its mandate, specified at the Williamsburg Summit in 1983, was to provide a stimulus to additional and improved international co-operation in science and technology, without developing additional permanent collaborative or administrative structures. (It should be recalled that the European Commission participates as a "guest" in all G-7 discussions and activities and thus forms a channel of communication to all EU member countries with respect to discussions and decisions that occur in the G-7 context.)

The TGE Working Group identified 18 areas of co-operation ("collaborative projects") where it thought guidance should be given in the future.[5] Among them were some which are today subject of discussions by the Megascience Forum.

It is worth noting that the Economic Summit recognised, without hesitation or restrictions, that basic research and large-scale science projects are of great importance for economic growth and employment – a fact which sometimes seems to be neglected in political decisions today.

One might argue that the TGE Working Group was just a platform for the largest countries and that non-participating countries were not involved. The Working Group was aware of this problem and therefore recommended a policy of openness in world-wide international co-operation:

"The Working Group confirms its general policy of enabling the participation of non-Summit countries in areas of cooperation wherever appropriate. The scope for wider participation is considered by the participants in the respective areas of cooperation and, in doing so account is taken of the potential mutual benefit. This approach is also evident in those areas in which training facilities have been provided to experts from developing countries and research of direct relevance to these countries' needs has been accelerated."[6]

The main areas of work within the 18 areas selected for collaboration were:

- to exchange information and experiences;
- to develop proposals for common research;
- to stimulate visiting and exchange programmes;
- to avoid unnecessary duplication of costly equipment and installations, and to enhance collaborative exploitation of existing research devices;
- to review and analyse trends in science and technology and the economic and legal aspects of its broad applications;
- to co-ordinate national programmes;
- to suggest common standards (where appropriate).

These tasks and activities are quite familiar to the OECD and the Megascience Forum.

In addition, the 1984 London Summit took up the subject of environmental research and technology. The Working Group then prepared and presented a "Report on Environment'', which describes the most important items of scientific and technical enquiry in six key areas of environmental research.[7]

The report surveyed current international collaboration in these areas, and noted gaps in knowledge that might best be filled by further international co-operation. It also identified the importance of appropriate, internationally recognised measurements. It suggested improvements in and harmonisation of techniques and practices of environmental measurement, particularly in the use of new and sophisticated methods. It assessed environmental activities already undertaken in existing international organisations and institutions, in consultation with the appropriate international bodies, in order to strengthen and complement their programmes.

During the 1980s, the G-7 TGE Working Group was a useful forum for discussion of world-wide co-operation in science and technology. Many of its findings and suggestions have been applied in international S&T decisions and practices. After some years of interest in S&T issues, new world-wide problems and challenges arose and the Sherpas, the high-level personal representatives of the heads of government, insisted that the G-7 focus its work on classic economic issues. Nevertheless, the G-7 TGE Working Group, which ceased its work in 1986, showed that many possibilities exist for enhancing international collaboration in science and technology projects/programmes.

3. Studies of success and failure

The problem of picking ''winners''

In light of discussions with members of the Megascience Forum, case studies of success (''winners'') and failure (''losers'') in megascience projects/programmes will not be presented. There are many possibilities and selecting a very few might give them excessive importance as ''positive'' and ''negative'' models. Furthermore, it is far easier to describe success stories than it is to analyse failures. The reasons for ''failures'' are usually more complex than the reasons for ''successes''.

Yet I would like to present a few facts and observations from my personal experience with the historic success story of the Institute Max Von Laue-Paul Langevin (and the High Flux Reactor ILL) in Grenoble in the 1950s and 1960s and the remarkable ''bargaining'' of the 1970s and 1980s for the realisation of the European Synchrotron Radiation Facility (ESRF), also in Grenoble, together with the European Transonic Windtunnel (ETW) in Porz/Cologne.

The high flux reactor at the Institut Laue-Langevin

The story of the HFR/ILL in Grenoble was shaped by the vision and efforts – whose source lay in personal and political experiences of the tragic years from 1933 to 1945 – of eminent physicists from France and Germany. Heinz Maier-Leibnitz recalls that:

"After the success of the first European undertaking, the CERN laboratory in Geneva, the idea was up in the air to establish more joint research institutions. To realise science in a way that assumes Europe is only one country seemed very attractive to many scientists, if not imperative in view of the smallness of the individual countries alone, in particular if one was not willing in the end to leave scientific leadership to the large nations, primarily to the USA."[8]

It was within the OECD (already in the early 1960s) that the idea emerged to seek projects that would force collaboration by their sheer size as the effort necessary was beyond the capacities of any single country. To quote Heinz Maier-Leibnitz again, "The size of the project was – as we see it today – certainly less decisive than the challenge of increasing scientific co-operation in Europe. Presenting size as an argument has greatly helped us to achieve the goals of intensifying European cooperation and advancing the emerging field of neutron research."

The OECD organised a working group consisting of research reactor and neutron experts. They provided the OECD Secretariat with the outline of and arguments for the construction of a modern HFR. The proposal failed because it was rejected by the United Kingdom, although leading British scientists had contributed substantially to the project.

Francis Perrin, at that time Chairman of the French *Commissariat à l'énergie atomique* (CEA) revived the project in 1963 and proposed to realise it as a bilateral Franco-German venture. A year later, Heinz Maier-Leibnitz from Munich and Louis Neel from Grenoble took up the idea, envisaged Grenoble as a possible site and Maier-Leibnitz as a significant contributor. A few months later (August 1964), during the Third International Geneva Conference on the Peaceful Uses of Atomic Energy, the French and German governments decided to advance the project and to prepare the final decision in Paris and Bonn. At the end of 1966, an Intergovernmental Agreement was signed between France and Germany, once the details of the new institution's statutes had been settled.

Building on the earlier scientific and technological (OECD) basis for the construction and use of the HFR, fewer than four years were needed to start the institute. The interaction between the two supporting countries, France and Germany, and the scientists, engineers, and government representatives responsible was close and friendly. A siting decision was unnecessary, as Grenoble was never questioned as an excellent site, and Heinz Maier-Leibnitz became the director of ILL.

Much valuable experience in joint undertakings was gained from the construction of the HFR, the designing and building of the neutron beam experiments, the later operation of the Institute and its organisational structures, the conflicts of interest that arose between member countries and member organisations, the legal constraints defined either by the statutes or by the application of the host country's regulations. To go into further detail would be to go beyond the scope and purpose of this chapter.

European Synchrotron Radiation Facility and European Transonic Windtunnel

Around 1983, the concerned R&D communities brought proposals for two new large experimental facilities – the ESRF and the ETW – to the attention of their governments, particularly in France and Germany. Both countries, in addition to Denmark, Belgium, the Netherlands and Italy, were interested in hosting the ESRF and both, along with the Netherlands, were also interested in hosting the ETW. Particularly in Germany, but also in France, there were lively discussions about national priority for the one or the other instrument among scientists, industrialists (aeronautics industries), and government officials. [In Germany, the chances of the ESRF were somewhat weakened by parallel plans to develop a Large Spallation Neutron Source (SNQ) in the Nuclear Research Centre at Jülich.]

The outcome of this complex and exciting battle for future investments was a decision to go ahead with both projects simultaneously, under similar financing conditions, with special contributions from the host country (see Section 2.12), and to select a German site for the ETW and a French one for the ESRF. The decision was a classic "package deal", fostered by the excellent quality and the seriousness of the two project proposals and the institutes, the industrial sector (for the ETW), and scientists and engineers identified with the proposals.

To prepare a "package deal", now also called "basket" or "multiple megascience approach", is an excellent strategy for easing decision making. However, it is often difficult to create conditions as favourable as those of the ESRF and the ETW.

4.   Lessons to be learned from the past/guidelines and suggestions for the future

Western Europe, confronted after the Second World War with monumental material and intellectual devastation, in science as elsewhere, had no choice other than to join its human and financial resources for the realisation of large projects in fundamental research. It therefore developed experience with a transnational "culture" of scientific co-operation. As a result, Europe learned the value of international partnership in megascience and of taking an intelligent approach to collaboration between large and smaller countries.

It is primarily science and scientists that initiate new projects/programmes. Eminent scientists in particular can launch successful initiatives, taking advantage of established contacts with the political and government sector as well as the respect they command within the science community. However, science and scientists would work in vain to realise their projects without a favourable political, social, and administrative environment.

Scientists have always been full of ideas, inventions, and plans for new large projects and programmes in science. Every country must give its own specific answers to the fundamental questions of science policy – to what extent it is justified in supporting science and research, particularly basic science; how weights and priorities for the different sectors of basic science should be established within the limits of available resources. For such decisions, every country must rely on its framework for, and practice of, consultation between government and the science sector, using expertise from home and abroad.

Today, megascience projects and programmes encounter difficulties arising from:

- intensified competition for limited public funding;
- diminishing public understanding and support for basic research;
- a general focusing on the short-term economic effects of science and technology;
- expectations of immediate solutions to problems of needs and lacks in the world, in countries and in societies.

However, governments would be ill-advised to judge the importance and merits of science on the sole basis of its present "usefulness".

Large co-ordinated science programmes, particularly those with social and political significance, are most likely to start from existing specialised smaller projects carried out in many places by many teams. Top-down approaches may be necessary to get such programmes established. However, the projects that form a large programme need serious review and assessment of their quality and expected merits.

All questions to be addressed by a megascience project/programme require time and patience, thorough preparation, experienced partners, and people who can carry out the necessary consultations and negotiations. Delegations should have very broad leeway to negotiate. All responsible governmental authorities and institutions should be included in national preparation and represented in national delegations.

The assistance and co-operation of dedicated and responsible members of national parliaments is of great advantage for realising scientific projects/programmes. Without reliable and long-term commitments from every partner government and parliament, large international projects/programmes cannot be developed. Should megascience projects/ programmes not also rely on organised international transboundary parliamentary interactions and support?

Megascience projects/programmes can employ different organisational approaches: a newly founded or an existing multinational/international organisation or institute; an already existing national organisation/institute; an *ad hoc* organisation. Each of these solutions has its merits.

In fundamental research, the regulation of the intellectual property rights (IPR) issue should, in principle, be less strict than in technological industry-relevant collaborations. The more matters are settled in a spirit of true partnership, of mutual understanding and trust, on the basis of clear rules and skilled negotiation, the less the issue of IPR will complicate the realisation of large projects/programmes.

The main obstacles to successful consultations, negotiations and agreements for large international projects and programme arise from the political positions of partners who are inexperienced, overburdened, or unwilling to co-operate in sharing work and responsibility. No participating country can impose its national and economic aims. World leadership and fair partnership participation in a megascience project/programme are incompatible. Co-operation in a megascience project should begin in the early planning stage, not when important decisions have already been made.

The transfer of national budgetary funds to an international megascience undertaking is meeting with growing resistance from national parliaments, governments, science and technology institutes, enterprises, and parts of the public. The issue is particularly sensitive when resources for national science programmes are on the same budgetary line as the international contribution. In addition, industrial returns from megascience contracts may be lower than expected or even promised. Using new approaches, solutions have been found to overcome these difficulties. The HERA model, in which contributions in kind and in personnel from abroad made it possible to realise a large machine for particle physics at the DESY laboratory in Hamburg, is a good example.

The supply of hardware and services for megascience projects/programmes by member country industries is important for general national support. Many different methods have been tried and are available for future megascience undertakings.

Hosting a megascience project/programme naturally results in economic gains for the relevant region and country. Therefore, discussions among governments about host-ing/siting a megascience project must be sound and sensitive. As the number of large international facilities in western Europe grew, the idea of asking host states for special contributions to the investment and operating budgets of large projects emerged, and some interesting models have been developed.

Participation in megascience projects/programmes is particularly difficult for smaller countries, but it offers opportunities that would not otherwise exist. The ''one country--one vote'' rule offers policy-making advantages to smaller countries, particu-larly when they co-ordinate their interests and actions. The relations between larger and smaller partner countries in a megascience project/programme, as well as their roles and interaction, need careful attention, particularly in the negotiation phase when statutes and rules are established.

The fact that contributions to megascience activities are related to countries' GNP may result in somewhat unbalanced expenditures in national R&D budgets in countries that spend a relatively small portion of GNP for R&D. This issue deserves further attention.

Owing to their powerful scientific and economic potential, larger states are now in a better position to become host countries for large scientific undertakings. This has not always been true, as the history of CERN shows.

Existing international organisations have experienced staff and well-established organisational structures and can collect and analyse megascience experiences, give advice for discussions and negotiations and offer – if relevant – their operating schemes, structures, and programmes for a new large scientific activity.

In the 1980s, the G-7 Working Group on ''Technology, Growth and Employment'' (TGE) was a useful platform for discussing world-wide co-operation in science and technology.

''Package deals'' or ''basket approaches'' for deciding on and choosing a site for two or more new megascience proposals is an excellent strategy. However, it may be difficult to create conditions as favourable as those that existed for the European Synchro-tron Radiation Facility (ESRF) and the European Transonic Windtunnel (ETW) in the 1980s.

It would be worthwhile extending the Megascience Forum's work to applications-oriented science and technology.

Annex 1 to the Convention

STATUTES of the EUROPEAN SYNCHROTRON RADIATION FACILITY

Société civile

Article 8
POWERS OF THE COUNCIL

1. The Council shall decide important issues of Company policy. The Council may issue instructions to the Director General.

2. The following matters shall require the unanimous approval of the Council:

   a) the admission of new Members;
   b) arrangements in accordance with Article 8 of the Convention;
   c) transfer of shares among Members of different Contracting Parties, and increase in the capital;
   d) the Council's rules of procedure;
   e) the financial rules;
   f) amendment of these Statutes;
   g) increases in the construction costs as set out in Article 5 of the Convention.

3. The following matters shall require the approval of the Council by a qualified majority:

   a) the election of its Chairman and Vice-Chairman;
   b) the medium term scientific programme;
   c) the annual budget and medium term financial estimates;
   d) the closure of the annual accounts;
   e) the appointment and termination of the appointments of the Director General and the Directors;
   f) the establishment and terms of reference of advisory or other committees, notably an Administrative and Finance Committee;
   g) the appointment of the chairman and the vice-chairman of each advisory or other committee;
   h) the Audit Committee's terms of reference and rules of procedure;
   i) the policy for the allocation of beam time;
   j) short and medium term arrangements for use of the ESRF by national or internationl scientific organisations;
   k) the *Convention d'Entreprise* (Company agreement on the conditions of service of its staff).

4. The Council shall take decisions on other matters by a simple majority.

Article 9
VOTING PROCEDURE

1. Each Contracting Party shall have a single indivisible vote exercisable by the delegate designated for the purpose by the relevant Members.

2. A "simple majority" means half of the capital, the number of unfavourable votes not exceeding half of the Contracting Parties.

3. A "qualified majority" means two-thirds of the capital, the number of unfavourable votes not exceeding half of the Contracting Parties.

4. "Unanimity" means at least two-thirds of the capital and no counter-vote of any Contracting Party, all Contracting Parties having an opportunity to vote.

5. In case of urgency, or at the request of any delegation, the Chairman shall submit an urgent proposal for decision to the Council by consulting delegates individually by correspondence. The proposal shall be approved if the required majority of delegations give their written assent. However, if any delegate promptly so requests, the question shall be remitted to the next meeting of the Council.

Notes

1. See Chapter 4.

2. See Chapter 4.

3. John Kriege, *History of CERN*, Vol. 1, North Holland, 1987.

4. Canada, France, Germany, Italy, Japan, the United Kingdom, and the United States.

5. Photovoltaic solar energy; controlled thermonuclear fusion; photosynthesis and photochemical conversion of solar energy; fast breeder reactors; food technology; aquaculture; remote sensing for space; high-speed trains; housing and urban planning in developing countries; advanced robotics; impact of new technologies on mature industries; biotechnology; advanced materials and standards; new technologies applied to culture, education, and vocational training (ANTEM); public acceptance of new technologies; basic biology; high energy physics; solar system exploration.

6. *Report of the TGE Working Group to the Bonn Economic Summit*, 1985.

7. Atmospheric pollution, toxic and radioactive wastes, marine pollution, pollution of soils and water, appropriate land husbandry, and climatic change.

8. *Journal of Franco-German Association for Science and Technology*, 1987.

Chapter 4

THE IMPLICATIONS OF HOSTING INTERNATIONAL SCIENTIFIC FACILITIES*

by

Katherine E. Barker
Programme of Policy Research in Engineering, Science and Technology (PREST)
University of Manchester, United Kingdom

Executive summary

This chapter addresses the issues that arise for the hosting of international scientific facilities. On the basis of a synthesis of recent documents, it provides a summary of key findings on the implications of hosting such facilities, both for the host nations and in terms of the management of co-operation for large scientific facilities.

There is usually fierce competition for the siting of new international facilities, because of the expectations of increased prestige and economic activity brought to the locality. Siting may be determined by the scientific credibility of the host, infrastructural or geographical requirements, but political considerations, such as the sharing of international organisations (scientific or not) among countries, are important.

Among the perceived benefits and disadvantages of hosting, the degree of influence over the facility is balanced against the impossibility for a host to exit, gaining a greater share of contracts against the costs of providing infrastructure, more employment of staff and cultural benefits to the locality in terms of internationalisation and scientific awareness against possible environmental costs in terms of destruction of a greenfield site.

Evidence for actual benefits is examined. Prestige and cultural effects are difficult to assess but are highly valued in some countries. Studies of the economic impact of large facilities show a net benefit to the host, even where the policy is to share high-tech contracts, because of the large volume of lower-tech contracts awarded to local firms.

* This chapter was prepared with the assistance of Mr. Mark Klein, formerly of PREST. It is based on work supported by the UK Economic and Social Research Council (grant L323 253005) under the Science Policy Support Group Programme "The European Context for UK Science Policy". The author would also like to thank those who have commented on the chapter.

Such studies assume that the facility does not displace other economic activity. The key determinant of the economic and industrial benefits for a host is the procurement system (open competition or sharing). More staff are usually employed from the host nation, particularly at non-scientific levels.

Options for balancing scientific and economic returns are examined. Simple mechanisms are payments in kind by the host, such as the provision of a site or discounted power, and the payment of a hosting premium, that is, an increased annual subscription. These may be an arbitrary way to achieve a balance of benefits, but are simple to operate. "Fair returns" mechanisms can be applied to employment, procurement and scientific access. Here, members gain in proportion to their contribution. These may be more accurate, but are laborious to administer, can compromise quality, and can increase costs of procurement.

Increasing attention is likely to be paid to the balancing of benefits among members, particularly after the much publicised dispute at CERN in 1994. A hosting premium is a simple way to redress host benefits and does not compromise quality or price. Facilities can actively encourage member nations' firms to tender for contracts. Governments should take a longer and broader view of international facilities, including their environmental impact and decommissioning costs. The balancing of benefits will remain important, as the benefits of a global facility to a host will increase the skew of benefits to the host, necessitating greater attention to balancing.

1. Introduction

Large scientific instruments required for certain fields of research have been built as internationally shared scientific facilities. European countries in particular have a long history of pooling resources to create joint facilities to allow their scientists to work at the leading edge of knowledge. There is little doubt among the scientists concerned that their success on the world stage is wholly dependent upon the availability of ever larger or more powerful equipment. Thus, they have been able to persuade their national governments to participate in international facilities, this of course requires entering into agreements, committing to subscriptions, and relinquishing sole control. If one looks at the history of international co-operative scientific facilities, one sees that, while undoubtedly enormously successful as a means to achieve scientific advances at a manageable cost, such co-operation is not without difficulties.

Scientists are now well accustomed to travelling to facilities abroad, working in internationally mixed teams and publishing discoveries jointly. Governments have developed administrative expertise in organising the negotiation of shared facilities, the participation of their scientists, and the political representation of their interests at those facilities. It has long been noticed that membership subscriptions for large facilities are very large, particularly in comparison with national science budgets in some countries. As public spending budgets come under increasing pressure, the value obtained from international facility subscriptions has come under question. The particular issue for scientific facilities (as opposed to a decentralised international research programme) concerns the difficulties of sharing the benefits among members, as these appear to be skewed towards the host.

Countries have not failed to notice that the host nation appears to gain most from the co-operation. The host nation (or region) may have donated the land and buildings to the co-operative facility, but its industry will gain most from its construction and furnishing and from the provision of basic goods and services during the facility's life time. Host nation scientists seem to have a natural advantage in gaining posts, to say nothing of clerical, technical and manual labour. Firms from the host nation also obtain the most contracts for procurement of sophisticated instruments and equipment. It is this kind of discrepancy which has led governments to question their contributions to shared facilities and to significant problems at a political level. The recently resolved (December 1994) dispute between members of the European Laboratory for Nuclear Research (CERN) over the financing of the Large Hadron Collider (LHC) was fuelled by both these concerns: that the proposed new machine, the LHC, was going to add to the already very large annual subscriptions and was difficult to justify in national terms, and that France and Switzerland, as hosts, would benefit the most from the expenditure on the machine, as they had in the past for both high-tech and lower-tech goods and services contracts. The dispute broadened to issues about general expenditure at CERN, and the LHC project was delayed for several months.

In many respects, CERN is not a representative example of a co-operative research facility, since it is so much larger than other shared facilities. However, it is important, because the financial levels at which international facility subscriptions come under scrutiny appear to be dropping, with the result that the notion of ''megascience'' is being applied to smaller activities (which may now be larger in proportion to national budgets for science). Scientific facilities which, in the past, would have been built by a single nation to serve its scientific community are increasingly being considered as suitable for cost-sharing projects across nations. This means that, more than ever, decision makers are in need of a rationale for deciding on the best location and management structure for new facilities in order to avoid such problems, and in need of guidance for solving disputes about fair contributions and returns at existing ones.

There has always been fierce competition for hosting international scientific facilities. Nations or regions have wished to attract what they perceive as prestigious organisations. While prestige is important, the investment effects, industrial and economic benefits accruing to a host nation of a large scientific facility, are also sought. However, hosting nations do not merely reap easy gains from a scientific facility. The host may have to invest in expensive infrastructure, such as roads, and could be left with an outdated facility to decommission at the end of its life time. This document aims to bring out and analyse the implications of hosting international scientific facilities. Experience to date will be used to indicate where the pitfalls lie and how problems, both for hosting and contributing nations, might be solved, or at least alleviated.

The starting point for addressing this complex topic will be a brief survey of how nations have negotiated siting decisions in the past. The types of debate entered into by collaborating nations should reveal something of decision makers' expectations for large facilities. Is the motivation for hosting expected scientific gain? Do anticipated opportunities for local high-tech industry drive the bid? Are regions competing for the facility as a cornerstone for technopole creation? Or are more general employment benefits being sought? This leads to a discussion of the perceived benefits and problems of hosting, and an examination of the evidence of actual benefits and disadvantages, their magnitudes, and their key determinants. In fact, in this policy area, perceptions carry greater weight than good quality evidence for the magnitudes of hosting effects. This makes it difficult to advise on workable solutions for sharing scientific facilities.

The document then goes on to review the mechanisms used for balancing the scientific and economic/industrial benefits across member nations. These include the payment of a larger subscription by the host nation (a hosting premium) and the operation of various types of fair return (*juste retour*) mechanisms whereby employment, procurement and scientific access are monitored and controlled in proportion to the contributions of members to the facility. The advantages and pitfalls of these mechanisms are debated. The concluding section explores the implications of initiating and operating internationally shared scientific facilities and sets out some points for policy makers in this field.

2.   Site negotiation

Deciding on the site of a new shared facility is a difficult process. Different factors are assessed at different levels, and the outcome is not determined by scientific factors alone. The political process most often starts with an invitation to interested parties (who must also be members of the co-operative project) to submit proposals for hosting. A set of criteria, both explicit and implied, is then used to produce a short list of contenders before the final decision is made. The negotiation process will be heavily influenced by how contending nations and regions, who may offer strong inducements such as provision of special facilities or discounted services, perceive the expected benefits from hosting a large facility. Indeed, the prestige of hosting an international scientific facility may motivate governments (national and regional) to offer attractive bids, on the assumption that the benefits that will flow to the area, including intangible ones, will make the offer cost-effective.

The considerations in these negotiations can be broadly classified as scientific/ technical, infrastructural, environmental and political. The first two are scrutinised in a generally similar way in all facility siting decisions and are described below, while the political considerations are more case-specific, as are the ways in which siting decisions are finally arrived at by partners.

Scientific and technical considerations restrict the number of potential sites for geographical reasons. These are significant in astronomy facilities and any involving radioactive installations. For example, telescopes are best located in the Southern Hemisphere in order to observe certain astronomical objects, such as the Milky Way, and longitude is crucial, as certain events can only be seen from certain land masses (this argument underpins the siting of the South African Large Telescope). They need to be at high altitude and in dry regions. The siting of large telescopes has recently been a source of controversy, and this causes difficulties because it is not easy to find alternative sites with the same geographical characteristics. The site of the European Southern Observatory's (ESO) Very Large Telescope (VLT) project is under a land rights dispute, and that of the planned Large Binocular Telescope at Mount Graham in the United States is subject to litigation from environmentalists who claim that the telescope will endanger the habitat of red squirrels. If these disputes concerned other types of large facility, it would be somewhat easier to find an alternative location. The seismic stability of the region can be critical if large instruments or nuclear reactors are being sited. This issue was recently highlighted by doubts over the absolute stability of the Cadarache site, where the French fusion effort is located.

The scientific and technological environment is important for the siting decision. The reputation of the candidate country's scientists in the field seems to play an important role. Whether this is for reasons of scientific credibility, or whether it is because an active scientific community can strengthen negotiating power is difficult to determine. Certainly, the scientific and technological support available in the form of skilled technicians and the presence of university departments likely to create a critical mass of activity around the facility may be taken into account. A significant technological environmental factor is the telecommunications infrastructure, as facilities need to make their data outputs rapidly available to scientists in the member nations. The siting of the European Centre for Medium-range Weather Forecasts (ECMWF) in the United Kingdom was determined by the need for high specification telecommunications links to transmit the weather data to all members after processing. The site, next to Reading University and the United Kingdom Meteorological Office, was close a very active existing community of meteorologists. Similarly, when the European Molecular Biology Laboratory (EMBL) was considering candidates for its Bioinformatics outstation, the scientific excellence of the Cambridge area in biosciences and the telecommunications infrastructure were considered crucial, owing to the need for high-speed data links between the institute and European universities.

While well-developed scientific and technological environments may favour placing international facilities in areas of existing strength, there now seems to be some thought that they should be sited in less developed areas, to act as an impetus for economic and technological development. Certainly, the European Union is concerned with cohesion and thus with reducing the scientific, technological and economic gaps among its members. As such, it may wish to see less developed member states siting international scientific facilities. The German candidate site for the ITER fusion experiment is not in a traditionally scientifically strong area, such as Jülich, but in former East Germany.

The infrastructural needs of new facilities can be severe. Apart from modern communications links there is often a demand for large quantities of electricity, usually at the cheapest possible price. The availability of large amounts of electrical power was a factor in the siting decisions for CERN and the Joint European Torus (JET). The ease of access to a facility, the availability of schools (particularly international education for the offspring of the expatriate staff), housing and quality of life have to be provided by the candidate host.

Environmental issues are becoming more important in the choice of site for new international scientific facilities. For example, if a greenfield site is considered, there will be disruption of the local environment, building of extra roads, and the destruction of habitats. A convincing case that environmental impact will be within acceptable limits will be necessary. This seems to apply particularly to new telescopes. As described above, by their very nature, they need to be built in remote locations without much human activity and where the local ecosystem may be designated of special value, as the recent controversy surrounding the construction of the Large Binocular Telescope on Mount Graham in Arizona illustrates. Opposition to this project has taken the form of an organised attack upon the facility's environmental "credibility". It has been claimed that the telescope threatens the survival of the local red squirrel population and also constitutes an offence to the San Carlos tribe of Apaches, who consider the mountain sacred. Local environmental impact will be important in local planning. After the site for JET was chosen, opposition arose when it was discovered that the facility was to be built on land designated as "green belt", i.e. safeguarded against construction. Planning permission was eventually granted, on condition that the site be returned to greenfield upon termination of the project.

A shortlist of sites that satisfy the basic technological and infrastructural criteria is usually drawn up (in the case of telescopes, as discussed above, there is often only one favoured site). Political factors are never remote in decisions about megascience, and they are influential. If the country already hosts an international facility, this may be a positive argument, since it implies that the technical and infrastructural criteria have already been met and that economies of scale can be achieved. However, countries may wish to have their "fair share" of international science sites, and thus existing facilities may be a negative factor. Smaller nations can sometimes benefit from their perceived neutrality, as was the case for the siting of CERN in Switzerland and the European Space Agency facility ESTEC in the Netherlands. However, their lack of political power in the negotiation process results in their marginalisation.

In reality the choice of site can be extremely complicated and time-consuming, involving high-level politicians. Scientific sites may be "traded" for the siting of other international organisation headquarters which bring prestige and economic benefits. For example, the ECMWF was sited in the United Kingdom as part of a deal whereby the European Patent Office went to Germany.

This brief examination of the processes of choosing a site for an international scientific facility shows that scientific and technological considerations are not the only ones, nor even the most important ones in some cases. Site choice is influenced by the members' perceptions of the expected direct and indirect benefits of a facility. The next section of this paper examines more systematically the expected benefits and problems of hosting.

3. Perceived benefits and disadvantages of hosting

Table 10 summarises many of the potential benefits and disadvantages arising from the location of a large scientific facility. These factors are often cited by politicians, policy makers and scientists as evidence that a facility will always be beneficial overall.

The following expansion of the table puts forward in greater detail some of the factors described above, and reflects common assumptions. The next section then investigates the extent to which many of these factors are actually observed.

Table 10. **The benefits and disadvantages of hosting**

Category	Potential benefit	Potential disadvantage
Political	• Prestige • Management control	• Increased difficulty of withdrawal
Economic	• Effects of salary spending and tax revenue • Regional development • Reduced travel costs	• Hosting premium • Creation of infrastructure • Decommissioning/closure costs
Industrial	• Contracting to local industry • Improved technology in industry • Technological spin-off	• Displacement from other economic activities
Scientific	• Creation of centre of excellence • Ease of access • Return from critical mass	• Opportunity cost to national programme
Employment & skills	• Local administration and maintenance staff • Higher proportion of national scientific staff • Prevention of brain drain • Training – PhDs, Tech., Eng.	• Possible salary differentials • Opportunity cost to employment • Skills/expertise left over when facility closes
Cultural	• European/international school • Science education/public understanding	
Environmental	• Sustainable development/green policies	• Destruction of greenfield site • Nuclear concerns

Source: Author, 1995.

Political

Prestige is said to be one of the most important benefits of a megascience facility. Chauvinism was evident in the aftermath of the Second World War and the cold war and involved using science as a symbol of scientific and technological superiority. The post-cold war environment is witnessing a greater emphasis on collaboration, with national prestige being sacrificed in favour of reducing costs, the host nation can use a megascience facility as a cost-effective means of obtaining scientific and political prestige.

However, the extent to which this is a benefit depends on the standing and visibility of science within the host nation.

It is also expected that the host nation will be able to exert a greater degree of control over a facility's operation. The only perceived political drawback to hosting is the impossibility of withdrawing from the facility. While nations competing for the site of an international scientific facility may lose sight of this potential disadvantage, they should not underestimate the long-term political commitments and obligations which hosting brings. A host cannot disengage from the co-operation, and it will be left with the obsolete installations and buildings if the facility is closed.

Economic

There are strong expectations that hosting a large scientific facility will bring broad economic benefits, and they partly underlie the desire to win the facility. The simple fact that (usually relatively large) salaries will be spent and that foreign funds will flow to the country raises expectations of economic gain for the region. This may be an important aspect of regional development plans (as in the relocation of German facilities to less favoured regions in the Eastern part of the country). The procurement of basic goods and services can create economic activity, particularly where the goods are necessarily locally provided. Funding bodies Treasuries may be find the prospect of avoiding fluctuations in exchange rates when paying foreign subscriptions attractive. The host's science funding agencies may see reduced travel costs for host nation scientists a valuable benefit as well.

Potential economic disadvantages should be mentioned. There may be a "hosting premium" to pay. This is an additional sum above the normal contribution and is charged to try and compensate the non-host members for the benefits gained by the host. As mentioned above, the host may have to promise expensive investments in the site and may be responsible for decommissioning and closure, costs which are unknown at the start of the facility's life. If the facility is sited in a region which is already economically prosperous, economic "overheating" might occur and activities might merely be displaced from elsewhere (with no overall net gain).

Industrial and economic

High-technology procurement for a megascience facility is expected to help create competitive advantage for the hosting nation, primarily through the technological spin-off resulting from carrying out industrial contracts. This procurement is also expected to raise standards and technological competencies in the host nation's industrial base.

Scientific

A host's scientific expectations include the effects of creating a scientific centre of excellence within a nation, which is expected to raise the standard of science in a particular field. This should be reinforced by the greater ease of access for host nation scientists (including students) and by the effects on the science base of the "critical mass" produced. A potential problem for the scientific community is that the benefits may be offset by reductions in national programmes, or that talented scientists are attracted away from the host country's national laboratories and university departments.

Employment and skills

A large facility is expected to generate employment, particularly for host nation scientists, as well as local jobs for administrative, service and support functions. Training benefits would also be expected for scientists (students preparing a Ph.D.) and technical staff (who are also likely to be predominantly local). When such staff is later recruited by national firms, they benefit.

Cultural

Cultural benefits might include the effects of having a European or international school located in the vicinity of a large facility. This will apply only if international companies are able to make use of the school. Other cultural factors are more intangible and include possible enhanced language skills and a more "international" outlook in the local community. The facility's role in enhancing public understanding of science and scientific education could be an important benefit if these aspects are exploited by the host, for example through a visitors' centre.

4. Evidence for actual benefits and disadvantages of hosting

The expected benefits and potential problems of siting a large international scientific facility have important consequences for its functioning. In fact, the evidence for the impacts of hosting is largely anecdotal, although some recent UK studies (OST, 1993; PREST, 1994) are used throughout the following section, as are some economic studies commissioned by international facilities themselves. The evidence will again be reviewed briefly, following Table 10.

Political

The effects of prestige have never been investigated, but it is obvious that withdrawing from a hosted facility is very difficult. The belief that the host nation has greater control over management of the facility was investigated to some extent in the PREST study (1994). This study showed that, at a primary level, the assertion is false: the committees that manage a facility seldom give the host any more votes than the next largest contributor. In addition, the director of a megascience facility need not be a citizen of the host nation. However, at a secondary level, it is clear that the administration of a facility may be dominated by host country nationals. Although this may mean that the host potentially dominates the day-to-day running of the facility, there is no evidence to that effect. As significant decisions are always made by committees, the effect is unlikely to be more than very slight. While has apparently been no systematic study of the influence of host nation administrative employees, the example of JET in the United Kingdom shows that there is some effect. The British do not seem to occupy the very senior positions on committees and in management, but they are very numerous in the administration owing to the need for excellent command of the English language and familiarity with British law and customs. This point is clearly related to employment effects (see below).

Economic and industrial

Some economic impact studies are available. Their quality and rigour vary, and it has proved difficult to verify and measure the expected broader economic benefits from hosting international facilities. The studies involve highly problematic judgements and difficulties in translating those judgements into shadow prices for economic analysis. The 1993 United Kingdom Office of Science and Technology report analysed the economic effects of salary spending and increased revenue from taxation for several different European facilities. It concluded that net positive returns were obtained from hosting a facility, but added that this assumed no displacement effects.

In 1991, a study was published on the economic benefits to the Netherlands of hosting the European Space Research and Technology Centre (ESTEC). Each guilder spent by ESTEC brought secondary effects (a multiplier of 1.8), and the Dutch contribution to ESA's non-R&D costs was returned over nine-fold. Other benefits (regional, employment, and technological) led to the conclusion that ESTEC was "good value for money". Information supplied by the European Centre for Medium-range Weather Forecasts has suggested a national return to the United Kingdom for its expenditure on the Centre of 4:1. Another study (Carter, 1993) examined the impact of the JET Joint Undertaking upon the United Kingdom, concluding that the nation received an overall financial return of 2.04.

The distribution of costs among infrastructure, fixed installations and operating costs would influence the results of such cost/benefit approaches, but these have not yet been tackled. Neither have attempts been made to value the environmental benefits and costs, although the ESTEC study did take into account the effects of the visitor's centre upon the image of its home town. Cost-benefit analysis techniques for placing a value on such intangibles exist, but they are controversial. If the economic values assigned to environmental, cultural and other effects are transparent, they could be added to the analysis of the host benefits. The time horizon for assessing the economic impact of a facility is of course crucial. In the case of JET, for example, while financial returns can be calculated (see above), the outcome for the host might be negative if the projected costs of decommissioning are included. Obviously, when planning a co-operative facility, all members should try to take a longer-term view than in the past. It must be true that analysis could be informed by approaches devised for appraising government investment in other major projects.

An important conclusion to be drawn from these reports concerns the technological level of the benefit. Carter's analysis of JET shows that the level of high-tech industrial return is much lower than that received through other types of procurement. This may be due to the UK's comparatively weak high-tech sector. However, it may also be that the higher the technical demands of the tender specification, the less transport costs are significant. For very sophisticated components, only a few companies world-wide have the capabilities to undertake the contract. The technical procurement committee of the facility, advised by its scientific and technical staff, will have a global or at least regional knowledge of potential candidate firms, and local presence of host nation firms will have little effect on such choices. This point is very important politically. It is unfortunate that there is little clear evidence on whether location or capability is important for winning high-tech contracts, but it seems that contractors for CERN have been predominantly Swiss or French, and French firms have done well in competing for ESRF and ILL work.

Other studies examining the effects on all members of high-tech contracts from large facilities have been carried out (Schmied, 1975, Schmied et al., 1984; Bach and Lambert, 1992). This work highlighted the direct and indirect benefits of high-tech contracts placed with industry. The extent to which the host nation will benefit depends on the procure-ment policy. If there is a *juste retour* (''fair return'') policy, the host nation is unlikely to receive more industrial high-tech benefit than other participants. (The fair return policies are discussed further in Section 5 below.) Where a fair return policy is applied to all aspects of procurement, low-tech contracts tend to receive a low weighting, and so the degree of absolute financial benefit obtainable by the host should remain high. An important finding of the ESTEC report is the considerable financial benefit obtained from provision of ''low-tech'' goods and services. (ESTEC has a fair return policy for high-tech contracts.) Argument over allocation of contracts to member firms concentrates at the high-tech end, because of the expected spin-off benefits to successful firms. Relatively less consideration has been given to the potentially significant economic impact of low-tech contracts which the host nation firms are in a good position to win.

Other key points here concern whether or not the main purpose of the facility includes industrial research and development. Unfortunately, facilities are diverse, and the separation is not clear-cut. For example, although the remit of CERN is fundamental research, a major part of this entails developing the detectors, computers and instruments that make the research possible. ILL and ESRF can be used for many types of research, and they can sell beam time to industrial firms. The presence of development work, either in instrumentation or as direct use of the facility, would be an important determinant of potential industrial effects. A related issue is the intellectual property policy of the co-operative facility. At ESA, the intellectual property rights for contract work are held by the industrial contractor, but a licence is retained for ESA member countries. ESRF retains the property rights for contracted work, but not for work paid for by a third party. Thus, the benefits to host nation firms, assuming that they are more successful in winning contracts, would depend upon whether they are in a position to exploit new developments arising from contract work. Even if they are not, the work of Schmied et al. (1975, 1984) suggests that the indirect benefits of undertaking contracts for facilities are still worthwhile.

Other economic effects of hosting are minor when compared with the above. Reduced travel costs prove not to be significant. In certain facilities (*e.g.* the ILL and ESO), travel costs are met by the facility. Where this is not the case, the argument carries more weight but remains unconvincing for Europe, since the costs (in both money and time) of travel between European countries (where the shared facilities tend to occur) are not high enough to be prohibitive. If the international facility in question is a global effort, then the possibility of the host's gain from reduced travel costs becomes greater.

The key determinant of the economic and industrial benefits to a host member is the procurement system. If it operates by open competition, then the host nation may receive more contracts than other participants, owing to advantages arising from geographical proximity, shared language, and the ease of maintaining contact with the administration and technical staff (however, no specific studies have been carried out on this last issue). There is evidence that the firms awarded high-tech contracts receive significant competitive benefits. Without fair return, the host nation does seem to benefit from more high-tech contracts, as statistics from CERN reveal. Certainly it seems that basic goods and services contracts will be predominantly won by the host, and in times of unemployment and recession these benefits should not be dismissed.

Scientific

Many of the factors indicated in the previous section are manifestly identifiable, but the advantage to the host is not as large as is commonly assumed. One erroneous assumption concerns the increased ease of access for scientists from the host nation, as experimental time at facilities is usually awarded in one of two ways. CERN uses a merit system, as does ILL, but ILL gives some attention to ensuring that participants' contributions are taken into account, so that no one nation can dominate the scientific access. The adoption of this new system of scientific access, which might seem to go against scientific principles of merit, has been a reaction to the United Kingdom's unilateral reduction in its contribution to the facility following its refurbishment. Despite reallocation of beam time from UK to French proposals, UK proposals have still won more time than those of any other country, and the ILL, France and Germany will no doubt continue to exhort the United Kingdom to restore its contribution level. In practice, some host nation scientists actively seek out collaborators from other nations in order to effectively increase their proportion of experimental time, but, in principle at least, host nation scientists receive no preferential treatment. The concept of slack time must also be considered: this is beam time that becomes unallocated, owing to a lack of proposals, last minute cancellations, or inefficient planning. It is assumed that host nation scientists are best placed to take advantage of slack time whenever it becomes available. However, experimental time is distributed well in advance, and slack time is very rarely available, and so cannot be considered as a major source of benefit. It may even be allocated among members, as it is at ESO. The scientific benefits appear to be the possibilities for informal contacts and access for students.

In order for the host nation to obtain more advantage than the other participants from the presence of a critical mass, the scientific staff must have a large complement of host nationals. Some facilities, such as CERN, recruit staff solely on a merit basis from many different countries. Others, such as ESA, recruit from their member countries on a fair return basis. Participating nations increasingly tend to insist that a certain number of their own personnel receive employment at the facility. Where there are already strong communities in the host country (as for meteorology in the United Kingdom) scientists do claim that the international facility helps to reinforce them. Of course, this depends on the host nation's willingness to maintain an adequately resourced and staffed national effort in the fields covered by the international facility. This may be politically difficult if the international facility is very visibly drawing upon the national science budget.

Employment and skills

The evidence gathered from examining the personnel profiles of international scientific facilities shows that the host member has the most employees. In order to avoid paying expensive international salaries to all staff, facilities usually differentiate between cadre staff (high technical, administrative and scientific grades) and non-cadre staff (covering clerical, manual and lower-grade technical staff). Non-cadre staff will usually be hired locally. Moreover, contract research and technical staff are usually drawn mainly from the host nation, probably because they are keen to work at an international facility without facing the disruption of a move abroad. Thus, employment benefits appear to be significantly in favour of the host. There do not appear to be studies of the longer-term impact of international facilities upon skills and training in the host region. In the European shared facilities examined by PREST the host did appear to gain a benefit in scientific positions for its nationals, but, as argued above, this can only be a benefit if it is not displacing talented scientists who otherwise would be employed in national laboratories or universities.

JET offers a striking example of the employment disadvantages for host nationals in a shared large facility. According to the agreement underpinning the joint undertaking, the UK staff remained employees of their atomic energy authority, while their colleagues from the rest of Europe are employees of Euratom and thereby enjoy far higher salaries and the right to move to other employment within the EU. This has caused a bitter dispute involving intervention from the European Parliament. The lesson here is that dual employment conditions should be avoided. The UK government has been unusual in considering that host nation employment benefits are not worthwhile, as they merely displace other employment. There is no evidence that this is the case.

Environmental and cultural

There is little thorough evidence on the environmental impacts of large scientific facilities. There are strong arguments against the environmental campaign which is seeking to stop the Mount Graham telescope. In the case of JET, environmental concerns about the dangers of low-level radioactivity have enormously raised the projected decommissioning cost, which the United Kingdom undertook to bear as part of its hosting agreement. Likewise, the cultural benefits of international facility sites to the region do not appear to have been studied, although, as mentioned above, there is no inherent reason why such effects could not be taken into account in a cost/benefit framework.

The above paragraphs have shown that there is evidence for host benefits from large scientific facilities and, in particular, that benefits other than high-tech benefits can account for a large portion of the overall economic/industrial effects. Not surprisingly, evidence of indirect and intangible benefits has not been found, but this does not mean that they do not exist. Where the host nation has a strong high-tech sector and the facility has no balancing mechanism, these firms benefit greatly from the presence of the facility. Section 5 now examines some possible balancing mechanisms.

5. Options for balancing scientific and economic return

Today, policy makers cannot ignore the fact that, in the absence of balancing mechanisms, benefits across members of an international scientific facility are likely to be very uneven. As pointed out above, the host nation may have certain disadvantages, such as investment in infrastructure and impact upon the natural environment and the need to dismantle outdated facilities. However, even the rather patchy evidence available clearly indicates that facilities operating in an unconstrained manner with respect to employment, procurement and access allow most returns to the host nation. Thus, existing facilities have felt pressure to adopt mechanisms to redress this balance, and in some cases member nations have threatened to withdraw funding. This section explores some options for balancing the benefits from shared facilities in order to avoid such damaging disputes.

Of course, the host nation (and the non-host members) are not able to predict the outcomes of the international facility with any real certainty. The uncertainty is scientific, technological and commercial. Circumstances change, particularly over the 15 to 20 years of the typically projected life of a shared scientific facility. An approach which focuses too narrowly on expected economic benefits will tend to underestimate the potential longer-term costs, which make hosting less attractive in economic terms, although local construction firms are likely to realise short-term benefits. It also means that the host nation might shoulder, for the non-host members, the burden of risk (of the facility's failure) and thus would not unreasonably expect to receive a greater share of (expected) benefits in return.

Payments in kind

As observed above, competition to host international scientific facilities is fierce, and bids usually include concessions from the nation or region to provide a site, buildings or discounted power. Naturally, the value of sites can vary considerably. Provision of buildings can represent a significant payment in kind. The decommissioning of JET, mentioned above, will be a very significant cost to the host. In its favour, payment in kind is simple to operate. However, such payments will be arbitrary in terms of achieving a balance of benefits, and unless non-host members constantly make demands, will be one-off occurrences.

Table 11. **Options for balancing scientific and economic return**

Option	Mechanism	Examples of use	Advantages	Disadvantages
Payments in kind	• Host provides goods and services for the facility outside its subscription/ contribution.	• Cheaper electricity provided to CERN. • Site and buildings provided for ECMWF. • United Kingdom responsible for closure and decommissioning of JET.	• Simple to operate, as such "payments" often form part of bids for siting.	• Arbitrary in relation to hosting benefits gained. • On-going donations may be needed to satisfy other members.
Hosting premium	• Host pays larger subscription.	• Joint European TORUS (United Kingdom pays extra 10 per cent). • ESRF (France pays extra but varying according to stage).	• Simple to operate. • Simple in negotiations for siting. • Recognises "low-tech" and "high-tech" host benefits.	• Arbitrary extra percentage – may be too low or too high.
Fair return (employment)	• Employment of facility personnel in numbers proportional to member inputs.	• Non-contract staff for ESA. • Loose examples include EMBL.	• Allows fair returns in scientific and technical employment. • Staff from all members present at facility to support visiting scientific teams.	• Requires active monitoring and control (overhead). • Costly to import technical and clerical staff and pay on international scales. • Could compromise staff quality.
Fair return (procurement)	• Flexibility on bids to give contracts to member nation firms in proportion to their inputs.	• ILL and ESRF (loose policy). • ESA (industrial progress weighed according to technological content).	• Avoids majority of contracts going to host, allows firms of less advanced members to work in "high-tech" areas, satisfies demands for fair industrial returns.	• Requires active monitoring and control (overhead). • Increase costs if more expensive bids chosen. • Could compromise quality of goods and services. • Does not distinguish high-and low-tech returns.
Fair return (scientific access)	• Scientists allowed access to facility in proportion to their nation's inputs.	• ILL (loose policy).	• Helps scientifically weaker or smaller members to gain maximum benefit from the facility.	• Requires active monitoring and control (overhead). • Could compromise scientific quality.

Source: Author, 1995.

193

Hosting premium

The hosting premium is the payment by the host member of an increased annual subscription. This is the case at JET, where the United Kingdom pays 10 per cent in addition to its indirect contribution to the European Commission and its part in the fusion programme. At the European Synchrotron Research Facility (ESRF), the host (France) pays a higher subscription, which varies according to the stage of the facility. During construction, the premium is 10 per cent of the construction cost, to take into account the region's benefits in construction contracts, once the facility is fully operational, the premium drops to 2 per cent with a possibility of further reduction. The figure for hosting premiums is not based upon well-accepted notions of the expected extent of host returns but is arbitrary. It might therefore be too low or too high. In its favour it is a simple mechanism to operate, and balances all different types of benefits which hosts gain.

The following three mechanisms are based upon the notion of fair return, *i.e.* that a member's benefits from the international facility should be proportional to what it pays into it.

Fair return (employment)

The question of fair distribution of scientific posts was raised at the European Molecular Biology Laboratory (EMBL). Italy threatened to withdraw, but has been appeased by the location of the mouse gene repository near Rome. Fair return in terms of employment would abate these concerns, however, it is widely practised in international facilities, probably because scientists are accustomed to using peer review processes for employment and promotion decisions. In its favour, it ensures that there are facility staff from all member nations to support scientific teams in their experiments. Against it, there are the overhead costs of implementation, the possibility of having to turn down excellent candidates on the grounds of national quotas, and the costs of importing technical and clerical staff (if fair return is extended to all levels). It would be sensible to limit the practice to cadre staff, in order to avoid paying expensive international salaries to all employees. Indeed, the European Space Agency, which practises fair return on employment, does not apply it to contract staff. For scientific employment, the question of fair return is related to the ability of the facility to be sufficiently attractive to non-residents, particularly for long-term appointments, and to attract the very best scientists to make use of the site.

Fair return (procurement)

In procurement, purchasing committees of the international facility use flexibility in awarding contracts so that returns to members ' firms are in line with their contributions. Since it is the direct economic benefit to hosts from contracts which has caused concern at several international facilities, this would seem an obvious way to avoid disputes. The most extreme example is ESA's industrial programmes. This is because ESA has an explicit industrial development goal, while other scientific facilities do not. ESA contracts are closely monitored and weighted according to technological content, and each member 's quota is monitored. This requires a heavy administrative overhead. ILL and ESRF use fair return for procurement loosely, mainly through maintaining a watch on contracts awarded, asking tenderers to resubmit at lower costs, and awarding bids with a degree of flexibility to prevent an unacceptably large bias towards French industry.

The significant disadvantages to this balancing mechanism for scientific facilities are high overhead costs and higher costs due to the need to accept more expensive bids. However, experience shows that it is unrealistic for less advanced nations to expect a fair return in very high-tech areas. When fair return is restricted to high-tech areas, no account is taken of the host's benefits in basic goods and services. Indeed, any measure of the industrial benefits to a host must scrutinise carefully the nature of the companies gaining contracts. For example, at CERN, many goods and services providers either establish or operate from a French or Swiss office, or set up a collaboration with a local firm that has the knowledge and ability to work to local laws and standards. This results in an immediate bias in the returns to host country firms. Such issues are examined by ESA's strict system but could be monitored in a looser way, provided that bidders are requested to clarify the component parts of their provision of goods and services. Fair return has evolved as a policy mechanism within Europe and might be less easily applied for global co-operative facilities, where distance would affect costs of contractors.

Fair return (scientific access)

Scientific access completes the possible types of fair return that could be adopted. In this case, access to the facility for experiments is awarded to scientists according to their national contributions. The only example found is ILL, which keeps track of access for members. As for employment of scientists, access by merit (peer review of proposals) is the normal way for scientists to organise themselves. In its favour, this form of fair return would allow scientifically smaller or weaker nations to gain maximum scientific benefit from the facility, which is exactly what their governments are buying with the subscription. As with the other forms of fair return, the overhead costs and the possible compromising of quality are serious drawbacks.

6. Conclusions and pointers for policy makers

This survey of the benefits and problems of hosting a large international scientific facility has shown that the issues are complex and not often illuminated by clear evidence. What experience with large shared scientific facilities clearly shows is that governments will no longer pay for them without asking hard questions. Although the aims of such facilities are primarily scientific, they are not without economic impact, both in general terms and in terms of support of the advanced technological competencies, products and processes which are so important for the competitive performance of nations. Unfortunately, this review has not unearthed any unequivocal results on the benefits of international facilities. Most are case-specific, and we are in a changing world where economic benefits are less and less tied to the location of R&D or to customers, and where the value nations place on science and leading-edge technological development varies greatly. Despite this, some points can be made for policy makers.

Because of past imbalances in favour of host nations (particularly via industrial contracts), governments increasingly press for rectification. They will give greater attention to questions of benefits and their balancing when negotiating new international facilities, and it is likely that the pressures on public expenditure in general will means closer scrutiny of their returns. An excellent illustration is the recently resolved difficulty in initiating the Large Hadron Collider at CERN. Unhappy at the projected costs of the new accelerator, Britain and Germany insisted on a cheaper solution. This was tied to a new financial package which explicitly recognised that the hosts gain disproportionately (on the construction costs). France and Switzerland will, in the combined package, now pay a 5 per cent (of the construction cost) hosting premium. In addition, there is a new procurement policy at CERN whereby a loose fair return is operated. Efforts are made to open the procurement system, encourage bidding from non-host companies, and allow some renegotiation of bids so that member states achieve a return coefficient target. CERN was anxious not to implement a system that is very costly to operate or that results in an increase in the price of its goods and services, and so has not adopted strict fair return. The premium cannot compensate for the many years during which the hosts gained large benefits from CERN but it shows that nations subscribing to international scientific facilities will no longer leave such issues unresolved.

Members of large international scientific facilities should recognise the disproportionate benefits accruing to the host nation and employ a balancing mechanism to prevent potentially damaging disputes.

The brief survey of the options for balancing returns from participation in international facilities indicates that overhead costs for ensuring a strict fair return are heavy. The resulting higher prices and potentially lower quality also argue against the adoption of strict fair return. On close examination, the mechanism is not always feasible, given the different characteristics of member nations' industrial firms and scientific communities. Employment or access to facilities according to national dues might be fairer, given that member nations are paying precisely in order to be able to participate in the science. However, this goes against the normal scientific ethos of merit-based recognition by peer review. Payments in kind are simple, but not consistent. A hosting premium, while it does not necessarily fully repay the host benefits, is a simple way to compensate other members on an annual basis.

A hosting premium should be considered as the simplest mechanism to balance benefits to hosts and non-hosts. The balance of access, staffing and industrial contracts should be loosely monitored by the facility in order to anticipate and redress large imbalances.

Imbalances can be checked if the facility and its members adopt policies to make the procedures for industrial tendering transparent and to encourage applications from firms and scientists from all members. They should also encourage collaborative (industrial and scientific) bids to allow inexperienced applicants to work with experienced ones.

This review indicates that we do not know the actual benefits and disadvantages arising from the siting of an international scientific facility. Governments' underlying motivations for attracting these organisations are not well understood and may be changing. The US government's rejection of the Superconducting Super Collider may have reverberations in the world of megascience. The notion of using large scientific facilities to stimulate regional development also calls for better understanding of their potential in this respect.

Governments should be well aware of why they wish to host an international scientific facility or what they expect to gain. They should balance short-term and local benefits by a longer-term perspective. Policy makers need more and better information when they form their views.

It seems clear that the longer-term implications of hosting a facility are not always appreciated. Fixed-term projects rarely stop, and hosts may be left with an obsolete facility and the expense of returning the location to a greenfield site. Moreover, the environmental impact of large scientific facilities is an increasing concern, and environmental concerns may start to outweigh the perceived economic and other benefits of hosting in the near future.

It is important to take a longer-term (life cycle) view of the siting of large facilities, with more attention to the environmental impact. In the longer term, gaining a site may be less attractive.

This review has concentrated on experiences of European shared facilities, since these have the longest history and are the most numerous. Information on regional facilities does not necessarily apply at a truly global scale where future possibilities for scientific co-operation in facilities increasingly lie. Whether the fusion experiments continue to the exploitation stage depends upon a global effort at a shared site, and the United States and Japan are looking towards possible co-operation in CERN's LHC.

Balancing benefits from international scientific facilities will soon include packages for broadening regional co-operation to global co-operation. The operation of global single-site megascience will increase the skew of economic benefits to the host, necessitating great attention to balancing, possibly through greater hosting premiums than those presently required.

References

BACH, L. and G. LAMBERT, (1992), "Evaluation of the Economic Effects of Large R&D Programmes: The Case of the European Space Programme", *Research Evaluation*, Vol. 2(1), April, pp. 17-26.

CARTER, P.D. (1993), "A Review of the Costs and Benefits of Hosting a Large International Scientific Facility: Experience from the Joint European Torus (JET)", MBA Thesis, Imperial College of Science, Technology and Medicine, London.

GENERAL TECHNOLOGY SYSTEMS (NETHERLANDS) B.V. (1991), *Analysis of the Economic, Technological, Scientific and Additional Benefits of the ESTEC Establishment for the Netherlands*, ESA, Paris.

KLEIN, M., K. BARKER, P. STUBBS, and R. BODEN, (1994), "The Implications for Host Nations of Transnational Research Facilities", Final Report to the Economic and Social Research Council, PREST, University of Manchester.

OFFICE OF SCIENCE AND TECHNOLOGY (1993), *Economic Impacts of Hosting International Scientific Facilities,* HMSO, London.

SCHMIED, H. *et al.* (1984), *Economic Utility Resulting from CERN Contracts,* CERN, Geneva.

SCHMIED, H. (1975), *A Study of Economic Utility Resulting from CERN Contracts*, CERN.

Chapter 5

COST, FUNDING, AND BUDGET ISSUES IN MEGASCIENCE PROJECTS: THE CASE OF THE UNITED STATES*

by

Albert H. Teich
Director,
Science and Policy Programs, American Association for the Advancement of Science
Washington, D.C.

Executive summary

This chapter examines how the United States supports megascience projects (both large capital facilities and distributed R&D efforts), in terms of cost, funding, and budget issues, and explores options for improving the system in order to facilitate participation in international efforts.

The federal budget and R&D

A fundamental aspect of the US budget process is the balance of power between the branches of government. Neither Congress nor the Executive Branch is in complete control, and outcomes depend on the interplay of many forces. There is no single budget for R&D; R&D programmes are carried within the budgets of many agencies and departments. These agencies are treated individually by different sections of the Office of Management and Budget (OMB) in the budget review process. Executive Branch co-ordination of R&D efforts and priority setting have long been problematical.

Congressional treatment of the budget is even more fragmented. Detailed considera-tion of programmes takes place at two levels, that of authorisations and that of appropria-

---

* The views and opinions contained in this chapter, prepared at the request of the OECD, are the author's and should not be taken to represent the position of the American Association for the Advancement of Science, its Board or its Council. The author wishes to thank Kathleen M. Gramp for her invaluable assistance in the preparation of the chapter.

tions. Authorisations of discretionary programmes (including R&D) provide programme guidance to the agencies and set ceilings for their appropriations. The authority to actually make expenditures comes through appropriations bills.

The current federal budget climate is one of austerity. The Budget Enforcement Act (BEA) of 1990 limits the amount that can be appropriated and expended for discretionary programmes in a given year. An additional package of tax and spending measures enacted in 1993 freezes outlays for discretionary programmes for five years at their FY 1993 level, eroding resources in real terms.

Megascience facilities in the current fiscal environment

Several characteristics of megascience facilities make it difficult to plan them and keep them on track: they are expensive, ranking among the largest federal non-defence investments; they are not easily divisible; their budgets are driven by construction and acquisition cycles; they often involve cost uncertainties; they are concentrated in a few federal agencies; their construction depends almost exclusively on federal financing; their operating costs are also borne by the federal government; and they involve interests that go far beyond science.

The way these characteristics influence the course of specific projects can be seen in case studies of: the Superconducting Supercollider (SSC), terminated by Congress in 1993 – a result of poor management, cost overruns, lack of international support, and unfortunate timing; the Space Station, with international participation, but without a clear mission; the Earth Observing System (EOS), a set of orbiting platforms studying global climate change, whose budget has been protected by Congress so far because of the priority of its mission; the Continuous Electron Beam Accelerator Facility (CEBAF); the Laser Interferometer Gravitational-Wave Observatory (LIGO); the National Aerospace Plane (NASP); and several proposed new starts.

Distributed projects in the current fiscal environment

Distributed megascience projects are handled more easily than facilities in the US system owing to several factors. While they are expensive, most of their costs are for conducting R&D rather than construction or equipment; their budgets are relatively stable from year to year; and their annual expenditure levels are adjustable (within limits) to suit budget constraints. Brief case studies of the Human Genome Project and the Global Change Research Programme, both of which have managed to stay more or less on track, show how these factors operate.

Key factors affecting project outcomes

Management. A project's management must inspire the confidence of its funding agency, its scientific or technical constituency and Congress. As noted above, the larger the scale of the project, the closer the scrutiny it receives, and the more its management must be above reproach.

Technical uncertainties and cost increases. Cost increases require project officials to re-open a decision that had already been made. Unless the predicted benefits of the project increase correspondingly, this changes the cost-benefit ratio for the project, weakens its justification, and undermines confidence in its management.

Clarity of mission. The importance of a clear mission for a megascience project is nicely demonstrated by the contrast between the relative ease with which the EOS programme has acquired and maintained congressional support and the erratic course of the Space Station.

Scale of expenditure. The more expensive a project is, the greater the benefits required to justify it, the more high-level support it must have to survive, and the more attractive a target it presents for "deficit hawks" and those who favour other priorities.

"Overbooking" of projects in an agency. A look at the histories of megascience projects suggests that some have fallen victim to budget constraints simply because their sponsoring agency has tried to carry out too many projects simultaneously.

Political factors. Political coalitions, sometimes based on geographical distribution of expenditures, may be an important factor in the success of megaprojects.

International participation. The failure of the Department of Energy (DOE) to obtain significant funding from international partners for the SSC was one of the reasons for its termination. International participation in the Space Station has helped it to survive so far, but in the absence of a compelling mission, it may not be enough to save the project in coming years.

Fiscal parameters. Since 1993, fiscal austerity has begun to exert unilateral pressure on federal investments in large R&D facilities and may well be the controlling factor in the future.

The future of megascience: prospects and alternatives

The fiscal conditions of the past several years are likely to continue. The climate for new starts for megascience facility projects during the next several years will not be hospitable, and even existing programmes will face very difficult times. Recent experience suggests that one tendency will be to stretch out construction and re-scope projects. Any money for new starts, such as the Advanced Neutron Source (ANS) or the International Thermonuclear Experimental Reactor (ITER), is likely to come with strings attached (*e.g.* cost sharing, commitment measures, milestones, etc.). Project terminations are also more likely.

Alternative budgeting techniques and devices. Some of the difficulties that megascience projects have encountered might be alleviated through the use of budgeting techniques and devices that have not previously been applied to such projects. Ideas include:

- *Advance appropriations*, through which the government makes an up-front commitment of budget authority for a programme. Under this approach, Congress appropriates money that does not become available until a future fiscal year. However, advance appropriations do not make spending "mandatory". The budget authority and outlays from an advance appropriation for an R&D project would be classified as discretionary and subject to the general pressures on such spending. The experience of the DOE's Clean Coal Technology Program indicates that advance appropriations do not guarantee predictability of programme funding.
- *"Full funding" and multi-year contracting*, used in the procurement of large weapons systems by the Department of Defense (DOD). In fact, the principles governing this practice already apply to civilian procurement and construction projects, but the results differ for R&D because of differences in what is being purchased. In the case of, say, a submarine, DOD is buying a complete and proven product with understood specifications. In the case of R&D projects, agencies usually are procuring parts of a larger, evolving system. As a result, procurement funding tends to involve a series of contracts that may be staggered over time and spread among contractors. For R&D projects, it is the sum of individual contractual commitments, not the project as a whole, that is "fully funded" by appropriations in any given year.
- *Milestone budgeting*, with which DOD has experimented when funding major R&D and weapons systems procurement. Under this concept, funding for a project is authorised – and sometimes appropriated – in advance for a multi-year period and revisited by policy makers only at certain milestones or at the end of a five-year period, whichever comes first. Results so far have not been impressive.
- *Trust funds*, which are financial devices used by the federal government to dedicate certain budgetary receipts to specific purposes. The appeal of this concept is that it allows the government to allocate the costs of certain programmes to the users and/or beneficiaries instead of the general public. Trust funds offer some protection for a programme's financing because federal laws prohibit the use of trust fund receipts for purposes other than those specified. However, expenditures from the highway, airway, nuclear waste, and Superfund trust funds are all discretionary. The amounts available each year are set by authorisation legislation and by annual limitations on obligations set by appropriations acts.

Budget process reforms. Two proposed reforms of the budget process might facilitate support of megascience projects.

- *Two-year budget cycles*, which would presumably provide greater stability in funding, reduce uncertainty and administrative burdens, and allow project managers to operate more efficiently. The benefits may be somewhat illusory, however. Despite legislation from the authorising committees enacted several years ago requiring DOD to submit two-year budgets, the appropriations committees have retained the annual appropriations cycle for DOD.

– *Separating the long term and the short term in the budget* by distinguishing between capital investment and operations. Following recommendations of the National Performance Review, OMB plans to divide the current unified budget into a capital budget, an operating budget, and a cash budget, beginning in FY 1996. The plan reportedly would couple capital budgeting with several related improvements in the planning and budgeting process for fixed assets, including the adoption of more flexible funding mechanisms to accommodate "spikes" in agency spending caused by capital acquisition processes.

Private-sector financing and tax incentives for megascience projects. One alternative that might offer some potential is that of authorising the sale of tax-free bonds to universities or other bodies which might use the proceeds to finance construction of megascience facilities and repay the debt by collecting user fees. While this is a novel and interesting proposal, it raises a host of questions that would need to be answered before it could be considered practicable. Perhaps the more likely trend would be an expansion of partnerships between the federal government and non-federal interests.

Implications for international co-operation

What can be done to improve the way in which the United States deals with megascience projects? The bottom line can be stated simply: There is no magic formula. Reforms and alternative budgeting techniques may help, but they cannot solve the basic problems of limited resources, poor planning, and short-sighted management.

Experience with past megascience projects – especially the SSC and the Space Station – suggests the fundamental importance of planning from the outset in a forthright, realistic manner. In the long run, the advocates of megascience projects will benefit from complete and honest cost estimates of all dimensions of a project, starting from its initial planning stages. The scale and timing of expenditures also must be realistic. Agency officials must be willing to make hard choices among projects in their early stages, rather than let them proceed simultaneously, knowing that their funding peaks are likely to overlap yet hoping somehow to muddle through the resulting budget conflicts.

Beyond planning, agency and project management needs to be strengthened. Better cost controls are needed to track spending and performance over the life of a project. Agencies must learn to manage projects – especially the largest ones – efficiently and effectively. The real problem for megascience projects is not the budget process, but the willingness of scientific leaders and government officials to reconcile their visions with political and economic reality.

1. Introduction

In many fields of science, research has become a highly complex and expensive endeavour. In the United States, a growing share of the more than $70 billion that the federal government spends annually for R&D is being devoted to what are termed "big science" or "megascience" projects – complex efforts that demand equipment and resources on a vast scale. Such projects are of two types: large-scale facilities that require major capital investments, such as particle accelerators, energy demonstration plants, and space vehicles; and large-scale distributed (co-ordinated) R&D efforts, such as the Human Genome Project and the Global Change Research Program.

The growing costs of such projects, combined with the ever-tightening constraints on the federal budget, have raised questions about the ability of the United States to continue to "go it alone" in megascience. At the same time, however, it is widely believed that the US political and budgetary system poses significant barriers to successful completion of megascience projects, and that it is particularly ill-suited to international collaboration in such efforts (President's Council of Advisors on Science and Technology, 1992). With the cancellation of the SSC, the matter has gained new urgency, and the time seems ripe to take a systematic look at how the United States supports megascience projects, in terms of cost, funding, and budget issues, and to see what options exist for improving the system of support in order to facilitate participation in international efforts.

What follows is a first attempt at such an examination. It looks at the federal budget process and at how that process affects the needs of R&D, and particularly megascience, projects. It analyses, on the basis of examples, the effects of the budget process and recent fiscal policies on megascience projects and suggests which factors most influence project outcomes. Finally, it explores a variety of alternatives for improving the way in which megascience projects are funded, including applying techniques used in non-R&D megaprojects, budget reforms, alternative financing arrangements, and international co-operation.

2. The federal budget and R&D

The federal budget process: how it works

Overview: a balance of power

Fundamental to the budget process, as to so many other aspects of government in the United States, is the balance of power between the branches. Under the US system, neither Congress nor the Executive Branch is in complete control. Budgetary outcomes depend on the interplay of many forces, and ultimately on accommodation, compromise, and negotiation.

The federal government currently spends money in two general ways. Some spending is the direct result of laws that guarantee payments to certain beneficiaries under specific conditions, such as social security, health care entitlements, and deposit insurance. Once written into law, these "mandatory" payments are largely beyond the control of either branch of government. On the other hand, programmatic activities, including R&D, are considered "discretionary" because the amounts spent are determined and adjusted on a regular basis. Since the 1970s, the budget process has been governed by procedures that ensure that the level of spending and receipts conforms with governmental fiscal policies. Laws enacted in 1990 went a step further, setting firm multi-year limits on spending for discretionary programmes and controls on the expansion of mandatory payments.

The federal budget process operates on an annual cycle. By the first Monday in February of each year, the President submits a consolidated request outlining his proposals for the operations of the federal government for the fiscal year beginning 1 October of that year. Congressional deliberations begin with the adoption of a concurrent budget resolution that specifies multi-year targets for federal spending (both mandatory and discretionary) and is enforced by various procedural mechanisms. This resolution is internal to the workings of Congress and does not require presidential approval.

In subsequent months, Congress pulls apart, scrutinises, and debates the details of the President's request, and ultimately approves a federal budget in the form of 13 separate appropriations acts. Appropriations acts specify the amounts that may be spent on discretionary programmes and estimate the amounts that will be spent on mandatory payments for the new fiscal year. Appropriations for discretionary activities usually follow the broad contours of the President's proposal, but may differ significantly in priorities, emphasis, and treatment of specific programmes and agencies. Congress may – and often does – delete programmes from the President's budget and add items that the President has not requested. If necessary, Congress enacts separate "authorising" legislation to reconcile the levels of direct spending and revenues to the limits set in the budget resolution.

Budget formulation in the Executive Branch

The fiscal and budgetary policies of the Executive Branch are orchestrated by OMB. Existing programmes form a baseline, and proposals for new starts generally receive the most scrutiny. Spending proposals may originate virtually anywhere in the federal government, but they must work their way up through the hierarchy of programmes, offices, agencies, and departments and eventually be approved by OMB in order to become part of the President's budget. In general, there are far more ideas and proposals than money, and the process therefore consists in winnowing out proposals to meet fiscal constraints.

Proposals for R&D programmes often originate outside of government, in advisory committees or among groups of researchers. Their incorporation into the President's budget depends on review and approval by the relevant agency, or, if they are of sufficient size and importance, by OMB or the White House. The Office of Science and Technology Policy (OSTP) has traditionally played a subordinate role in the budget process for R&D, serving principally as an advisor to OMB; it sits in on the hearings at which agencies present their proposed budgets and helps OMB evaluate these proposals.

There is no single budget for R&D in the federal government. Rather, R&D programmes are carried within the budgets of many agencies and departments. These agencies are treated individually by different sections of OMB in the budget review process, so that cross-agency co-ordination of R&D efforts and setting of priorities among them have long been problematical. During the Bush Administration, OSTP began to take on a somewhat larger role in the budget process. Under President Clinton, its role has been further strengthened in an effort to improve co-ordination and priority setting among R&D agencies through a new National Science and Technology Council.

The congressional budget process

Congressional treatment of the budget is characterised by fragmentation and diffusion of power. Spending measures are reviewed at three levels, in two chambers, by a majority and minority party in each, by a welter of committees and subcommittees. Operating at the highest level of aggregation are the House and Senate budget committees, which are responsible for formulating the budget resolution. In addition to setting targets for total spending and revenues, the resolution recommends spending priorities for the coming fiscal year. While the allocations in the budget resolution are not binding, the fact that they are negotiated and adopted by Congress makes them an important barometer of congressional priorities.

Detailed consideration of programmes takes place at two levels – authorisations and appropriations. Authorisation laws enable government units to spend money for particular purposes and are the purview of the committees that have legislative responsibility for the various agencies. These committees develop special expertise and are deeply involved in the substance of agency programmes. Authorisation of discretionary programmes does not directly result in spending, but rather provides programme guidance to the agencies and sets ceilings for their appropriations.

For discretionary programmes like R&D, the authority to actually make expenditures comes only through appropriations bills, which are enacted yearly. [However, it is possible to enact an appropriation for an agency or programme in the absence of an authorisation under certain procedures (*e.g.* waiver, continuing resolution, etc.)] The power to craft these bills resides in the Appropriations Committees of the House and the Senate. These committees take the total amount approved for the fiscal year in the budget resolution and divide it among their 13 subcommittees.

The separation of the budget into 13 appropriations bills limits the extent to which it is possible to trade off increases and decreases in agency R&D budgets in the congressional process. For example, three R&D agencies – the National Science Foundation (NSF), the National Aeronautics and Space Administration (NASA), and the Environmental Protection Agency (EPA) – come under the jurisdiction of the Subcommittee on Housing and Urban Development, Veterans Affairs, and Independent Agencies. Appropriations of the National Institutes of Health (NIH) are decided by the Subcommittee on Labor, Health and Human Services, and Education, while the Department of Energy (DOE) is handled by the Subcommittee on Energy and Water Development. This meant that the money saved by cancelling the SSC at DOE could not readily be transferred to R&D programmes in NSF or NIH.

The federal budget: current realities

The current federal budget climate is one of virtually unprecedented austerity, the result of compromises reached in response to the rising tide of federal debt. Budget deficits are not new to the federal government, but their size and persistence were exacerbated in the early 1980s by a rapid build-up in defence spending and a major reduction in taxes. After a series of failed attempts to reduce the deficit, Congress passed the Budget Enforcement Act of 1990 (BEA), which has two principal features: first, limits ("caps") on discretionary spending and second, a "pay-as-you-go" (PAYGO) requirement for mandatory programmes and taxes. The caps limit the amount that can be appropriated and expended ("budget authority" and "outlays", respectively, in federal budget parlance) for discretionary programmes in a given year. The PAYGO provision requires that authorisation legislation that would cost the government money – by expanding entitlements or reducing taxes – provide offsetting savings through other entitlement cuts or tax increases in order not to increase the deficit.

An additional package of tax and spending measures enacted in 1993 will lead to an even harsher budget climate for most federal agencies. Outlays for discretionary programmes were frozen for five years at their FY 1993 level, eroding resources in real, inflation-adjusted terms. Spending on discretionary programmes is projected to fall in relation to the economy, declining from 9 per cent of gross domestic product (GDP) in 1992 to 6.5 per cent by the year 2000.

One aspect of BEA bears particular mention, since it may have an important effect on funding for capital projects, including megascience facilities. Restricting annual outlays, which are the cash disbursements during a given year resulting from prior obligations, is a relatively blunt instrument of fiscal policy (US General Accounting Office, 1990). Fixed limits on outlays favour programmes with relatively stable expenditure patterns rather than capital projects whose needs fluctuate from year to year in response to construction and acquisition cycles. Under the BEA outlay caps, temporary increases in the funding for capital projects will squeeze the amounts that can be spent on other programmes in certain years, forcing policy makers to cut spending elsewhere to accommodate the cyclical surge in disbursements. This is true even for capital projects funded with multi-year appropriations, because there are separate spending caps for appropriations and outlays.

3.   Megascience facilities in the current fiscal environment

Megascience facilities: what makes them different?

The current fiscal environment in the federal government has made the task of planning a megascience facility and keeping it on track through several years of construction and implementation enormously complex and difficult. Even in the best of times, however, federal funding for large-scale R&D facilities is not easily won or sustained.

The budget process and the diffusion of power in the US system work against such projects. Several characteristics of megascience facilities contribute to this situation.

First, megascience facilities are expensive. While this almost goes without saying, it is important not to overlook the obvious. The costs associated with some of the better-known megascience projects rank among the largest non-defence investments made by the federal government. They truly are "big-ticket" items: the estimated (current dollar) $27.3 billion for the space station, $11 billion estimate for the SSC, and the $7.3 billion cost of EOS all outstrip the federal investments in most other civilian physical investment projects (US Congressional Research Service, 1994). There are some civilian infrastructure projects of a similar scale – the federal share of the 103-mile Metro system in Washington, D.C. is expected to total $5.7 billion over its 30-year construction period, and the upgrade of the national air traffic control system is projected to require at least $24.8 billion from 1996 to 2005. However, most of the money spent on non-defence public physical infrastructure [$50.2 billion in FY 1994, including R&D facilities (US Office of Management and Budget, 1994a)] dispersed among thousands of smaller projects. Such sizeable financial commitments mean that the decision to proceed with a megascience facility is a major one that must be taken at a high level. Formal initiation of both the SSC and the Space Station required a Presidential decision. These decisions also require careful and continuing scrutiny, which means that congressional interest will be especially strong.

Second, megascience facilities are not easily divisible. Simply put, you cannot buy half an SSC. The commitment to such projects is, generally, an all-or-nothing proposition, creating what some observers term "mortgages" on the budget – commitments that limit flexibility in future years. Most other civilian projects, in contrast, can be tailored to fit available resources. Extensions of subway lines can be postponed or shortened and air traffic control systems can function with obsolete computers (albeit less than optimally). While ways to reduce the cost of megascience facilities sometimes exist, they are limited and can have undesirable effects on the programme (US Congressional Budget Office, 1991). This restricts the range of options available to decision makers. It may deter minor budget cuts, but under some circumstances it may mean that only full funding or termination are viable options.

Third, megascience facility budgets are driven by construction and acquisition cycles. Most agencies' operating budgets are fairly stable from year to year, a characteristic that is compatible with the incremental nature of the federal budget process. In contrast, the funding requirements of megascience facilities, like those of other capital projects, are cyclical and driven by the pace of acquisition or construction – digging foundations, pouring concrete, assembling spacecraft, etc. Many programmes that finance other types of civilian infrastructure are able to blend the ebbs and flows of individual projects in a manner that enables agencies to show fairly smooth funding trends. Much of the government's investment in transportation is distributed through formula grants, which puts the onus of juggling project spending on states and localities. The year-to-year variability of megascience projects exposes them to special scrutiny, especially during those years when significant increases are required.

Fourth, megascience projects often involve cost uncertainties. By their nature, most megascience projects are one-of-a-kind facilities that depend on technologies designed specifically for the project. In this respect, they are like major weapons systems, for which technology and production proceed concurrently. The Hubble Space Telescope depended on the development of specialised mirrors, the SSC on superconducting magnets, and the National Aerospace Plane on advanced materials that do not yet exist. Analysts suggest that while concurrency does not necessarily lead to unusual cost increases, it can sometimes do so and has contributed to significant cost overruns in a number of defence projects (US Congressional Budget Office, 1988).

Fifth, megascience projects are concentrated in selected federal agencies. The fact that megascience funding is concentrated in a few agencies can affect the likelihood of project support. For years it was taken for granted that NASA's mission dictated that the agency's budget must grow faster than most others and it did. This made it possible for NASA to develop several spacecraft or facilities simultaneously (e.g. the Hubble Space Telescope and the Gamma Ray Observatory in the 1980s). In today's fiscal environment, there are de facto ceilings on agency spending, which may limit the ability of NASA or DOE to pursue multiple projects even if offsetting savings could be found elsewhere in the government.

Sixth, megascience project construction traditionally depends almost exclusively on federal financing. The federal government's general revenues are the principal source of funding for megascience projects. This stands in contrast to federal investments in highways, transit, and aviation which are financed mainly by dedicated user taxes and fees. These and other infrastructure programmes also leverage non-federal resources by requiring cost-sharing with project recipients or beneficiaries. Because of the diffuse and long-term benefits of fundamental research, the federal government has traditionally been its major sponsor, although in recent years, states that directly benefit from the construction of large science facilities have contributed resources to those projects (e.g. Texas for the SSC and Florida for the National Magnet Laboratory).

Seventh, the operating costs of megascience projects are often borne by the federal government. It is obvious, but must be remembered, that to reap the benefit of the investment, facilities must be used by researchers. If the federal government owns the facility, it usually bears most of its operating expenses (e.g. maintenance, staffing, repairs, etc.). The government also underwrites most of those using facilities that support research in the fundamental sciences. While the government also subsidises some users of other capital investments (e.g. low-income housing), the beneficiaries of most civilian infrastructure projects are generally expected to pay the operating costs associated with the facility (e.g. highways and other transportation systems).

Finally, megascience facility projects involve interests that go far beyond science. Because much of the money spent on megascience facilities goes into construction and fabrication, the projects become financially important to large engineering and construction contractors for whom the scientific purpose of the project is not of primary importance (although the technological aspects might be). These firms provide large numbers of jobs and can have a significant impact on a community. And there are also losers in such projects: advocates of sites not selected, those whose property may be condemned for use by the project, and those who see negative impacts deriving from the project. These people can oppose the project, though their reasons may have little to do with science.

Recent experience with megascience facility projects

The ways in which these characteristics influence the course of megascience facility projects can be seen in a number of brief case studies.

The Superconducting Super Collider

The SSC was conceived by the scientific community in the early 1980s as the world's most powerful proton-proton collider, which would enable scientists to test theories about the fundamental structure of matter and energy. DOE's High Energy Physics Advisory Panel (HEPAP) recommended the SSC as a new start in 1983, and the project was formally proposed by President Reagan in 1987. As originally proposed, the SSC would have been a predominantly American venture to be completed by 1996 at an estimated cost of $4.4 billion (in 1988 dollars). The concept was well received by Congress and the scientific community, and the project received $33 million in FY 1988 and $98.6 million the next year for site selection and design. A 25-state competition for the siting of the facility ended the day after the inauguration of George Bush in 1989, who announced selection of Waxahachie in his home state of Texas. The contract for managing the project was awarded to Universities Research Association (URA). Congressional support came with the stipulation that one-third of the costs be derived from non-federal partners, who were expected to use and benefit from the facility.

By the time Congress gave the go-ahead for construction of the SSC in FY 1990, the project's projected costs had risen to $5.9 billion, which DOE said would be the "absolute final cost" (Vaughan, 1990). Soon thereafter designers encountered a series of technical problems with the superconducting magnets and other items. While the technical problems were surmountable, they added costs and delays. Figures also had to be revised to include elements omitted from the original projections, such as the cost of certain buildings and systems. Government auditors reported that even the conventional construction activities for the SSC had exceeded projected costs and deadlines, and this raised concerns about the project's management (US General Accounting Office, 1993c, p. 36). By 1991, the SSC was behind schedule and its projected cost had risen to an estimated $8.25 billion. Within the scientific community, there were rumblings about the SSC draining resources from other projects and about conflicts between the project managers at URA and DOE.

DOE also had problems in raising the one-third share from non-federal partners. Texas pledged $875 million for the project (plus in-kind contributions such as land), but the $1.7 billion needed from international partners was not forthcoming. The DOE plan relied on a contribution of over $1.3 billion from Japan, but issues such as the internationalisation of the project had not been resolved by the end of 1992 (US General Accounting Office, 1992b, p. 9). When the Clinton Administration came into power in 1993, estimates of the SSC's costs were adjusted once again, this time to reflect the shortfall in non-federal payments that added $1.2 billion and a revised, lengthened timetable for completion that added $1.6 billion (US General Accounting Office, 1993*d*, p. 2). Government auditors reported that the project's system for tracking costs was ineffective, and that URA had improperly billed expenses for social and office functions to the SSC project. Thus, as the project approached its peak expenditures (FY 1994), its projected costs had escalated to $11 billion, it lacked significant foreign commitments, its support from the scientific community had waned, and its management was under fire.

These issues came to a head in the summer of 1993. Congress was engaged in an intense battle over an Administration proposal to raise taxes and cut spending to reduce the deficit. Lawmakers were loathe to touch taxes. The House passed its version of the budget with only a six-vote margin of victory and the Senate by virtue of a tie-breaking vote cast by the Vice-President. Within 24 hours of the hotly contested Senate vote on the deficit-reduction package, the House took up appropriations for FY 1994 and came within six votes of cancelling the space station. On the following day, the House voted by a two-to-one margin to terminate the SSC. Senate appropriators tried to restore the project's funding, but rank-and-file members of the House rejected the proposed compromise and forced DOE to cancel the SSC.

The fate of the SSC hinged on the interplay of many factors, but four stand out: poor management, cost overruns, lack of international support, and unfortunate timing. On the one hand, the project was caught in the downdraft of the "we had to kill something" fervour of the 1993 deficit reduction legislation (American Association for the Advancement of Science, 1993, p. 18). On the other hand, a long-time congressional supporter of the project summed up his vote for cancellation saying, "There should be some penalty for promising and not performing." (Taubes, 1993)

The space station

The space station concept originated within NASA as the "next step" in manned exploration of the solar system (this section is greatly indebted to McCurdy, 1990). The idea had been discussed within the agency since its inception, but was not fully developed until the early 1980s as work wound down on the space shuttle. The project faced several hurdles within the government, notably the opposition of key defence officials (whose support had been critical to the success of both the mission to the moon and the space shuttle), the President's science advisor, and OMB. Lacking a mandate for the project, NASA officials worked to form a coalition of interested users, including international partners. Most negotiations focused on potential uses of a manned research facility rather than on the technical, legal, and cost implications of a diverse constituency. It was felt that the project could be developed incrementally, with components added or dropped to suit the needs of users.

In 1984, NASA took the concept forward for presidential approval. The agency had no formal designs but presented "band" estimates of its federal cost, opting to present the $8 billion that would buy the minimum, basic components of the system as well as political support. The station fit President Reagan's personal vision of space and technology policy, and he announced his support for the project in January 1984. The European Space Agency (ESA), Canada, and Japan formally agreed to participate in the spring of

1985, and negotiations began on the provision of systems, modules, and operating support in exchange for the opportunity to share in the resources provided by the project.

Once it had permission to go ahead, NASA began melding the sometimes conflicting missions of the project's constituencies into a coherent design. Congress appropriated the amounts requested for this definitional and advanced technology phase, which lasted from FY 1985 through FY 1987. Cost estimates escalated as NASA reconciled project demands with technical requirements, and had nearly doubled to about $14.5 billion by 1986. Even at this level, NASA was criticised for having excluded costs associated with launching components, in-house personnel, and initial operations, which the agency treated as embedded costs.

NASA claimed the space station would achieve many objectives, most of which were technological in nature: it would provide a permanently manned research facility in low Earth orbit, improve the ability to live and work in space, stimulate robotics and automation technologies, and provide manned and unmanned platforms for long-term scientific and operational observations (US National Aeronautics and Space Administration, 1988, p. RD 1-8). As the specifications evolved, projected costs rose to a total of an estimated $26 billion in 1988. The project had strong supporters in Congress, but many legislators were sceptical of its justification and cost.

The development phase of the station – and its political and fiscal instability – began in FY 1988. Internally, NASA had to reckon with the technical and managerial complexities of the project. Congress, for its part, was being asked to provide $767 million for the station in a year when the government was forging a fiscal response to the stock market "melt-down" of October 1987. The result was a $367 million appropriation that slowed the pace of the project, but was enough to allow NASA to begin awarding contracts to major aerospace and related industries across the country. Lawmakers moved haltingly forward with a $900 million appropriation in FY 1989 by delaying the availability of much of the money to give the President the opportunity to terminate the project. Congress also rejected the Administration's request for "advance appropriations" for FY 1990 and 1991 of $2.1 billion and $2.9 billion, respectively.

The Bush Administration put forth an ambitious space agenda, proposing a moon base and a piloted mission to Mars as sequels to the newly christened "Space Station Freedom." Bush's FY 1990 request went full tilt towards developing the station, proposing $2.1 billion for FY 1990 and advance appropriations of $3 billion and $3.5 billion for the subsequent two years. Lawmakers continued to react cautiously, delaying NASA's ability to obligate nearly half of the $1.7 billion appropriated for FY 1990 and denying the request for advance appropriations. Congress was in the midst of negotiating a major deficit reduction package when it took up the station's FY 1991 request, and had misgivings about the project's escalating costs (which then stood at $37 billion, including launch and associated costs through 1999) and its unresolved problems with power requirements, scientific capabilities, overhead rates, and management. Congress appropriated $1.9 billion for continued development of the station, but directed NASA to rescope the project so that its peak funding levels would not exceed $2.5 billion to $2.6 billion in any given year. This led to substantial changes in the station's design and assembly sequence.

The resources for the station began to have a discernible impact on other NASA priorities in FY 1992, the first full budget cycle after the 1990 discretionary caps took effect. NASA asked for a 16.7 per cent increase in its R&D budget for that year, but received an annual gain of only 3.3 per cent. House appropriators wanted to cancel the space station to make funding available for other initiatives, but, after intense lobbying by the White House, Congress agreed to provide $2 billion. This left too few dollars for other projects on NASA's agenda, forcing delays in some [e.g. the Comet Rendezvous and Fly-by (CRAF)/Cassini missions and the Advanced X-ray Astrophysics Facility] and cancellation of others (e.g. the Space Infrared Telescope Facility). Criticism mounted in FY 1993 over the project's overhead costs and drain on other NASA programmes [the cost remained near $30 billion despite the 1991 reconfiguration (US General Accounting Office, 1993b)]. However, concern about the effect on the economy – especially the 75 000 jobs it provided – helped deflect termination proposals.

President Clinton sent NASA back to the drawing board in 1993, because Space Station Freedom was "unaffordable in light of total constraints on NASA's budget". NASA was told to redesign the project "to greatly reduce programme costs while still providing significant research capabilities" (Padron, 1993). NASA selected a simplified design that would initially emphasize human-tended capabilities and evolve into a perma- nent base for extended human operations. Assembly was projected to begin in 1997 and be completed in the year 2002 at an estimated cost of $17 billion (excluding the $9 billion already spent). While this configuration was recommended by a blue-ribbon panel, it cut into the geographic network of jobs, and this further eroded political support for the station. That summer, the House came within six votes of cancelling the space station. International participation, especially the addition of Russia as a partner in 1993, was among the factors credited with its survival.

As part of the final compromise on its $1.9 billion appropriation for FY 1994, Congress directed NASA to combine its two manned space flight programmes into a single account which would be subject to its own spending caps. While funding for the new account fell in FY 1995, all of the cuts were taken from the shuttle programme, leaving the newly named "International Space Station Alpha" the full amount of its request for the current year.

Earth Observing System

EOS was conceived in the early 1980s as one of several space-based platforms for studying Earth processes which affect climatic changes. It was proposed as a new start in FY 1991, the centrepiece of NASA's contribution to the US Global Change Research Program. The companion data and information system (EOSDIS) being developed to process and distribute the data generated by EOS and other existing satellites in NASA's "Mission to Planet Earth" will require the largest civilian data management system ever built (US General Accounting Office, 1992d, p. 1). EOS differs from some megascience projects in that its scientific output is expected to have a direct bearing on public policy.

NASA's initial design called for six polar orbiting platforms, instruments on the space station, and US instruments on Japanese and European polar platforms. Congress enthusiastically embraced NASA's goals for the Mission to Planet Earth, but new starts were hard to sell in a year in which all eyes were focused on a deficit reduction bill. NASA received $155 million as a first instalment towards the $16 billion EOS project in FY 1991, but was directed to concentrate on additional studies and slow the pace of developing observatories. Faced with newly enacted outyear limits on all discretionary spending, appropriators told NASA in FY 1992 that it would have to cap expenditures for EOS at $11 billion through the year 2000, forcing the agency to downsize platforms, rely on more but smaller satellites, delay various instruments and launch plans, and delete some instruments from the programme (US General Accounting Office, 1992a). Under the revised plan, Japan and Canada were among the international participants supplying selected instruments, and some US instruments were to use international spacecraft.

Lawmakers demonstrated their commitment to EOS and EOSDIS in FY 1993 by earmarking $391 million exclusively for the projects and setting a "floor" of $8 billion for EOS development costs (after adjusting for certain transfers, the project total drops to $7.25 billion). While this theoretically ensures that NASA will preserve the project at this minimum level, the floor is also a *de facto* ceiling in today's fiscal environment. NASA has had to drop plans for instruments related to the middle and upper stratosphere and solid Earth geophysics to stay within this lower limit. In an effort to protect the quality of the programme, appropriators have initiated cost-control measures of their own, directing NASA to set caps on the development costs of all instruments once they are under contract so that both the agency and Congress can better evaluate which ones exceed estimates. Congress has also sought to protect EOS from escalating demands from other agencies, programmes, and users (US Senate, 1993, pp. 151-53). Under these terms and conditions, funding for EOS and EOSDIS rose to $507 million in FY 1994 and $775 million in FY 1995, which has enabled NASA to proceed with developing and procuring the instruments and spacecraft.

Continuous electron beam accelerator facility

Soon to go on-line in Newport News, Virginia, CEBAF is a relatively small accelerator in an era of giant machines (sources for this section are Mukerjee, 1993; von Baeyer, 1994; and Crawford, 1986). Initiated in 1983, the facility will make available a beam of electrons for high energy nuclear physics studies in the range of 0.5-4.0 GeV. While this energy is low compared to the largest machines, the continuous beam will provide a significant advantage over other accelerators whose particles are emitted in short bursts. The project is being constructed by the Southeast Universities Research Association (SURA) with DOE funding. SURA, which had developed the plans for the machine, won the contract in competition with several other, more experienced groups, on the basis of its design and its promise to create 35 new faculty positions for physicists in its member institutions. Construction delays and an early redesign raised the cost of the machine from an original estimate of $225 million to $515 million (plus another $39 million for additional detectors to be completed after the facility opens in early 1995).

The project survived several early congressional tests and the initial opposition of Senator Bennett Johnston (Democrat, Louisana), who chaired DOE's appropriations subcommittee and was concerned about the original design. CEBAF's assets have included effective management (under a new director brought in after the project's shaky start); relatively modest costs; the special role it plays for universities in the region, which have not traditionally been strong in high energy physics; a contribution from the host state, Virginia; and technical features that make its capabilities particularly appealing to experimenters. Nevertheless, DOE, hard pressed by other demands on its budget, failed to request operating funds for FY 1995, when CEBAF is to be completed and commissioned. Congress scolded the administration and added nearly $9 million to DOE's request for this purpose.

Laser interferometer gravitational-wave observatory (LIGO)

LIGO is a high-risk project designed to detect the existence of gravitational waves predicted by Einstein's theory of general relativity (sources for this section are Waldrop, 1990; Travis, 1993; Anderson, 1994; and Mervis, 1994). Modestly priced, by DOE and NASA standards, at $365 million (the most recent cost estimate for its construction and four years of operation) the facility is the most expensive project ever attempted by the predominantly little-science NSF. LIGO will consist of two nearly identical facilities, one in Hanford, Washington, the other in Livingston, Louisiana, each with a pair of 4 km long vacuum tubes joined in an L-shape incorporating a highly sensitive laser measurement device. LIGO is the brainchild of a team of Caltech and MIT physicists who developed plans for it in the early 1980s on the basis of studies conducted over the previous decade.

LIGO's "big science" character and its cost relative to the NSF budget and the Foundation's primary role as a supporter of academic "little-science" research have been its principal liabilities. Although NSF approved the conceptual design in 1989 and requested funds for LIGO as a new start in FY 1991, LIGO did not receive congressional approval until FY 1993 – when its construction request was cut from $38 to $20 million. Subsequent management problems led to the replacement of the project's director in 1993 and, more recently, to directions from NSF's Senate appropriations subcommittee to freeze LIGO's FY 1994 and FY 1995 funding until a new management plan and a revised cost estimate were approved. The new plan, submitted in November 1994, raises the cost estimate for construction by $85 million owing to a timetable stretched from four to seven years, as well as additional contingency funding, more staff, and upgraded detectors. The project has had support from powerful Democratic members of Congress from Washington and Louisiana. However, given the new Republican congressional majority and concerns about the project's budgetary impact on other NSF programmes, particularly in view of plans to renovate NSF's South Pole station to build the millimetre array (MMA) radio telescope, its future prospects in an era of financial constraint are somewhat uncertain.

National aerospace plane

NASP is a joint programme of the Department of Defense and NASA to develop technologies to provide a foundation for future aerospace vehicles (see US General Accounting Office, 1992e). Efforts have focused on building and testing an experimental flight vehicle able to take off from and land on a runway, attain a speed of Mach 25, and reach a low Earth orbit. Begun in 1982 as a classified study known as "Copper Canyon", the programme was formally established by the Secretary of Defense in December 1985. At that point (the end of Phase I) about $5.5 million had been spent in order to define the technical concept, evaluate key technologies, identify technical risks, and develop approaches to reducing these risks. Phase II, which began in 1985, included efforts to develop design concepts and to design and test engine and airframe components. More recent work (Phase IID), begun in 1991, has sought to carry the development efforts further towards building a prototype vehicle. During the period FY 1986-93, total project funding was $1.67 billion, of which DOD's share was $1.27 billion and NASA's was $0.4 billion. Not included in these figures are NASA's personnel, facilities, and utilities costs (budgeted separately and estimated at $450 million) and industry contributions (about $736 million).

The programme's ambitious aims have been controversial since its early days, and the NASA component was criticised and finally cut by Congress in FY 1993. Subsequently, the programme was restructured to focus on technology development rather than development of an operational vehicle, but even in that guise (labelled as a joint NASA-DOD hypersonic R&D effort), congressional hostility remains. Appropriators cut $8 million from the $40 million request and warned NASA not to proceed with such joint projects without their oversight (American Association for the Advancement of Science, 1994, p. 33). Although DOD's efforts are continuing, NASP's highly demanding technological requirements and its uncertain and potentially large costs loom as obstacles to success. Programme advocates have so far been unable to demonstrate that there is a reasonable prospect of building such an aircraft at a price that is consistent with any currently envisaged military or civilian mission.

Proposed new starts

Apart from EOS and LIGO, the federal government has initiated few new large R&D facilities since discretionary spending caps were first adopted in 1990. In its request for FY 1994, DOE proposed beginning the construction of a $2.9 billion Advanced Neutron Source Facility which would support research in condensed matter physics, biology, chemistry, and materials sciences. While strongly supporting the project, appropriators have postponed funding for construction, making it contingent upon the development, by DOE, of credible designs, schedules, and cost estimates, and a site selection process. Among other congressional concerns are the availability of funding for research in the related disciplines and the "outyear mortgage" for its long-term costs. Congress has also been wary of building new fusion facilities (either one for experiments on the tokamak concept or ITER, the International Thermonuclear Experimental Reactor) in the absence of a clear national commitment. In 1994, Senate appropriators said there needs to be an "eyes-wide-open debate and commitment to an international effort in order for such a project to realistically proceed.... To proceed without such a commitment is to invite another SSC debacle." (US Senate, 1994, p. 88). What this implies is that the Administration and Congress are committed in principle to these projects, but the terms under which they will be conducted have not yet been fully worked out.

The terms governing NASA's new National Aeronautical Facilities programme suggest that Congress will insist on stronger commitments, cost controls, and cost sharing before committing large sums for future R&D facilities. Acting upon the findings of a blue-ribbon panel, Congress created a new programme in FY 1995 for the construction of two wind tunnels needed to test transonic and subsonic aircraft. The $400 million appropriated for the project, which is expected to cost $2.5 billion to complete by 2002, came with some unprecedented warnings. The entire appropriation will be rescinded automatically after nine months unless NASA demonstrates its commitment to the project by recommending an equal amount for FY 1996 and meeting other conditions. Other requirements include cost sharing by the private sector, cost sharing by other federal agencies, and a comprehensive plan for site selection and cost management.

4.   Distributed megascience projects in the current fiscal environment

Budget characteristics of distributed megascience projects

Although they are often discussed together with megascience facility projects, the political and budgetary characteristics of distributed megascience projects differ in important ways. As a consequence, distributed projects are handled more easily in the US system, especially in the current fiscal environment.

In the first place, while distributed megascience projects are expensive, most of their costs are for conducting R&D rather than building facilities or purchasing equipment. This characteristic is a double-edged sword. Distributed projects are often treated more like conventional R&D activities than like megaprojects. They have less political visibility and less budgetary emphasis, and their advocates tend to be less fervent. However, for the same reasons, they are also less controversial. Unlike facility projects, they do not derive support from those who see them primarily as a vehicle for construction contracts and jobs in their local area. They do not attract the same kinds of coalitions and opposition, and they are not subject to the criticism of being ''pork barrel'' projects.

Second, instead of being cyclical, budgets for distributed projects are relatively stable from year to year. This means that they do not place excessive demands on agency budgets in certain years because of construction-related cost peaks, and their budgets fit in more easily with those of other programmes. Increases (and decreases) in programme levels may be phased in gradually, rather than abruptly, as often occurs for facilities.

Finally, annual expenditure levels for distributed megascience projects are adjustable (within limits) to suit budget constraints. Unlike facility projects, distributed megascience projects are divisible. They do not represent all-or-nothing commitments. If less money is available, they can be scaled down as needed. While downsizing may have negative effects on the project, these effects need not be fatal.

Some would argue that distributed megascience projects do not really belong in the same category as megascience facilities, that they are collections of co-ordinated ''little science'' projects rather than true ''big science'' efforts. Nevertheless, distributed megascience projects represent a departure from other forms of research in several respects: in the degree of top-down management involved; in the cultural shift required of the researchers in the project; and in their deliberate dedication to certain specified goals.

Furthermore, by justifying their budgets in "big science" terms and presenting them as line items, the advocates of these projects essentially define them as megascience.

Recent experience with distributed megascience projects

The Human Genome Project

In the words of two of its leading figures, "the US Human Genome Project is part of an international effort to develop genetic and physical maps and determine the DNA sequence of the human genome and the genomes of several model organisms" (Collins and Galas, 1993). The project, jointly funded by the National Institutes of Health (NIH) and DOE, was initiated in FY 1991, after several years of discussions in the scientific community. As recommended by the National Research Council (NRC), it is intended to run for 15 years at a cost of approximately $200 million a year (in 1991 dollars). Although funding has consistently fallen somewhat short of that level in inflation-adjusted terms, the project is widely regarded as productive and largely on track.

Although the level of funding that HGP has received is unprecedented for a single project in the biomedical arena, the effort has been relatively non-controversial. Some concerns have been raised by researchers in adjacent fields about the potential squeeze on funding for research initiated by individual investigators. The project's strategy, however, has been to distribute the work among a large number of research teams and genome centres at institutions in various parts of the country, giving it the appearance of a collection of little science projects. Co-ordination, both within the United States and internationally, has taken place largely at the field level rather than from the top down, and a number of important breakthroughs have been attributed to the effort. The major limitation on the growth of the project has been the overall situation of budget austerity, which has limited increases at both NIH and DOE. Despite these constraints, however, the project has managed to do reasonably well financially. In the FY 1995 budget cycle Congress granted the NIH component the 20 per cent increase (to $153 million) requested by the Administration and increased DOE's share by nearly 8 per cent to $70 million.

Global Change Research Program

The US Global Change Research Program co-ordinates the vast array of studies and missions undertaken by federal agencies to examine and understand the natural and anthropogenic processes affecting climate change. Unlike megascience facilities, and even the Human Genome Project, this effort involves research in many disciplines addressing a wide range of scientific issues. Although it involves fundamental research, the project is expected to support national and international decision making and address "practical problems of economic development and environmental stewardship" (US Office of Science and Technology Policy, 1993, p. 1). What it shares with megascience projects is its scale – funding in FY 1994 totalled $1 billion, excluding NASA's EOS component – and its thematic co-ordination.

When the interagency effort began in FY 1989, it covered only a small portfolio of programmes at seven agencies, which was valued at an estimated $133.9 million. By

FY 1991, its reach had expanded in terms of participating agencies, programmes, and funding. From its $753.6 million level that year (again excluding EOS and EOSDIS), funding for the global change programmes rose by an average of about 9 per cent annually through FY 1993 (the last year for which actual figures are available). Funding trends have varied over time, with growth surging early in the programme (*e.g.* FY 1991-92) and tapering off in the following years. Growth rates have also varied among agencies, generally reflecting overall trends for the individual agencies rather than the merits or popularity of the global change projects. Mission-oriented agencies like EPA, the National Oceanic and Atmospheric Administration (NOAA), and the Geological Survey are relatively small players and have received only modest resources and growth compared to agencies such as NSF and DOE.

5. Key factors affecting project outcomes

These case studies point to a number of factors affecting the outcome of megascience projects.

Management

For a megascience project to succeed, its management must inspire the confidence of its funding agency, its scientific or technical constituency, and Congress. As noted above, the larger the scale of the project, the closer the scrutiny it receives, the more its management must be above reproach. Megascience projects are, by definition, large and complex. They place substantial demands on managerial skills; opportunities to make mistakes are legion. Cost increases, project redesign, delays, misspent funds – whatever the cause of these problems, management takes the blame. A series of failures – such as those suffered by NASA in the Challenger disaster, the Hubble Space Telescope, and the Galileo mission – can tarnish an agency's reputation, diminish confidence in its management, and invite micro-management by Congress. CEBAF was strengthened by a new director whose management style impressed important members of Congress; the SSC was weakened by a series of management issues, including internal conflicts and friction between the contractor and DOE.

Technical uncertainties and cost increases

Uncertainties affect the cost of a megascience facility project in a number of ways (US General Accounting Office, 1992*f*). If such facilities are to be ''state-of-the-art'', they sometimes require technologies that are not fully developed when the project is being conceptualised and planned. In order not to delay the project, detailed planning (and sometimes construction) are allowed to proceed while R&D on these technologies continues, a process widely employed in military systems procurement and termed ''concurrency''. The risk is that R&D will not yield the needed technology in time or that its cost will rise beyond the original estimating parameters.

Cost increases force programme officials to reopen a decision already made. Unless the predicted benefits of the project increase correspondingly, this changes the cost-benefit ratio for the project and weakens its justification. Whatever the reasons behind the increase, it is viewed as a failure on the part of a project's management and therefore tends to undermine confidence in the competence of that management. It may also raise suspicions that the project's advocates have used the "foot-in-the-door" approach to gain support – deliberately underestimating a project's costs in order to get the project started in the expectation that support will build as the project progresses, as NASA officials reportedly did in the case of the Space Station (McCurdy, 1990, p. 66).

Clarity of mission

The importance of a clear mission for a megascience project is nicely demonstrated by the contrast between the relative ease with which the EOS programme has acquired and maintained congressional support and the erratic history of the Space Station. EOS was designed to study terrestrial processes associated with global climate change – a high priority mission. The Space Station seems to many observers a technology in search of a mission. Characterised as the "next step" in manned space exploration, the project has never succeeded in developing a clear sense, beyond this rather vague idea, of what it is intended to do. Scientific experimentation, defence, manufacturing, and testing technological concepts have all been proposed, but none of these, individually or in combination, has really persuaded sceptics that the project's substantial cost is justified.

Scale of expenditures

Without wishing to belabour the obvious, the overall cost of a project is crucial to its treatment in the political process. The more expensive a project is, the greater the benefits required to justify it, the more high-level support it must have to survive, and the more attractive a target it presents for "deficit hawks" and those who favour other priorities. The multi-billion dollar estimated cost of the SSC meant that its rather esoteric potential benefits could be compared with those of a great many other possible uses to which such a vast amount of money could be put. Resources at this level demand excellence; management errors can have enormous consequences. Furthermore, by eliminating a large item in single stroke, deficit-conscious members of Congress can point to substantial savings. To achieve such savings by other means might require cutting or eliminating many other programmes, a process that could entail much larger political costs.

"Overbooking" of projects in an agency

A look at the histories of megascience projects suggests that some have fallen victim to budget constraints simply because their sponsoring agency tried to carry out too many projects simultaneously. NASA seems particularly prone to this problem (US General Accounting Office, 1992c). Several of its missions – the CRAF mission and the Space Infrared Telescope come to mind immediately – seem to have been terminated simply because there was not enough money in the budget to do everything the agency wanted to do. These projects were progressing satisfactorily, but priorities had to be set, and some projects had to be abandoned. Flexibility is a virtue in such circumstances: if a project can be deferred or its timetable can be lengthened without incurring disproportionate additional costs, it is more likely to survive such budgetary competition from other projects. Distributed projects have an advantage in this regard.

Political factors

Political coalitions, sometimes based on geographical distribution of expenditures, are an important factor in the success of megaprojects. It is widely believed, for example, that congressional support for the SSC weakened markedly once a site was selected and members from the states and localities that were rejected lost interest. NASA is reported to be particularly effective in assuring that contracts for its largest projects are widely distributed around the country and that relevant members of Congress and their constituents are aware of the jobs that depend on these projects. LIGO has been helped by the location of its facilities in Washington and Louisiana, states represented by powerful members of the last Congress.

The association of the SSC with Texas politics was an important factor in both its life and its death. Then Vice-President George Bush's Texas roots were an important element in the power of the coalition backing the Texas site. Speaker of the House Jim Wright (Democrat, Texas) was another key figure, and his resignation marked a milestone in the downfall of the project. Other Texas politicians also played important roles. When the House first voted to terminate the project in 1992 (a decision subsequently reversed by the Senate), it was widely believed that the negative vote of many liberal Democrats was in fact a vote against Rep. Joe Barton (Democrat, Texas), in whose district the project was located. Barton, a fiscal conservative, had campaigned hard to force a vote on a balanced budget amendment, something which liberal Democrats were trying hard to avoid. The absence of strong support for the SSC from President Clinton was probably another factor. While the President indicated he favoured the project, neither he nor his staff lobbied very hard for it, and – significantly – no one seemed to regard the SSC's cancellation as a defeat for his Administration.

International participation

The international character of a project, or its absence, may be influential in its outcome, although not necessarily in predictable ways. Congressional science policy leaders have called repeatedly for federal agencies to seek international participation in megascience projects. The failure of DOE to obtain significant funding from international partners for the SSC was one of the reasons for its termination. It is likely that substantial contributions to the project from other nations would have strengthened domestic support for the project, both because it would have reduced its cost to the federal government and because it would have been a tangible demonstration of confidence in the project by other governments. In addition, it would have added another cost to a termination decision

– that of provoking the displeasure of the international partners. Nevertheless, in view of its other liabilities, it is not certain that international participation would have saved the project. International participation in the Space Station has helped it to survive so far, but in the absence of a compelling mission, it may not be enough to save the project in coming years.

Fiscal parameters

While cost has been a long-standing impediment to large infrastructure projects, the phenomenon of declining resources is relatively recent. Prior to the 1990s, project terminations were largely the result of technical constraints (*e.g.* the ISABELLE accelerator) or ideological shifts regarding the government's mission *vis-à-vis* the civilian economy (*e.g.* synthetic fuels projects) (US Congressional Research Service, 1994). The budgets of civilian programmes such as the space station and EOS fared well in the early 1990s, because the end of the cold war made it possible for Congress to achieve most of the desired savings by cutting defence spending. Even the FY 1994 budget, which cancelled the SSC, provided a year-to-year increase of 5 per cent for non-defence R&D. However, starting in 1993, the year in which a newly elected President and Congress enacted a massive tax and spending measure, fiscal austerity began to exert clear and somewhat unilateral pressure on federal investments in large R&D facilities. The bad news is that this austerity seems likely to be the controlling factor in future decisions about megascience projects.

6. The future of megascience: prospects and alternatives

Budget outlook for the next five to ten years

The 1994 election provides a strong indication that the fiscal climate of the past several years is likely to continue and that deficit reduction efforts, resistance to increased taxes, and pressures to reduce discretionary spending will probably intensify. The capture of both houses of Congress by the Republican Party for the first time in several decades means a move toward greater fiscal conservatism and a reduction in the size and scope of federal programmes.

This does not necessarily mean a reduction in political support for basic research, which has had bipartisan backing for many years. On the other hand, increased funding for science programmes will doubtless come up against the wall of fiscal constraints in view of the promises to cut spending and reduce taxes. The Republican "Contract with America", in fact, contains several provisions that will have profound implications for megaprojects if they are enacted. In the short term, key science agencies, including NSF and NIH, may be among the agencies and programmes targeted for level funding or budget cuts in the name of deficit reduction. In the longer term, there are the Balanced Budget Amendment and the "line-item veto".

The Balanced Budget Amendment, a constitutional measure that would require that the deficit be brought down to zero by early in the next century, would put enormous pressure on the government to control expenditures and have a chilling effect on new programme starts, including megascience projects. The line-item veto proposal would allow a President to reject individual items within an appropriations bill, a change that could affect the traditional structure of budgetary politics in unpredictable ways. How it would affect megascience projects is not clear.

It does appear that, whatever the fate of these proposals, the climate for new starts for megascience facility projects during the next several years will not be at all hospitable, and even existing programmes, such as the Space Station, will face a bitterly competitive budgetary environment. Some of the measures discussed below may have the potential for improving the odds a bit, but none of them will change these basic parameters.

Current budget strategies

As the level of resources available for government investment in civilian discretionary programmes continues to shrink, policy makers are likely to make adjustments to the budgets of megascience projects. Recent experience suggests that some of the likely actions will be to stretch out construction and re-scope projects. Any money for new starts, such as the Advanced Neutron Source or ITER, is likely to come with strings attached (*e.g.* cost sharing, commitment measures, milestones, etc.).

Setting longer timetables for construction is politically relatively easy. This presumably does not change the nature of the project but nearly always results in higher overall cost. Political leaders are usually willing to accept the increased long-term cost in order to gain the short-term savings. Re-scoping the project is more difficult, and may sometimes be impossible. The Space Station and EOS are examples of megascience projects that have been repeatedly re-scoped in order to bring costs down. A major risk of re-scoping, as the Space Station experience demonstrates, is that it undermines the project's rationale. Another is that it introduces significant delays and, if done for reasons of political expediency, it can also weaken the technical soundness of the project.

Finally, when these measures fail, and savings cannot be achieved within the project's existing scope and schedule, the decision to terminate a project remains as the final option. The current fiscal environment has made this option – which in the past was often ruled out as wasteful when a project was in mid-stream – much easier to exercise. The SSC experience is the best-known example in recent years, but other instances include NASA's Advanced Solid Rocket Motor (ASRM) which was also terminated in FY 1994.

Alternative budgeting techniques and devices

It has been suggested that some of the political and budgetary difficulties that past megascience projects have encountered might be alleviated by using budgeting techniques and devices that have not previously been applied to these kinds of projects. Ideas that might have some potential include advance appropriations, full funding and mile-stone budgeting, and trust funds.

Advance appropriations

Advance appropriations are one way the government makes an early commitment of budget authority for a programme. Under this approach, Congress appropriates money that does not become available until a future fiscal year. The budget authority provided by an advance appropriation is scored (*i.e.* counted) in the year in which the money becomes available for obligation. Thus, if a programme receives an advance appropria-tion of $1 billion that will be obligated in equal amounts over the following two years, the programme will show budget authority of $500 million in each of those years rather than a lump sum in the year it is appropriated. Advance appropriations have no effect on a programme's outlays, because expenditures depend on the timing and nature of the obligations and activities, not on when the money is deposited in the account. Likewise, having an advance appropriation does not alter the character of a programme, so it does not make the spending "mandatory". The budget authority and outlays from an advance appropriation for an R&D project would be classified as discretionary and subject to the general pressures on such spending.

In practice, advance appropriations do not guarantee predictability of programme funding. The experience of the Clean Coal Technology Program at DOE is a case in point. President Reagan initiated this programme in 1987 in response to an agreement between the United States and Canada on acid rain. After an initial regular appropriation of $398 million, Congress agreed to provide advance appropriations totalling $2.4 billion for the next four rounds of solicitations for cost-shared R&D on technologies to improve the environmental and economic performance of coal use. The money was appropriated in three different appropriation acts ($575 million in FY 1988, $575 million in FY 1989, and $1.2 billion in FY 1990), with timetables for obligations tied to the projected pace of the solicitations. Since then, however, availability has been repeatedly adjusted by Con-gress and DOE to accommodate not only programme needs but the outlay limits on discretionary spending.

"Full funding" and multi-year contracting

During the defence build-up in the 1980s, it was common to see multi-billion dollar appropriations for DOD procurement of weapons systems. Some have suggested that having advance lump-sum appropriations for large R&D facilities might reduce funding instability and thereby lower programme costs and improve efficiency. In fact, the principles governing the DOD practice already apply to civilian procurement and con-struction projects, but the results differ for R&D because of differences in what is being purchased.

Federal budget guidelines require all agencies to provide "full funding" of the entire cost of major procurement and construction programmes (US Office of Manage-ment and Budget, 1994*b*, p. 16; 1978). For defence projects, this includes not only the cost of the items being purchased, say 100 F–16 aircraft, but the cost of all spare parts and components needed for initial operation and the amount specified in the contract for a buyout in case of termination. This policy is designed to protect the interests of both the government and the supplier. By initially setting aside enough money, the acquisition should meet expected quality standards (*e.g.* enough spare parts to function for one year) and not drain resources for future projects. The supplier is assured that the government will make good on its promises, or will pay the penalty.

In a limited number of cases, DOD is authorised to negotiate multi-year procurement contracts, which can markedly affect budget authority in the year the money is appropriated because of the full-funding requirement. Studies have shown that such multi-year contracts may yield savings and promote stability (US Congressional Budget Office, 1986). To be eligible for a multi-year contract, the project must involve the purchase of "economic order quantities" (*e.g.* 100 planes a year for five years) and satisfy various risk, cost, and military criteria. In 1987, only about 6 per cent of DOD's procurement funding supported multi-year contracts. Appropriations for multi-year contracts can either be provided in lump sums (*e.g.* $5 billion in one year) or annually (*e.g.* $3 billion one year, and $1 billion for each of the next two years). Either way, however, the programme's funding is subject to authorisation and appropriation oversight each year, and the government retains the right to cancel or adjust the order, subject to the penalties in the contract. The outlay effects are also the same, but the appropriations will be "scored" against the year in which they are provided.

NASA, DOE, and other civilian agencies are subject to the same "full-funding" rules as DOD for major procurement and construction projects. Thus, when buying components for a particle accelerator or spacecraft, agencies are required to budget the full amount needed to cover the cost of all of the items under contract. Agencies have, however, the latitude to decide which projects are "major", and this can lead to uneven application of the policy among agencies.

There is an important difference between weapons procurement and megascience projects. In the case of a submarine, DOD is buying a complete and proven product with understood specifications. Full funding may not be requested until the planning of a project has reached the point at which it is certain that the contract will be awarded in the current budget year. In the case of R&D projects – whether defence or non-defence – agencies usually are procuring pieces of a larger, evolving system. As a result, procurement funding tends to involve a series of contracts that may be staggered over time and spread among contractors. For R&D projects, it is the sum of individual contractual commitments, not the project as a whole, that is "fully funded" by appropriations in any given year.

Some have suggested extending the full-funding concept to whole projects, not just the individual procurement and construction components. Under this scenario, agencies would be required to estimate the complete range of costs associated with a project and budget that amount initially as a lump sum. In theory, this would enable policy makers to make more informed judgements about alternative ways of investing the government's limited discretionary dollars. While this strategy could provide greater certainty for the projects that get approved, it is unclear how unanticipated cost increases, which are always a risk in R&D projects, would be handled. History also shows that appropriations are not entitlements, and can and will be rescinded or adjusted if needs or perceptions change.

Milestone budgeting

During the 1980s, DOD was authorised to experiment with an alternative approach to funding major R&D and weapons systems procurement called "milestone budgeting" (US Congressional Budget Office, 1987). Under this concept, funding for a project would be authorised – and perhaps appropriated – for a number of years ahead and only be re-examined by policy makers at certain milestones or at the end of a five-year period, whichever came first. This approach was suggested by several prominent advisors as a means of improving programme stability and reducing costs resulting from the lengthening of programme timetables. There are potential problems as well: depending on the number and size of the projects involved, it could limit DOD's budgetary flexibility if several programmes reached key milestones concurrently. Its effectiveness could also be diluted if it only applied to project authorisation and not appropriations. The fact that milestone budgeting was endorsed by authorisers and resisted by appropriators suggested that implementation would encounter obstacles.

Milestone budgeting had a brief and inauspicious trial run. DOD suggested three weapons systems as candidates in 1987 and proposed funding them annually rather than in lump-sum amounts. In its first test, milestone budgeting was tried as an overlay on the normal authorisation and appropriations process rather than as a stand-alone method of financing. The dual system proved cumbersome, and authorisation for the experiment was repealed.

Trust funds

Trust funds are financial devices used by the federal government to dedicate certain budgetary receipts to specific purposes. According to the General Accounting Office (GAO), receipts are classified as belonging to a trust fund if they have two attributes: if they are dedicated by law to a particular programme or set of programmes; and if they are dedicated to accounts designated by law as "trust fund" accounts (US General Accounting Office, 1988, p. 4). Trust funds have accounted for approximately one-third of the government's outlays in recent years. Examples are the Social Security Trust Fund (the largest by far, funded by Social Security taxes), the Highway Trust Fund (funded by gasoline excise taxes), the Airport and Airways Trust Fund (supported principally by taxes on airline tickets), the Superfund (for clean-up of hazardous waste sites, financed by taxes on selected industries), and the Nuclear Waste Trust Fund (for the development and construction of a permanent repository for civilian nuclear wastes, financed by fees paid by electric utilities). The appeal of the trust fund concept is that it allows the government to allocate the costs of certain programmes to the users and/or those who benefit from the programmes instead of the general public (US Congressional Budget Office, 1992).

Trust funds offer some protection for a programme's financing because federal laws prohibit using trust fund receipts for purposes other than those specified. Trust fund financing does not change the character of a programme, however, so it does not confer "mandatory" status on the spending. Expenditures from the highway, airport, nuclear waste, and Superfund trust funds are all discretionary. The amounts available each year are set by authorisation legislation and by annual "limitations on obligations" set by appropriations acts. Also, expenditures need not match receipts in a given year. In some cases, this occurs for technical reasons: the Nuclear Waste fund had accumulated a $4 billion surplus by FY 1994 because progress on a repository has been delayed by technical and political factors. Political factors have also come into play in other ways, with spending being constrained so that the surplus receipts offset the deficit or other discretionary spending.

Establishing a trust fund for a megascience facility project would, in theory, provide a mechanism for assuring it a dedicated and possibly predictable source of money. Such a trust fund could be supported in a variety of ways: by charging user fees to scientists working at the facility (or to their parent institution or granting agency); by a dedicated tax on related products (*e.g.* computers or consumer electronics) that presumably derive benefits from federally funded research; or by some other kind of dedicated tax, such as a tax on energy which could be used to support energy-related megaprojects. While there have been occasional discussions of such ideas in Congress, the notion of a megascience trust fund does not seem to have very broad appeal.

The primary difficulty for using a trust fund to support basic science megaprojects (such as particle accelerators or astronomical observatories) is the lack of a set of users or identifiable beneficiaries who could be charged fees on a scale sufficient to be useful. Even if beneficiaries could be identified, they would probably oppose a special levy. In addition, as experience with existing trust funds has shown, trust fund outlays are far from immune to spending constraints, and the existence of a megascience trust fund could not guarantee that money for projects would be made available when needed. Nevertheless, one area where the idea might have some potential is energy-related megaprojects (for example in nuclear fusion) where there are identifiable beneficiaries with the ability – if not the willingness – to pay.

Prospects for budgetary alternatives

In principle, none of these mechanisms would be especially difficult to implement – although a trust fund would require authorising legislation that included a dedicated tax or user fee, and its expenditures would still be limited by the caps on discretionary spending. Full funding and advance appropriations for specific projects may be used whenever Congress chooses. The main barrier to their use is Congress's traditional reluctance to surrender the degree of control over a project that such a decision involves.

In any case, trust funds, "full funding", milestone budgeting, and advance appropriations do not address two difficulties associated with the federal budget system. First is the problem of annual outlays. As mentioned above, the federal deficit is measured in terms of annual cash flow, and the principal deficit control measures of the Budget Enforcement Act are imposed in terms of outlays. This means that even if a project has adequate budget authority, Congress or the administration may still withhold expenditures because of conflicting demands and the need to meet deficit targets. Second is the issue of oversight and accountability. The larger, more visible, and more important a project is, the more Congress feels it must maintain close watch. This is, of course, consistent with its constitutional role and a vital part of the US system. This oversight will be exercised regardless of advance appropriations and can easily result in budget and programme changes. In a very real sense, therefore, budget issues are never really settled.

Budget process reforms

Two proposed reforms of the budget process might facilitate the support of megascience projects. These include the adoption of two-year budget cycles and changing the budget process to provide for separate consideration of long-term investment and short-term consumption.

Two-year budget cycles

Adoption of a biennial budget to replace the annual cycle has been advocated from time to time as a means of streamlining the budget process. The idea was endorsed by the Bush Administration in FY 1991 and 1992 and surfaced most recently as a proposal of Vice-President Gore's "National Performance Review" (popularly known as the "Reinventing Government Initiative") (US Executive Office of the President, 1993). Presumably, a biennial budgeting system would provide greater stability in funding and, by reducing uncertainty and administrative burdens, would allow project managers to operate more efficiently. This would seem to be especially beneficial to megascience projects.

The benefits of two-year appropriations may be somewhat illusory, however. Despite legislation from the authorising committees enacted several years ago requiring DOD to submit two-year budgets, the appropriations committees have retained the annual appropriations cycle. In essence, this gives Congress the best of both worlds: they receive official statements of DOD's future plans and yet still keep the agency on the "short leash of annual appropriations" (Shapley, 1992, pp. 56-57).

The discipline required by a biennial budget would not come easily either to Congress or the Executive Branch. Congress will still want to exercise annual programme oversight and not wait an extra year to intervene in politically important issues. The Administration and the executive agencies, likewise, may prefer not to wait two years to propose new initiatives and may also choose to retain the flexibility of making their own internal budget allocations on an annual basis. Given the difficulties facing two-year budgets, an intermediate step might be to require agencies to submit two-year budget estimates to Congress and have appropriations committees "mark up" (that is, make committee recommendations on) the second year's figures, but not take final action on them (Shapley, 1992, pp. 56-57). Such a procedure might provide additional stability without formalising the biennial budget process. It could have modest salutary effects on the management of megascience projects.

Separating the long term and the short term in the budget

Other budget reform proposals which offer some potential for improving the treatment of megascience projects involve the notion of distinguishing between long-term and short-term spending. In general, these proposals would separate capital investment from operations. Some would go further and seek to identify all forms of investment (not just capital expenditures) and separate them from consumption spending. As with the biennial budget proposal, proponents cite the positive experience that many individual states have had with separate capital and operations budgets.

Following recommendations of the National Performance Review (NPR), OMB plans to divide the current unified budget into a capital budget, an operating budget, and a cash budget, beginning in FY 1996. One goal would be to improve the way in which the government acquires capital assets. The NPR plan would not seek to exempt the capital budget from the BEA outlay caps. In this respect it differs from other proposals that would include only depreciation of the capital asset in a given year's operating budget. However, the plan would couple capital budgeting with several related improvements in the planning and budgeting process for fixed assets. These include a long-term planning and analysis process for capital assets in each agency; adaptations in the budget process to take account of these plans; and adoption of more flexible funding mechanisms to accommodate ''spikes'' in agency spending caused by capital acquisition processes (US Office of Management and Budget, 1994a, pp. 114-16).

The idea of a capital budget may receive additional impetus from the debate on the Balanced Budget Amendment. In general, the capital budget concept seems likely to be beneficial to megascience projects. Although advocates of such projects would still need to justify their costs in terms of potential benefits, inclusion in a capital investment budget would make it possible to assess the merits of the project on a more equitable basis. The broader concept of an investment budget is also attractive in the sense that it could, in theory, place most R&D (including R&D for distributed megascience projects as well as small science programmes) in a separate category from consumption expenditures. The weakness of the investment budget, as opposed to the capital budget, lies in the fact that the term ''investment'' cannot be defined as precisely as ''capital investment'' and may more readily be abused in order to serve political ends.

Private sector financing and tax incentives for megascience projects

The federal budget, of course, is not the only source of funding for large capital investments that serve public purposes. The recently completed Keck Observatory in Hawaii was built with private money through a $145 million foundation grant to a group of universities. Private philanthropical institutions in the United States have traditionally supported individual investigators and centres and institutes that house such investigators, but they could, conceivably, also fund smaller megascience projects. The annual budget for the Human Genome Programme, for example, is well within the funding capabilities of the privately funded Howard Hughes Medical Institute – which is, in fact, supporting a considerable amount of related work. On the other hand, projects the size of the Space Station and the SSC are clearly beyond the financial capabilities of any entity other than the federal government.

A related alternative that might offer some potential is to authorise the sale of tax-free bonds by universities or other bodies which would use the proceeds to finance construction of megascience facilities and repay the debt by collecting user fees. This is a novel and interesting proposal, but it raises a host of questions that would need to be answered before it might be considered practical. These include: the willingness of universities to take on additional debt for this purpose, in view of their existing infrastructure needs; the willingness of financial institutions to underwrite the debt; the need for someone (most likely the federal government) to guarantee sufficient income to cover the capital investment; and the availability of funds for continued operation of the project, once construction is complete. There is also another federal budget issue involved. Tax-free bonds represent foregone revenue – a "tax expenditure" for the federal government. Under the PAYGO provisions of the Budget Enforcement Act, any tax expenditure must be offset by an increase in another tax or an entitlement reduction. The method, while perhaps less costly to the government than an ordinary appropriation, is not cost-free. It still involves federal resources – and the need to offset it could well make it hard to sell.

The more likely trend might be expansion of partnerships between the federal government and non-federal interests. Facility projects typically involve in-kind and financial contributions from the host states that stand to benefit from the jobs and infrastructure created by the megascience projects (*e.g.* SSC, CEBAF). The scales have begun to tip even more towards external contributions in recent years, with state money becoming one means of competing for federal science facilities. For example, in 1990, with the aid of $66 million in state funding, Florida State University wrested the National Magnet Laboratory away from MIT (Celis, 1994). Projects with recognised beneficiaries, such as aeronautical facilities, are likely to be undertaken only if the user community is willing and able to share in the costs of the facilities.

7.   Implications for international co-operation

The United States has done and will continue to do some megascience projects successfully. But, as pressures on the federal budget increase, so does the interest of US scientists and policy makers in international co-operation. Sharing the costs of megascience facilities and distributed projects makes both economic and political sense, as the nations of Western Europe have long recognised. Yet, the same factors that pose obstacles to domestic megascience projects have made the United States an unreliable partner in international efforts. Unless these factors can be addressed, international co-operation in megascience will not be a viable option for the United States.

What, then, can be done to improve the way in which the United States deals with megascience projects, especially those involving large-scale facilities? The bottom line can be stated simply: There is no magic formula. The reforms and alternative budgeting techniques described above may help, but none of them can solve the basic problems of limited resources, poor planning, and short-sighted management. The United States has not just been a difficult partner internationally, it has been erratic in conducting megascience projects at home. To avoid wasting its increasingly scarce resources on projects that never reach fruition, the nation needs to do a better job of planning, budgeting, and carrying out such efforts. This will require adjustments in the style of operations in the scientific community and in Congress, but most of all, it will demand a new approach on the part of the federal agencies that sponsor these projects. These agencies – especially NASA, DOE, and NSF – have the essential responsibilities of planning and management of megascience projects. They have to "clean up their acts".

The experience with the projects described above – notably the SSC and the Space Station – suggests the fundamental importance of planning from the outset in a forthright, realistic manner. The foot-in-the-door strategy has its attractions, and it is easy to be overly optimistic about the ability to solve technological problems. But problems can and do arise after the foot is in the door, and the consequent delays and cost overruns diminish confidence in a project's management. In the long run, the advocates of megascience projects will benefit from complete and honest cost estimates for all dimensions of a project from the initial planning stages. In general, and especially in view of the current budgetary emphasis on controlling cash flow (budget outlays), the scale and timing of expenditures have to be realistic. Agency officials must be willing to make hard choices among projects in their early stages, rather than let them proceed simultaneously, knowing that funding peaks are likely to overlap and hoping somehow to muddle through the resulting budget conflicts.

Beyond planning, agency and project management needs to be strengthened. Better cost controls are needed to track spending and performance over the life of a project. There are legitimate differences of opinion on how this can best be done. Some argue that agencies would be more efficient if freed from layers of bureaucratic oversight; others think the problems are rooted in agencies' lack of rigour in following existing guidelines and procedures for project management. Federal agencies like NASA and DOE understand the need for change and are trying to reform their management, procurement, and institutional cultures (US General Accounting Office, 1993a; US Congressional Budget Office, 1994). Whatever strategy they adopt, these agencies must learn to manage projects – especially the largest ones – efficiently and effectively.

It is certainly possible to improve the federal budget process, to make it more "rational" and incorporate tools that facilitate decision making on long-term investments. The real problem for megascience projects, however, is not the budget process, but the willingness of scientific leaders and government officials – in the federal agencies as well as in Congress – to reconcile their visions with political and economic reality. If the United States is able to move in this direction, it can become a more reliable and desirable partner for international megascience projects. Then, the current situation of fiscal adversity might become an opportunity to enlarge the scope of international scientific collaboration to the benefit of the entire world.

References

AMERICAN ASSOCIATION FOR THE ADVANCEMENT OF SCIENCE (1993), *Congressional Action on Research and Development in the FY 1994 Budget*, AAAS, Washington, D.C.

AMERICAN ASSOCIATION FOR THE ADVANCEMENT OF SCIENCE (1994), *Congressional Action on Research and Development in the FY 1995 Budget*, AAAS, Washington, D.C.

ANDERSON, Christopher (1994), "LIGO Director Out in Shakeup", *Science*, 11 March, p. 1366.

CELIS, William 3rd (1994), "The Big Stars on Campus Are Now Research Labs", *The New York Times*, 4 December, p. A–1.

COLLINS, Francis and David GALAS (1993), "A New Five-year Plan for the US Human Genome Project", *Science*, 1 October, p. 43.

CRAWFORD, Mark (1986), "Johnston Drops Opposition to CEBAF", *Science*, 9 May, p. 707.

MCCURDY, Howard E. (1990), *The Space Station Decision: Incremental Politics and Technological Choice*, The Johns Hopkins University Press, Baltimore, Maryland.

MERVIS, Jeffrey (1994), "LIGO's Price Rises as NSF Debates Big-ticket Items", *Science*, 25 November, pp. 1314-1315.

MUKERJEE, Madhusree (1993), "CEBAF Readies Its Electron Beam for Studies of Nucleons and Nuclei", *Physics Today*, August, pp. 17-19.

PADRON, Joanne (1993), "NASA in the FY 1994 Budget", in American Association for the Advancement of Science, *AAAS Report XVIII: Research and Development FY 1994*, AAAS, Washington, D.C., p. 103.

SHAPLEY, Willis H. (1992), *The Budget Process and R&D: A Consultant Report*, April, Carnegie Commission on Science, Technology, and Government, New York.

TAUBES, Gary (1993), "The Supercollider: How Big Science Lost Favor and Fell", *The New York Times*, 26 October, p. C1.

TRAVIS, John (1993), "LIGO: A $250 Million Gamble", *Science*, 30 April, pp. 612-614.

US CONGRESSIONAL BUDGET OFFICE (1986), "Alternative Strategies for Increasing Multiyear Procurement", Staff Working Paper, July, CBO, Washington, D.C.

US CONGRESSIONAL BUDGET OFFICE (1987), *Assessing the Effectiveness of Milestone Budgeting*, July, CBO, Washington, D.C.

US CONGRESSIONAL BUDGET OFFICE (1988), *Concurrent Weapons Development and Production*, August, CBO, Washington, D.C.

US CONGRESSIONAL BUDGET OFFICE (1991), *Large Nondefense R&D Projects in the Budget: 1980-1986*, July, CBO, Washington, D.C.

US CONGRESSIONAL BUDGET OFFICE (1992), *Paying for Highways, Airways, and Waterways: How Can Users Be Charged?*, CBO, Washington, D.C.

US CONGRESSIONAL BUDGET OFFICE (1994), *Reinventing NASA*, March, CBO, Washington, D.C.

US CONGRESSIONAL RESEARCH SERVICE (1994), *Big Science and Technology Projects: Analysis of 30 Selected US Government Projects*, 94-687 SPR, 24 August, CRS, Washington, D.C.

US EXECUTIVE OFFICE OF THE PRESIDENT, *Creating a Government That Works Better and Costs Less*, Report of the National Performance Review, 7 September, Washington, D.C.

US GENERAL ACCOUNTING OFFICE (1988), *Budget Issues: Trust Funds and Their Relationship to the Federal Budget*, GAO/AFMD-88-55, September, GAO, Washington, D.C.

US GENERAL ACCOUNTING OFFICE (1990), *Capping Outlays Is Ineffective for Controlling Expenditures*, GAO/AFMD-90-111, September, GAO, Washington, D.C.

US GENERAL ACCOUNTING OFFICE (1992a), *Changes to the Scope, Schedule, and Estimated Cost of the Earth Observing System*, GAO/NSIAD-92-223, July, GAO, Washington, D.C.

US GENERAL ACCOUNTING OFFICE (1992b), *Foreign Contributions to the Superconducting Super Collider*, GAO/RCED-93-75, December, GAO, Washington, D.C.

US GENERAL ACCOUNTING OFFICE (1992c), *NASA: Large Programs May Consume Increasing Share of Limited Future Budgets*, GAO/NSIAD-92-278, September, GAO, Washington, D.C.

US GENERAL ACCOUNTING OFFICE (1992d), *NASA Needs to Reassess Its EOSDIS Development Strategy*, Testimony of Samuel W. Bowlin, 27 February, GAO, Washington, D.C.

US GENERAL ACCOUNTING OFFICE (1992e), *National Aerospace Plane: Restructuring Future Research and Development Efforts*, GAO/NSIAD 93-71, December, GAO, Washington, D.C.

US GENERAL ACCOUNTING OFFICE (1992f), *Space Missions Require Substantially More than Initially Estimated*, GAO/NSAID-93-97, December, GAO, Washington, D.C.

US GENERAL ACCOUNTING OFFICE (1993a), *NASA: Major Challenges for Management*, GAO/NSIAD-94-18, 6 October, GAO, Washington, D.C.

US GENERAL ACCOUNTING OFFICE (1993b), *Space Station: Program Instability and Cost Growth Continue Pending Redesign*, GAO/NSIAD-93-187, May, GAO, Washington, D.C.

US GENERAL ACCOUNTING OFFICE (1993c), *Super Collider is Over Budget and Behind Schedule*, GAO/RCED-93-87, February, GAO, Washington, D.C.

US GENERAL ACCOUNTING OFFICE (1993d), *Super Collider – National Security, Similar Projects, and Cost*, GAO/RCED-93-158, 13 May, GAO, Washington, D.C.

US NATIONAL AERONAUTICS AND SPACE ADMINISTRATION (1988), *Budget Justification for FY 1989*, NASA, Washington, D.C.

US OFFICE OF MANAGEMENT AND BUDGET (1978), *Statement of W. Bowman Cutter Before the Task Force on Budget Process of the House Budget Committee*, 22 February, OMB, Washington, D.C.

US OFFICE OF MANAGEMENT AND BUDGET (1994a), *Budget of the United States Government, Fiscal Year 1995: Analytical Perspectives*, US Government Printing Office, Washington, D.C.

US OFFICE OF MANAGEMENT AND BUDGET (1994*b*), *Circular A-11: Budget Preparation and Submission of Estimates*, OMB, Washington, D.C.

US OFFICE OF SCIENCE AND TECHNOLOGY POLICY, FEDERAL COORDINATING COUNCIL FOR SCIENCE, ENGINEERING AND TECHNOLOGY (1993), *Our Changing Planet: The FY 1994 US Global Change Research Program*, OSTP, Washington, D.C.

US PRESIDENT'S COUNCIL OF ADVISORS ON SCIENCE AND TECHNOLOGY (1992), *Megaprojects in the Sciences*, December, OSTP, Washington, D.C.

US SENATE (1993), *Senate Report 103-137*, 9 September, US Government Printing Office, Washington, D.C.

US SENATE (1994), *Senate Report 103-291*, US Government Printing Office, Washington, D.C.

VAUGHAN, Chris (1990) "A long, long way to Waxahachie's dream machine", *The New Scientist*, 10 March, p. 32.

VON BAEYER, Hans Christian (1994), "Sweet Little Accelerator", *Discover*, August, pp. 52-58.

WALDROP, M. Mitchell (1990) "Of Politics, Pulsars, Death Spirals – and LIGO", *Science*, 7 September, pp. 1106-1108.

234

Acronyms

AEC   Atomic Energy Commission (United States)
AMPTE   Satellite programme for magnetosphere and plasma physics (United States, Germany, United Kingdom)
ANS   Advanced Neutron Source (cancelled, United States)
ASTEC   Australian Science and Technology Council
AXAF   Advanced X-Ray Astrophysics Facility

BCRD   Civilian Research and Development Budget (France)
BEA   Budget Enforcement Act (1990) (United States)
BMFT   Bundesministerium für Forschung und Technologie (Federal Ministry for Research and Technology, Germany)

CEA   Commissariat à l'énergie atomique (Atomic Energy Commission, France)
CEBAF   Continuous Electron Beam Accelerator Facility Laboratory (Newport, News, Virginia, United States)
CERN   European Organisation for Nuclear Physics (Geneva)
CNES   Centre national d'études spatiales (National Centre for Space Research, France)

DESY   Deutsches Elektronensynchroton (Hamburg)
DNW   Deutsch-Niederländischer Windkanal (Emmelord, Netherlands)
DOD   Department of Defense (United States)
DOE   Department of Energy (United States)

ECFA   European Committee for Future Accelerators
ECMWF European Centre for Medium Range Weather Forecasts (Reading, United Kingdom)
EFBR   European Fast Breeder Reactor
ELF   European Laser Facility
EMBL   European Molecular Biology Laboratory (Heidelberg)
EMBO   European Molecular Biology Organisation
EOS   Earth Observing System
EOSDIS Earth Observing System Data and Information System
EPA   Environmental Protection Agency (United States)
ESA   European Space Agency
ESO   European Southern Observatory
ESRF   European Synchrotron Radiation Facility (Grenoble)
ESS   European Spallation Source (project)
ESTEC   European Space Research and Technology Center (Noordwijk, Netherlands)
ETW   European Transonic Windtunnel (Porz, Germany)
EU   European Union

GAO   General Accounting Office (United States)

GDP	Gross domestic product
GEMINI	Collaboration for two 8 m optical telescopes (United States, United Kingdom, Canada, Argentina, Brazil, Chile)
GIOTTO	ESA satellite for the exploration of Halley's Comet
GOOS	Global Ocean Observing System
GRIP	Greenland Ice-core Project
HERA	Hadron-Elektron-Ringbeschleuniger-Anlage bei DESY, Hamburg
HGP	Human Genome Project
HUGO	Human Genome Organisation (European Union, United States)
ICSU	International Council of Scientific Unions
IGBP	International Geosphere-Biosphere Programme (ICSU)
ILL	Institut Laue-Langevin (Grenoble, France)
INSU	Institut national des sciences de l'Univers (National Institute for Sciences of the Universe) (CNRS, France)
IOC	Intergovernmental Oceanographic Commission (UNESCO)
ISIS	International Spallation Neutron Source (Rutherford-Appleton Laboratory, Didcot, United Kingdom)
ISR	Intersecting Storage Ring (CERN)
ITER	International Thermonuclear Experimental Reactor
JET	Joint European Torus (Culham, United Kingdom)
JINR	Joint Institute for Nuclear Research (Dubna, Russia)
KAON	K meson factory (cancelled, Vancouver)
KTB	Kontintentales Tiefbohrprogramme (Germany)
LEP	Large Electron-Positron Ring (CERN)
LHC	Large Hadron Collider (CERN)
LIGO	Laser Interferometer Gravitational Wave Observatory (United States)
LOFT	Loss of fluid test for water-cooled power reactors (Germany, EURATOM, United States)
MIT	Massachussets Institute of Technology
MMA	MilliMeter Array (project, NSF)
NASA	National Aeronautics and Space Administration (United States)
NASP	National AeroSpace Plane (United States)
NIH	National Institutes of Health (United States)
NRC	National Research Council (Canada)
NSF	National Science Foundation (United States)
NuPECC	Nuclear Physics European Collaboration Committee
ODP	Ocean Drilling Program
OMB	Office of Management and Budget (United States)
ORGEL	Early heavy water moderated organically cooled prototype reactor (EU-Joint Research Center, Ispra, Italy)
OST	Office for Science and Technology (United Kingdom)
OSTP	Office of Science and Technology Policy (United States)
PAYGO	"PAY-as-you-GO" (United States)
PS	Proton Synchrotron (CERN)
ROSAT	Röntgen-Satellit (Max-Planck-Institut für Extraterrestrische Physik, Garching)
SEFOR	Southwest Experimental Fast Oxide Reactor (Germany, EURATOM, United States)
SLAC	Stanford Linear Accelerator Center (Stanford, California, United States)

SSC	Superconducting Super Collider (cancelled, Texas, United States)
SURA	Southeast Universities Research Association
TGE	Très grand équipement (very large facility)
TRISTAN	Electron-Positron Collider Ring in the Japanese National High Energy Physics Laboratory (KEK) (Tsukuba)
UNEP	United Nations Environment Programme
VIRGO	Ultrasensitive Interferometer for the detection of gravitational waves (France, Italy)
VLA	Very Large Array (United States)
VLT	Very Large Telescope (Eso, Chile)
WCRP	World Climate Research Programme (ICSU and WMO)
WHO	World Health Organisation
WMO	World Meteorological Organisation (United Nations)

MAIN SALES OUTLETS OF OECD PUBLICATIONS
PRINCIPAUX POINTS DE VENTE DES PUBLICATIONS DE L'OCDE

ARGENTINA – ARGENTINE
Carlos Hirsch S.R.L.
Galería Güemes, Florida 165, 4° Piso
1333 Buenos Aires   Tel. (1) 331.1787 y 331.2391
                     Telefax: (1) 331.1787

AUSTRALIA – AUSTRALIE
D.A. Information Services
648 Whitehorse Road, P.O.B 163
Mitcham, Victoria 3132   Tel. (03) 873.4411
                          Telefax: (03) 873.5679

AUSTRIA – AUTRICHE
Gerold & Co.
Graben 31
Wien I   Tel. (0222) 533.50.14
            Telefax: (0222) 512.47.31.29

BELGIUM – BELGIQUE
Jean De Lannoy
Avenue du Roi 202 Koningslaan
B-1060 Bruxelles   Tel. (02) 538.51.69/538.08.41
                    Telefax: (02) 538.08.41

CANADA
Renouf Publishing Company Ltd.
1294 Algoma Road
Ottawa, ON K1B 3W8   Tel. (613) 741.4333
                      Telefax: (613) 741.5439
Stores:
61 Sparks Street
Ottawa, ON K1P 5R1   Tel. (613) 238.8985
211 Yonge Street
Toronto, ON M5B 1M4   Tel. (416) 363.3171
                       Telefax: (416)363.59.63

Les Éditions La Liberté Inc.
3020 Chemin Sainte-Foy
Sainte-Foy, PQ G1X 3V6   Tel. (418) 658.3763
                          Telefax: (418) 658.3763

Federal Publications Inc.
165 University Avenue, Suite 701
Toronto, ON M5H 3B8   Tel. (416) 860.1611
                       Telefax: (416) 860.1608

Les Publications Fédérales
1185 Université
Montréal, QC H3B 3A7   Tel. (514) 954.1633
                        Telefax: (514) 954.1635

CHINA – CHINE
China National Publications Import
Export Corporation (CNPIEC)
16 Gongti E. Road, Chaoyang District
P.O. Box 88 or 50
Beijing 100704 PR   Tel. (01) 506.6688
                     Telefax: (01) 506.3101

CHINESE TAIPEI – TAIPEI CHINOIS
Good Faith Worldwide Int'l. Co. Ltd.
9th Floor, No. 118, Sec. 2
Chung Hsiao E. Road
Taipei   Tel. (02) 391.7396/391.7397
                   Telefax: (02) 394.9176

**CZECH REPUBLIC – RÉPUBLIQUE
TCHÈQUE**
Artia Pegas Press Ltd.
Narodni Trida 25
POB 825
111 21 Praha 1   Tel. 26.65.68
                      Telefax: 26.20.81

DENMARK – DANEMARK
Munksgaard Book and Subscription Service
35, Nørre Søgade, P.O. Box 2148
DK-1016 København K   Tel. (33) 12.85.70
                       Telefax: (33) 12.93.87

EGYPT – ÉGYPTE
Middle East Observer
41 Sherif Street
Cairo   Tel. 392.6919
                   Telefax: 360-6804

FINLAND – FINLANDE
Akateeminen Kirjakauppa
Keskuskatu 1, P.O. Box 128
00100 Helsinki
Subscription Services/Agence d'abonnements :
P.O. Box 23
00371 Helsinki   Tel. (358 0) 121 4416
                      Telefax: (358 0) 121.4450

FRANCE
OECD/OCDE
Mail Orders/Commandes par correspondance:
2, rue André-Pascal
75775 Paris Cedex 16   Tel. (33-1) 45.24.82.00
                        Telefax: (33-1) 49.10.42.76
                        Telex: 640048 OCDE
Internet: Compte.PUBSINQ @ oecd.org
Orders via Minitel, France only/
Commandes par Minitel, France exclusivement :
36 15 OCDE
OECD Bookshop/Librairie de l'OCDE :
33, rue Octave-Feuillet
75016 Paris   Tel. (33-1) 45.24.81.81
                     (33-1) 45.24.81.67
Documentation Française
29, quai Voltaire
75007 Paris   Tel. 40.15.70.00
Gibert Jeune (Droit-Économie)
6, place Saint-Michel
75006 Paris   Tel. 43.25.91.19
Librairie du Commerce International
10, avenue d'Iéna
75016 Paris   Tel. 40.73.34.60
Librairie Dunod
Université Paris-Dauphine
Place du Maréchal de Lattre de Tassigny
75016 Paris   Tel. (1) 44.05.40.13
Librairie Lavoisier
11, rue Lavoisier
75008 Paris   Tel. 42.65.39.95
Librairie L.G.D.J. - Montchrestien
20, rue Soufflot
75005 Paris   Tel. 46.33.89.85
Librairie des Sciences Politiques
30, rue Saint-Guillaume
75007 Paris   Tel. 45.48.36.02
P.U.F.
49, boulevard Saint-Michel
75005 Paris   Tel. 43.25.83.40
Librairie de l'Université
12a, rue Nazareth
13100 Aix-en-Provence   Tel. (16) 42.26.18.08
Documentation Française
165, rue Garibaldi
69003 Lyon   Tel. (16) 78.63.32.23
Librairie Decitre
29, place Bellecour
69002 Lyon   Tel. (16) 72.40.54.54
Librairie Sauramps
Le Triangle
34967 Montpellier Cedex 2   Tel. (16) 67.58.85.15
                             Tekefax: (16) 67.58.27.36

GERMANY – ALLEMAGNE
OECD Publications and Information Centre
August-Bebel-Allee 6
D-53175 Bonn   Tel. (0228) 959.120
                      Telefax: (0228) 959.12.17

GREECE – GRÈCE
Librairie Kauffmann
Mavrokordatou 9
106 78 Athens   Tel. (01) 32.55.321
                      Telefax: (01) 32.30.320

HONG-KONG
Swindon Book Co. Ltd.
Astoria Bldg. 3F
34 Ashley Road, Tsimshatsui
Kowloon, Hong Kong   Tel. 2376.2062
                      Telefax: 2376.0685

HUNGARY – HONGRIE
Euro Info Service
Margitsziget, Európa Ház
1138 Budapest   Tel. (1) 111.62.16
                      Telefax: (1) 111.60.61

ICELAND – ISLANDE
Mál Mog Menning
Laugavegi 18, Pósthólf 392
121 Reykjavik   Tel. (1) 552.4240
                      Telefax: (1) 562.3523

INDIA – INDE
Oxford Book and Stationery Co.
Scindia House
New Delhi 110001   Tel. (11) 331.5896/5308
                      Telefax: (11) 332.5993
17 Park Street
Calcutta 700016   Tel. 240832

INDONESIA – INDONÉSIE
Pdii-Lipi
P.O. Box 4298
Jakarta 12042   Tel. (21) 573.34.67
                      Telefax: (21) 573.34.67

IRELAND – IRLANDE
Government Supplies Agency
Publications Section
4/5 Harcourt Road
Dublin 2   Tel. 661.31.11
                      Telefax: 475.27.60

ISRAEL
Praedicta
5 Shatner Street
P.O. Box 34030
Jerusalem 91430   Tel. (2) 52.84.90/1/2
                      Telefax: (2) 52.84.93
R.O.Y. International
P.O. Box 13056
Tel Aviv 61130   Tel. (3) 546 1423
                      Telefax: (3) 546 1442
Palestinian Authority/Middle East:
INDEX Information Services
P.O.B. 19502
Jerusalem   Tel. (2) 27.12.19
                      Telefax: (2) 27.16.34

ITALY – ITALIE
Libreria Commissionaria Sansoni
Via Duca di Calabria 1/1
50125 Firenze   Tel. (055) 64.54.15
                      Telefax: (055) 64.12.57
Via Bartolini 29
20155 Milano   Tel. (02) 36.50.83
Editrice e Libreria Herder
Piazza Montecitorio 120
00186 Roma   Tel. 679.46.28
                      Telefax: 678.47.51
Libreria Hoepli
Via Hoepli 5
20121 Milano   Tel. (02) 86.54.46
                      Telefax: (02) 805.28.86
Libreria Scientifica
Dott. Lucio de Biasio 'Aeiou'
Via Coronelli, 6
20146 Milano   Tel. (02) 48.95.45.52
                      Telefax: (02) 48.95.45.48

JAPAN – JAPON
OECD Publications and Information Centre
Landic Akasaka Building
2-3-4 Akasaka, Minato-ku
Tokyo 107   Tel. (81.3) 3586.2016
                      Telefax: (81.3) 3584.7929

KOREA – CORÉE
Kyobo Book Centre Co. Ltd.
P.O. Box 1658, Kwang Hwa Moon
Seoul   Tel. 730.78.91
                      Telefax: 735.00.30

MALAYSIA – MALAISIE
University of Malaya Bookshop
University of Malaya
P.O. Box 1127, Jalan Pantai Baru
59700 Kuala Lumpur
Malaysia   Tel. 756.5000/756.5425
                           Telefax: 756.3246

MEXICO – MEXIQUE
Revistas y Periodicos Internacionales S.A. de C.V.
Florencia 57 - 1004
Mexico, D.F. 06600   Tel. 207.81.00
                           Telefax: 208.39.79

NETHERLANDS – PAYS-BAS
SDU Uitgeverij Plantijnstraat
Externe Fondsen
Postbus 20014
2500 EA's-Gravenhage   Tel. (070) 37.89.880
Voor bestellingen: Telefax: (070) 34.75.778

**NEW ZEALAND
NOUVELLE-ZÉLANDE**
GPLegislation Services
P.O. Box 12418
Thorndon, Wellington   Tel. (04) 496.5655
                           Telefax: (04) 496.5698

NORWAY – NORVÈGE
Narvesen Info Center – NIC
Bertrand Narvesens vei 2
P.O. Box 6125 Etterstad
0602 Oslo 6   Tel. (022) 57.33.00
                           Telefax: (022) 68.19.01

PAKISTAN
Mirza Book Agency
65 Shahrah Quaid-E-Azam
Lahore 54000   Tel. (42) 353.601
                          Telefax: (42) 231.730

PHILIPPINE – PHILIPPINES
International Book Center
5th Floor, Filipinas Life Bldg.
Ayala Avenue
Metro Manila   Tel. 81.96.76
                         Telex 23312 RHP PH

PORTUGAL
Livraria Portugal
Rua do Carmo 70-74
Apart. 2681
1200 Lisboa   Tel. (01) 347.49.82/5
                         Telefax: (01) 347.02.64

SINGAPORE – SINGAPOUR
Gower Asia Pacific Pte Ltd.
Golden Wheel Building
41, Kallang Pudding Road, No. 04-03
Singapore 1334   Tel. 741.5166
                         Telefax: 742.9356

SPAIN – ESPAGNE
Mundi-Prensa Libros S.A.
Castelló 37, Apartado 1223
Madrid 28001   Tel. (91) 431.33.99
                         Telefax: (91) 575.39.98

Libreria Internacional AEDOS
Consejo de Ciento 391
08009 – Barcelona   Tel. (93) 488.30.09
                           Telefax: (93) 487.76.59

Llibreria de la Generalitat
Palau Moja
Rambla dels Estudis, 118
08002 – Barcelona
             (Subscripcions) Tel. (93) 318.80.12
             (Publicacions) Tel. (93) 302.67.23
                           Telefax: (93) 412.18.54

SRI LANKA
Centre for Policy Research
c/o Colombo Agencies Ltd.
No. 300-304, Galle Road
Colombo 3   Tel. (1) 574240, 573551-2
                         Telefax: (1) 575394, 510711

SWEDEN – SUÈDE
Fritzes Customer Service
S–106 47 Stockholm   Tel. (08) 690.90.90
                           Telefax: (08) 20.50.21

Subscription Agency/Agence d'abonnements :
Wennergren-Williams Info AB
P.O. Box 1305
171 25 Solna   Tel. (08) 705.97.50
                           Telefax: (08) 27.00.71

SWITZERLAND – SUISSE
Maditec S.A. (Books and Periodicals - Livres
et périodiques)
Chemin des Palettes 4
Case postale 266
1020 Renens VD 1   Tel. (021) 635.08.65
                           Telefax: (021) 635.07.80

Librairie Payot S.A.
4, place Pépinet
CP 3212
1002 Lausanne   Tel. (021) 341.33.47
                           Telefax: (021) 341.33.45

Librairie Unilivres
6, rue de Candolle
1205 Genève   Tel. (022) 320.26.23
                           Telefax: (022) 329.73.18

Subscription Agency/Agence d'abonnements :
Dynapresse Marketing S.A.
38 avenue Vibert
1227 Carouge   Tel. (022) 308.07.89
                           Telefax: (022) 308.07.99

See also – Voir aussi :
OECD Publications and Information Centre
August-Bebel-Allee 6
D-53175 Bonn (Germany)   Tel. (0228) 959.120
                           Telefax: (0228) 959.12.17

THAILAND – THAÏLANDE
Suksit Siam Co. Ltd.
113, 115 Fuang Nakhon Rd.
Opp. Wat Rajbopith
Bangkok 10200   Tel. (662) 225.9531/2
                           Telefax: (662) 222.5188

TURKEY – TURQUIE
Kültür Yayinlari Is-Türk Ltd. Sti.
Atatürk Bulvari No. 191/Kat 13
Kavaklidere/Ankara   Tel. 428.11.40 Ext. 2458
Dolmabahce Cad. No. 29
Besiktas/Istanbul   Tel. (312) 260 7188
                           Telex: (312) 418 29 46

UNITED KINGDOM – ROYAUME-UNI
HMSO
Gen. enquiries   Tel. (171) 873 8496
Postal orders only:
P.O. Box 276, London SW8 5DT
Personal Callers HMSO Bookshop
49 High Holborn, London WC1V 6HB
                           Telefax: (171) 873 8416
Branches at: Belfast, Birmingham, Bristol,
Edinburgh, Manchester

UNITED STATES – ÉTATS-UNIS
OECD Publications and Information Center
2001 L Street N.W., Suite 650
Washington, D.C. 20036-4910 Tel. (202) 785.6323
                           Telefax: (202) 785.0350

VENEZUELA
Libreria del Este
Avda F. Miranda 52, Aptdo. 60337
Edificio Galipán
Caracas 106   Tel. 951.1705/951.2307/951.1297
                           Telegram: Libreste Caracas

Subscription to OECD periodicals may also be
placed through main subscription agencies.

Les abonnements aux publications périodiques de
l'OCDE peuvent être souscrits auprès des
principales agences d'abonnement.

Orders and inquiries from countries where Distribu-
tors have not yet been appointed should be sent to:
OECD Publications Service, 2 rue André-Pascal,
75775 Paris Cedex 16, France.

Les commandes provenant de pays où l'OCDE n'a
pas encore désigné de distributeur peuvent être
adressées à : OCDE, Service des Publications,
2, rue André-Pascal, 75775 Paris Cedex 16, France.

                                          7-1995

OECD PUBLICATIONS, 2 rue André-Pascal, 75775 PARIS CEDEX 16
PRINTED IN FRANCE
(92 95 08 1) ISBN 92-64-14557-5 - No. 48157 1995